MAKING USE PHYSICS

for GCSE

R. Kibble

© R. Kibble 1989

All rights reserved. No reproduction, copy or transmission of this publication may be made without written permission.

No paragraph of this publication may be reproduced, copied or transmitted save with written permission or in accordance with the provisions of the Copyright Act 1956 (as amended), or under the terms of any licence permitting limited copying issued by the Copyright Licensing Agency, 33–4 Alfred Place, London WC1E 7DP.

Any person who does any unauthorised act in relation to this publication may be liable to criminal prosecution and civil claims for damages.

First published 1989

Published by
MACMILLAN EDUCATION LTD
Houndmills, Basingstoke, Hampshire RG21 2XS
and London
Companies and representatives
throughout the world

Printed in Hong Kong

British Library Cataloguing in Publication Data
Kibble, R.
    Making use of physics for GCSE
    1. Physics.
    I. Title
    530

ISBN 0–333–46926–7

CONTENTS

Preface	vii
Acknowledgements	ix
Introduction – GCSE, Physics and You	1
1. Speed, force, acceleration	5
2. Gravity	17
3. Atoms, molecules and models	29
4. Stretching solid materials	39
5. Modern materials	51
6. Work, energy and power	61
7. Heating things	71
8. Pressure	81
9. Practical work	93
10. Mathematical skills	103
11. Investigations	115
12. Vibrations and waves	125
13. The Electromagnetic Spectrum	135
14. Radioactivity	141
15. Electrons and electricity	153
16. Electromagnetism	163
17. Supplying electrical energy	173
18. At home with electricity	179
19. The energy business	187
20. Introducing electronics	197
21. Electronic systems	205
22. Assessments	215
23. Practice assessment questions	221
Appendix I: Answers to all numerical questions	231
Appendix II: Formulae and relationships	235
Index	237

PREFACE

This book has been written during a period of considerable change and innovation in education. Two changes are particularly relevant. The first is the principle of *science for all*. As embodied in the National Curriculum, 'science for all' will result in more students studying science but probably fewer students studying physics as a single subject before the age of 16. For many students, physics will be a subject studied for the first time in the sixth form or in college. The second change concerns assessment. There has been a gradual move towards school-based methods of assessment ever since I started teaching. Initiatives such as BTEC Science, CPVE, and GCSE have incorporated the notion of '*coursework*' into their patterns of assessment.

This book responds to both the changes outlined above. It provides students, many meeting physics for the first time, with a useful support text. As well as covering the basic subject matter, the book has been written in a style which is designed to appeal to the more mature student who has grown out of cartoons and crosswords but who still needs a sympathetic first physics textbook. It also gives advice and helpful hints on how to cope with a physics course involving coursework assessments with a greater emphasis on processes and practical skills.

This is not a book to be read from cover to cover, nor is it a course in itself. The units are unlikely to follow any one particular teaching sequence. Some Units, particularly the first two, will require a considerable amount of practical assistance in order to clarify such difficult concepts as force, acceleration, mass and weight. Others may serve as useful revision Units. The Units on mathematical and practical skills and on assessments will prove helpful early on in the course. The practice assessment questions are probably best left until shortly before the time for written assessments. Each Unit ends with progress questions which tend to be of graded degrees of difficulty. These questions, together with the related reading passages, might form the basis of work to be done at home.

I should like to thank those people who helped with the book. In particular, Jean Cook for the coffee and Nigel Duffin, for his watchful eye and professional advice.

Bob Kibble

ACKNOWLEDGEMENTS

The author and publishers wish to acknowledge, with thanks, the following photographic sources:

Aerofilms: page 128 (bottom)
BBC Hulton Picture Library: pages 11 and 141 (bottom right)
Camera Press: pages 48, 57 and 82
Mary Evans Picture Library: page 141 (top)
ICI Mond Division: page 59
Science Photo Library: pages 24 (NASA), 36 (photograph Lawrence Berkeley) and 151 (bottom) (CNRI)
Technigraph Studio, Inc.: page 151 (top)
Alan Thomas: pages 5, 52, 67, 128 (top) and 128 (bottom left).

All other photographs courtesy of the author.

The publishers have made every effort to trace the copyright holders, but if they have inadvertently overlooked any, they will be pleased to make the necessary arrangement at the first opportunity.

INTRODUCTION

GCSE (the system), *Physics* (the subject), *You* (the student)

GCSE (the system)
Your GCSE course will have been designed following nationally agreed criteria. This means that all GCSE physics courses will cover some common content. If you do well in your GCSE course you will be equipped to study physics at a higher level, take a vocational course such as BTEC or move into the world of work. A physics qualification is held in high regard by employers. Following the **national criteria**, assessment on your course will take place during as well as at the end of the course. You will be given the opportunity to demonstrate your knowledge and understanding of physics and your practical skills.

An important element in all GCSE assessments is **positive achievement**. No two physics students are the same. Some are good at explaining ideas, others are good at calculations. Some are good at practical work, others are best at remembering facts. Some students are good at all of these. The GCSE will allow credit for students who show what they can actually do. To enable students of different abilities to show what they can do in the assessments, all GCSE physics courses will offer a choice of examination papers. This is called **differentiation**. Ask your teacher to explain how these choices are to be offered in your particular course.

Physics (the subject)
Physics, together with biology and chemistry are the areas of study which most people call science. Science also includes other areas such as astronomy, earth science and botany. What do all these subjects have in common? What makes them all sciences?

Scientists do not all agree on exactly what science is. It is often thought that science is what scientists do and in particular how they do it. This has been called the scientific method and it covers the process of taking an idea, testing it with experiments, and discovering some 'facts' about it or even disproving it. In real life, science is more complex than this simple model. Scientists often disagree about ideas and experimental results. Progress can be very slow and new ideas can take years to become accepted.

One of the exciting things about physics is that there is always room for new ideas to challenge old ones. Once the Earth was flat, now it is round. Once there were just atoms, now there are muons, gluons, protons, photons and whatevernextons. The Sun used to move around the Earth, now the Earth moves around the Sun. Physics is a subject which is alive and its ideas are constantly changing. It deals with topics like forces and motion, atoms and materials, temperature changes, electricity and electronics.

To enable you to join in this arena of lively ideas you will have to start by learning some basic rules. The language of physics needs to be understood. Some words have **definitions**, for example, *power*. We might say that a swimmer has a powerful stroke but in physics power has a special definition:

Power is the rate at which energy is transformed

When definitions appear in this book they will be explained and picked out so that you notice them.

You will need to know how to deal with **relationships** between quantities. One example is the relationship between the pressure and the volume of a gas covered in Unit 8:

'the pressure of a gas is inversely proportional to the volume'

or pressure $\propto 1/\text{volume}$

or $P = \dfrac{\text{constant}}{V}$

The relationship is written like a mathematical equation so that measured values can be used and numbers put in the place of symbols.

Some ideas are not easily explained by an equation. The idea of energy is an example. We call such ideas **concepts**. Everyday examples of concepts are the ideas of 'loyalty' and 'beauty'. You will have to be patient with concepts as they become clear for the student only after regular use in a variety of different situations.

Physicists make sense of the world by using **models**. A model is a way of representing a difficult idea to make it easier to understand. Some models take the form of diagrams, such as the models of atoms in Unit 3. Sometimes the best model is mathematical, as is the case in Unit 4 with Hooke's law.

This section ends with a final word of advice. Although physics can be interesting with its models, theories and definitions, it is important that these ideas are seen to apply outside the physics laboratory. Physics does relate to everyday experiences and as a student you need to become aware of the many applications of physics in engineering, medicine, other sciences and in your own home.

You (the student)

As the reader of this book you are likely to be older than sixteen and studying in a sixth-form college or college of further education. You may have studied physics before but this is not a necessary requirement for success in physics 'mature'. Your course is probably a one-year course which, with time for assessments, leaves about two and a half terms for you to learn your physics. Your teacher will advise you on the exact order of topics to be covered during this time. It is your job to find this out.

With such a short course you will be expected to take a greater responsibility for your own learning. This extra responsibility comes with your 'mature' status and should be welcomed. This book will help you succeed in this task in several ways. First, the book will provide a reference for you to use should you need to go over a topic covered in lessons. Use the book as if it were a personal tutor. Do not read it from cover to cover, rather dip into it when and where you need to. Secondly, the book provides you with advice on mathematical skills, practical skills and examinations techniques. These sections will help you to best show what you can do when coursework assessments arrive. Finally, the book includes many questions. Use some to check your progress on a unit and others to prepare yourself for timed answers in the examinations.

A final word of advice. This book is not a complete course. It is no substitute for your physics lessons. Attend all lessons and be on time. Ask the teacher if you have difficulties; remember the teacher is paid to help you, not to scare you! Use your friends to help share any problems. A good way to test your understanding is to explain something to a friend. Use all these resources together with this book. Enjoy your physics and good luck.

SPEED, FORCE, ACCELERATION

1.1 Distance and time

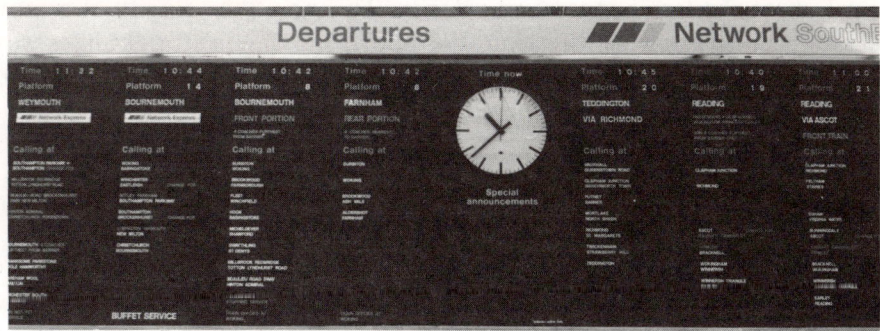

Figure 1.1

Question: "How far is it from London to Brighton?"

Answer: "About 50 miles."...a geographer

Answer: "About 5 hours." ...a cyclist

Answer: "About an hour."...a train driver

The first answer to the question is correct. Brighton is about 50 miles from London. The other two answers are perhaps less 'correct' but are more useful to a traveller. They include an assumption of how fast you will be moving. This unit is about speed of travel, distance travelled and time taken.

How fast is the London to Brighton train? How fast is the cyclist's speed? The speed of an object is related to the distance travelled and the time taken by the relationship:

$$\text{speed} = \frac{\text{distance travelled}}{\text{time taken}}$$

or

$$v = s/t$$

The symbols v, s and t are used instead of speed, distance travelled and time taken. Take care not to confuse them. In particular, remember that s represents the distance travelled.

For the train:

$$v = \frac{s}{t} = \frac{50 \text{ miles}}{1 \text{ hour}} = 50 \text{ mph}$$

For the cyclist:

$$v = \frac{s}{t} = \frac{50 \text{ miles}}{5 \text{ hours}} = 10 \text{ mph}$$

This relationship is included in Unit 1 because it is one of the most used of all physics relationships. Physics is full of situations where movement needs to be measured and speeds need to be known:

The speed of sound in air is about 330 m/s.
The speed of an electron in a television tube is about 40 000 000 m/s.
The speed of an air molecule in this room is about 400 m/s.
The speed of light is about 300 000 000 m/s.

(You will meet the terms **speed** and **velocity**. To know the velocity of a moving object you need to know its direction. For bodies moving in straight lines we can consider speed and velocity to be the same. As you are probably more used to the word speed, it will be used where possible in this book.)

1.2 Units and measurement

In Section 1.1 speed was measured in miles per hour (mph), and metres per second (m/s). Millimetres per year (mm/yr) and kilometres per hour (km/hr) are also units for speed. All units for the measurement of speed will have the form: **unit of distance/unit of time**. In physics, metres, m, and seconds, s, are used whenever possible.

You should try to become familiar with kilometres, metres, centimetres and millimetres. A metre rule will help you to get a 'feel' for these metric units. The thickness of your thumb is about two centimetres. Once around an athletics track is 400 m or 0.4 km. A very tall person is about 2 metres tall.

How fast is a speed of 12 m/s or 20 km/hr? You should practice thinking about speeds. A watch (or clock) and metre rule are all you need to start measuring speeds. Measure walking speed and jogging speed. Carry out a traffic speed check if there is a safe road nearby. Take care to read your clock or watch accurately. Digital watches are easy to read but stopwatches may have each second divided into smaller units. Unit 9 gives some advice.

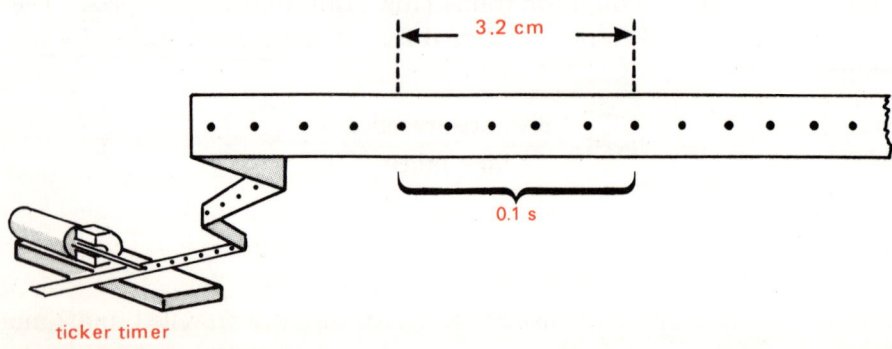

ticker timer

Figure 1.2

Ticker tape is often used in school and college laboratories for measuring speed. The time interval between dots is 1/50 second and the distances may be measured with a ruler.

For the tape shown in Figure 1.2:

$$\text{speed} = \frac{s}{t} = \frac{3.2 \text{ cm}}{0.1 \text{ s}} = \underline{32 \text{ cm/s}}$$

1.3 Calculations using the speed relationship

Relationships and equations may be rearranged to enable calculations to be made. (See Unit 10 for advice on mathematical skills.) The speed equation can become three equations:

$$\text{speed} = v = \frac{s}{t}; \text{ distance travelled, } s = vt; \text{ time taken, } t = \frac{s}{v}$$

Here are some examples. Try the last ones for yourself.

a. **How fast** is a cross-channel ferry which travels 20 km in two hours?

$$v = \frac{s}{t} = 20 \text{ km/2 hr} = \underline{10 \text{ km/hr}}$$

b. **How far** will an electron go if it moves at a speed of 18 mm/s for a minute?

$$s = vt = 18 \text{ mm/s} \times 60 \text{ s} = \underline{1080 \text{ mm}}$$

c. **How long does it take** a fly to cross a room 4 m wide if its speed is 0.8 m/s?

$$t = \frac{s}{v} = 4 \text{ m}/0.8 \text{ m/s} = \underline{5 \text{ s}}$$

d. A physics student takes four minutes to wander along an 80 m corridor to her lesson. **What is her speed?**

e. An atom in a gas has an average speed of 410 m/s. **How far would it go in an hour?**

f. **How long does it take** a spacecraft moving at 8 km/s to make the 500 000 000 km journey from Mars to Jupiter?

1.4 Using graphs to show motion

A graph is one of many ways of displaying information. Becoming familiar with graphs and learning how to read the information they carry is a skill which you should aim to develop. (Unit 10 gives some practice with graphical skills.)

Let us consider the case of a train which moves at a steady speed of 40 m/s. The graph of Figure 1.3 shows this constant speed, for a time of 90 s, by a horizontal line.

Now consider the shaded area. The area under the line carries useful

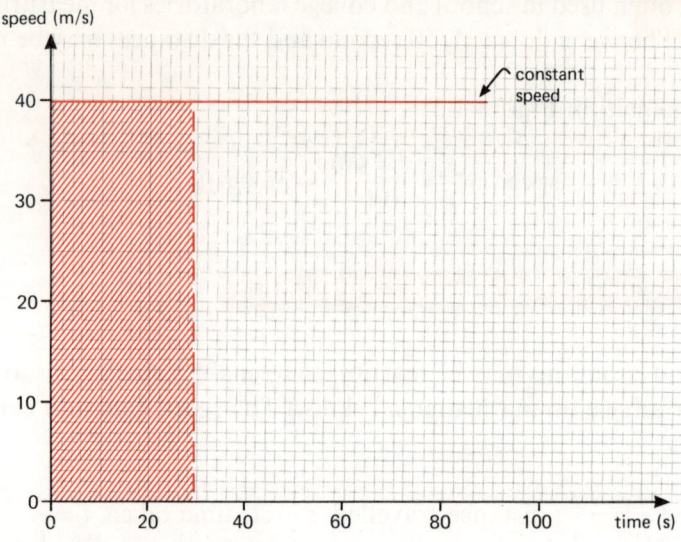

Figure 1.3 A constant speed of 40 m/s for 90 seconds

information. The area of the shaded rectangle is:

area = length × breadth   This is the distance
= 30 s × 40 m/s   travelled by the train
= 1200 m   in 30 s. Calculate how far
                           the train goes in 90 s.

Let us suppose that the train makes a stop, picks up passengers and continues up a sloping track to the next station. The speed/time graph for the journey would probably be as shown in Figure 1.4.

Check that you can find answers to these questions using the graph:

a. How long did the train wait at the station?
b. How far was it between the two stations?
c. What evidence is there that the train was moving uphill?

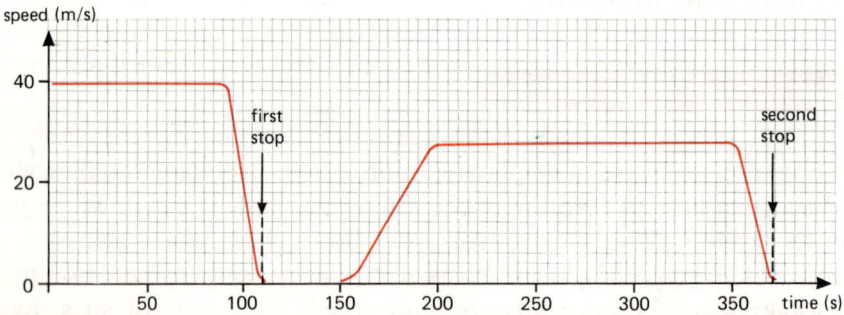

Figure 1.4 Speed/time graph for a stopping train

1.5 Acceleration

Consider the speed/time graph shown in Figure 1.5. It has a constant slope. The speed increases steadily. In physics, speeding up is called **acceleration**.

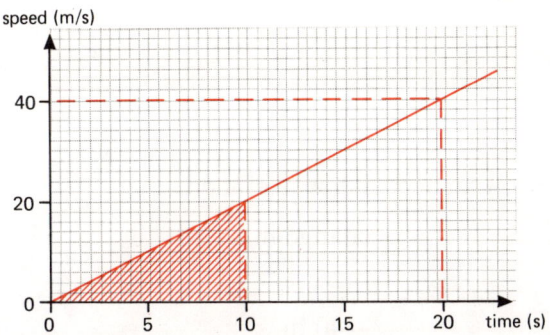

Figure 1.5 This graph shows constant, or uniform, acceleration

The graph shows that in each 10 s the speed has changed by 20 m/s.
The rate of change is 20 m/s in 10 s, or 10 m/s in 1 s.
This rate of change of speed is the **acceleration**, a. So

$$a = 10 \text{ m/s every second}$$

or

$$a = 10 \text{ m/s}^2$$

It is helpful to remember the relationship

$$\text{acceleration} = \frac{\text{change in speed}}{\text{time taken}}$$

$$a = \frac{\text{change in speed}}{t}$$

The units for acceleration are m/s^2

change in speed $= a \times t$

How far does an accelerating object go? Look at the areas under the slope in Figure 1.5.
In the first 10 s the area is the area of a triangle,

$$\frac{1}{2} \text{ base} \times \text{height} = 100 \text{ m}$$

In the next 10 s the area is greater, 300 m. This is not surprising as the train goes further in 10 s as it moves faster!
Of course, all objects which have speeded up can slow down. This is called **deceleration**. The rate of change of speed has a negative sign.

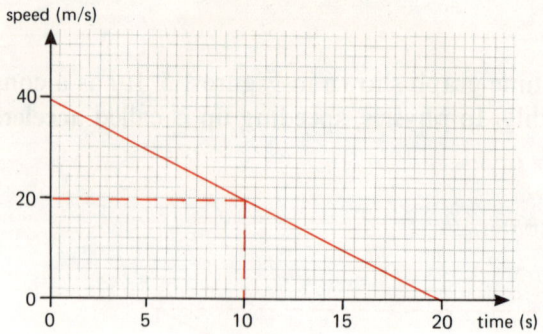

Figure 1.6 A graph showing constant deceleration

$$a = \frac{\text{change in speed}}{t}$$

$$= \frac{-40 \text{ m/s}}{20 \text{ s}}$$

$$= \underline{-2 \text{ m/s}^2}$$

Ticker tape can be used to study acceleration. Two average speeds need to be calculated and the time between them measured. An example is shown in Figure 1.7 (not to scale).

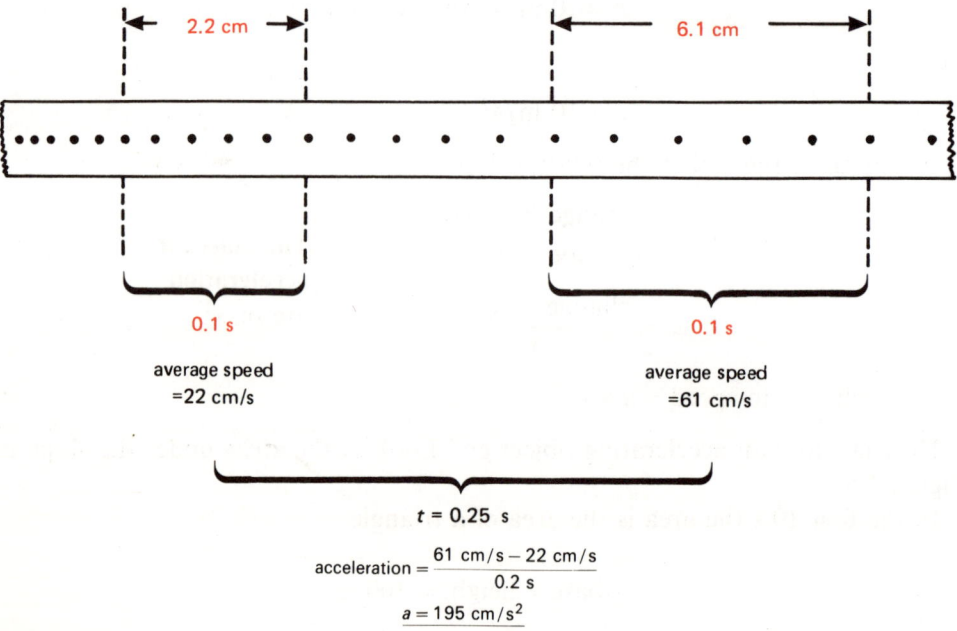

Figure 1.7

You could use ticker tape to investigate the acceleration of a trolley pulled by an elastic cord or of a trolley rolling down a slope. A simple experiment to start with would be simply to pull a piece of tape through a timer by hand.

Figure 1.8 Sir Isaac Newton

1.6 Force and motion

As you read this book you may be forcing it to hold it up. You are probably forcing down on your seat and on the floor, forcing air out of your lungs and even forcing yourself to read this book. Apart from the last one, these are all examples of what we call forces. A force can push, pull, twist or stretch. Forces like these are measured using a force meter, usually containing a spring. The unit of force is the newton, N (named after Isaac Newton, 1642 to 1727). One newton is about the weight of an apple. Pushing a car at a steady slow speed requires about 600 N.

The size of one newton force is determined by the effect it has on a 1 kg mass. If a single force has the effect of accelerating a 1 kg mass at a rate of 1 m/s^2 then the force is one newton. Isaac Newton realised that to produce larger accelerations greater forces were needed. To summarise this relationship, known as Newton's second law of motion, one can write

Force (N) = mass (kg) × acceleration (m/s^2)

$$F = m \times a$$

If no forces act on a body then it will not accelerate (both sides of the equation above = 0). This hardly ever happens. Perhaps in deep space, away from any influences, an object might have zero force acting on it. In this situation a space vehicle, once moving, would continue moving in a straight line at the same speed.

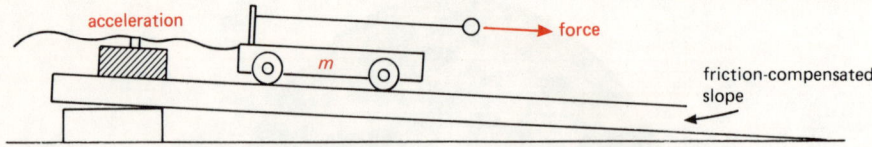

Figure 1.9   Investigating accelerations in the laboratory

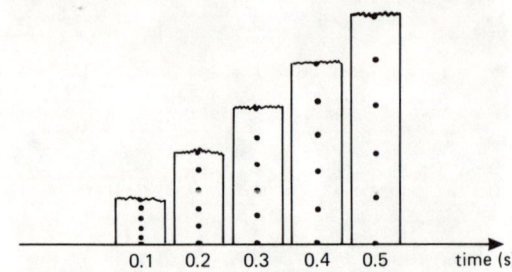

Figure 1.10   Ticker tapes showing acceleration

Here on Earth it is possible to find situations where all the forces on an object cancel out to give the same effect as no force at all. In all such cases there is no resulting force and so no change in speed. Newton's first law of motion describes this. **An object will remain at rest or continue to move at a steady speed in a straight line unless it is forced to do otherwise.**

1.7 Related reading: Physics and the *Highway Code*

Many road accidents are caused by a driver being too close to the vehicle in front. An emergency stop can lead to a multiple crash if cars are too close. The *Highway Code* gives a table of shortest stopping distances to help avoid such accidents.

A stopping distance is the sum of two parts, the thinking distance and the braking distance. To stop a car, the driver has first to make a quick decision to apply the brakes. During this 'thinking time', about 0.8 s for an alert mind, the car continues to move forward at a constant speed. Once the brakes are applied the car will decelerate and stop some time later.

A speed/time graph will show the overall stopping distance for a car travelling at 13 m/s (about 30 mph).

Figure 1.11 shows that at 13 m/s a car will come to rest 18.2 metres after the place where the driver first started to react. You might like to try to sketch a similar graph for a car at 31 m/s (70 mph) to see how the overall stopping distance increases with speed (assume that the deceleration is the same as for the slower speed).

Now let us consider two cars both needing to stop. The first driver will apply his brakes and at the same time the second driver will see the brake lights. After thinking for 0.8 s the second driver will then apply his own brakes. Although the

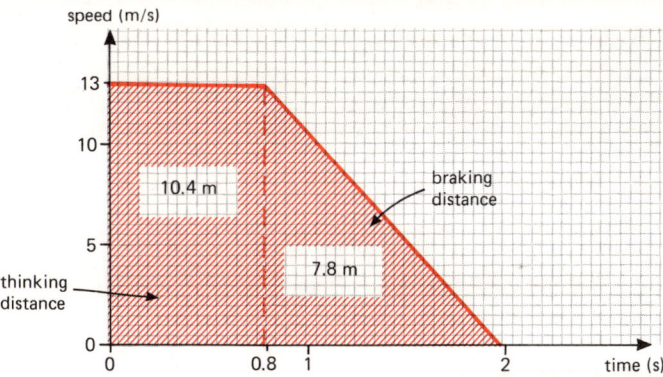

Figure 1.11 For a car moving at 13 m/s, the thinking distance is greater than the braking distance

second car takes 18.2 m to stop, the first car keeps moving through its braking distance to 7.8 m during this time. The smallest distance between the two cars at a steady speed of 13 m/s (30 mph) is therefore 10.4 m if they are to avoid impact.

It must be said that these figures are based on an assumption that the drivers are alert, the brakes are in order and that road conditions are perfect. On many occasions this is not the case and so it is safer to leave more than this minimum distance between your car and the car in front.

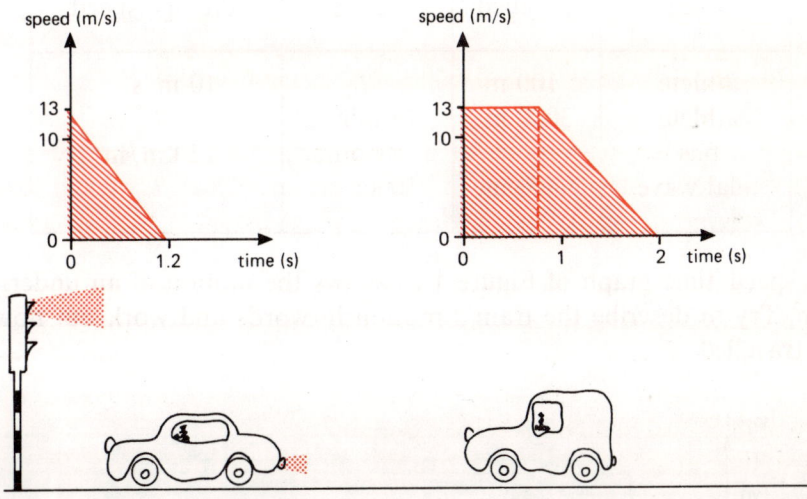

Figure 1.12 What is a safe distance between cars?

1.8 Summary

- Average speed (velocity) (m/s) = $\dfrac{\text{distance travelled (m)}}{\text{time taken (s)}}$
- The area 'under' a speed/time graph shows distance travelled.

- The slope of a speed/time graph shows acceleration.
- Acceleration is the rate of change of speed and can be negative.

$$\text{acceleration (m/s}^2\text{)} = \frac{\text{change in speed (m/s)}}{\text{time taken (s)}}$$

- To make a body accelerate, it must be acted on by an unbalanced force.

$$\text{force (N)} = \text{mass (kg)} \times \text{acceleration (m/s}^2\text{)}$$

- If there are no unbalanced forces on a body it will remain at rest or continue to move in a straight line. There will be no acceleration.

1.9 Progress questions

1. (a) How many metres are there in 3 km?
   (b) How many seconds are there in two hours?
   (c) Which is faster, 2 km/hr or 2 m/s?
2. How far would a stray cat go if it continued to wander on its own?
   (a) If a cat takes 12 s to travel 10 m, how long would it take to travel 5 m?
   (b) How long would it take to travel 1 km?
   (c) How far would it travel in an hour?
3. Copy this table and fill in the blank spaces:

Object	Distance travelled	Time taken	Average speed
athlete	100 m	?	10 m/s
athlete	3000 m	13 min	?
bus	?	4 hours	12 km/hr
tidal wave	400 m	50 s	?

4. The speed/time graph of Figure 1.13 shows the motion of an underground train. Try to describe the train's motion in words and work out how far it has travelled.

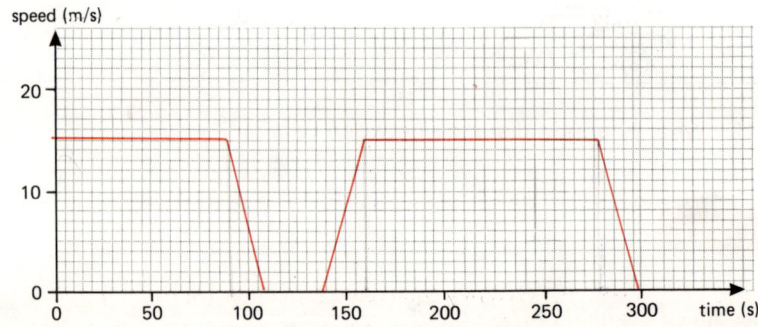

Figure 1.13

5. The speed/time graph of Figure 1.14 shows how a circus clown might move as she is fired from a circus cannon.

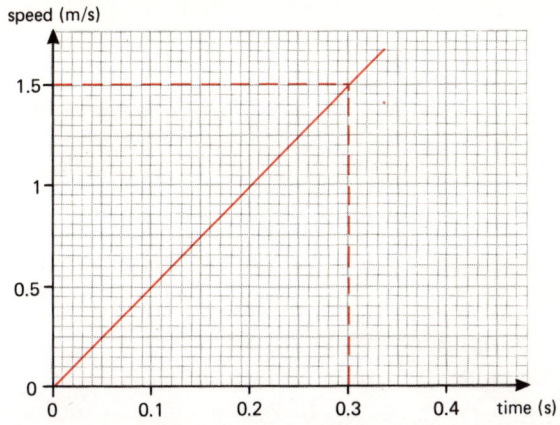

Figure 1.14

(a) Describe the clown's motion in words.
(b) How far does the clown travel in the first 0.1 s?
(c) Calculate the acceleration of the clown.
6. In Section 1.7, Related reading, Figure 1.11 shows the speed/time graph for a car braking. If the car's mass were 1050 kg, how much force would be needed to make the car decelerate as shown by the graph?
7. Try this exercise. Sit in a quiet place and think about being still. Think about the forces acting on your body. How many forces are acting? What is their effect? Sketch a diagram to show these forces acting on your body.

GRAVITY 2

2.1 The idea of gravity

What keeps an arrow moving once it leaves the bow?
Why do objects fall to the ground?
How fast do they fall?

These questions were asked, and answered in his own way, by the Greek Aristotle about 400 BC. As well as having philosophical value, the questions were important to hunters and soldiers. Today ski-jumpers or astronauts might ask similar questions. In this Unit on gravity you will become aware that modern physics has its own history and that today's ideas have evolved from simple beginnings and will continue to change.

For Aristotle, objects fell because their natural place was on the ground. He said that solids and liquids had 'gravity'. Much later, about 1600, Galileo, an Italian experimenter, found by measurement that all objects fell at the same rate. You do not need to go to Pisa to repeat Galileo's measurements. A table and chair provide enough height for you to drop two different rubber bungs.

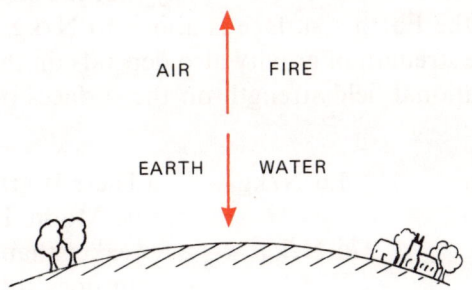

Figure 2.1 For Aristotle, earth and water possessed 'gravity'

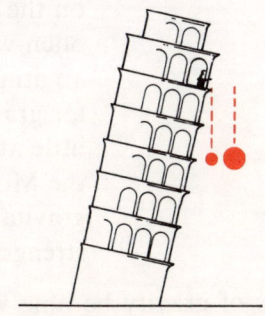

Figure 2.2 Experimenting with gravity

It was Isaac Newton in 1687 who provided a mathematical account of gravitation. Newton's theory of universal gravitation included falling apples as well as the motion of the Moon. He realised that all objects attracted all other objects through the force of gravity. There are attractive forces between you and this book! Gravity is responsible for keeping the Sun from exploding, for the paths of 'shooting stars' and for the struggle we have when climbing stairs.

Physics students, however, should note that despite all the successes of gravitational theory there is still no explanation as to exactly how gravity works. How can the Earth attract the Moon without even touching it? How can a book attract a banana? Perhaps there exist some invisible particles which transmit the force of attraction between all objects. We just do not know. The story is incomplete and that is what makes physics so challenging.

2.2 How strong is gravity?

Gravitational forces are weak forces. The force of attraction between a book and the reader is so small we do not notice it. In the 18th century an object the size of a mountain was needed before any effect was noticed on a delicate pendulum. Even an object like the Earth still has only a weak effect on a banana. Just lift up a banana and feel how easy it is to overcome gravity! The strength of gravity at any place can be measured by finding its effect on an every day mass like a banana. A 1 kg mass is used as a standard mass.

You can check the strength of your local gravity, given the symbol g, using a newton balance and a 1 kg mass. You will find that the Earth's gravity attracts a 1 kg mass with a force of about 10 N. We say that the strength of the Earth's gravitational field on the Earth's surface is about 10 N/kg. The actual value is almost 9.81 N/kg. The strength of gravity also depends on the mass of the object causing it. The gravitational field strength on the surfaces of some of our Solar System neighbours are:

The Moon	1.6 N/kg	(There **is** gravity on the Moon. It is weaker than on Earth but does still cause an attractive force. Things are **not** weightless on the Moon. It is often wrongly thought that an atmosphere is needed for gravity. There is little atmosphere on the Moon but there is a gravitational field strength of 1.6 N/kg.)
The Sun	274 N/kg	
Jupiter	25 N/kg	

Newton realised that the forces of gravity became weaker as objects moved apart. The effect of the Earth's gravity gets weaker the further we move away from the Earth's surface. Most of the fuel in space rockets is used in the early stages when the Earth's gravitational attraction is strongest.

2.3 Mass and weight

Here are two terms which are often confused. They are not the same thing. A good physics student should know the difference. Every object has its own **mass**. We measure mass in kilograms (kg). A hammer's mass is related to the number and type of atoms from which it is made. Small carpet-tack hammers (about 0.5 kg) are less **mass**ive than large 'club' hammers (about 2 kg). In the example of Figure 2.3, the more massive hammer will have a greater effect on a nail.

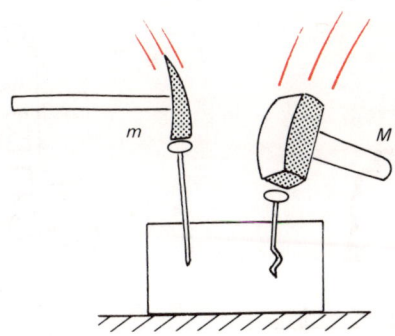

Figure 2.3 The effect of a hammer's mass

Although we could in principle use this same test to find the mass of any object, we choose to compare masses by measuring the force needed to accelerate the mass. Larger masses need larger forces to accelerate them. Newton's second law of motion says exactly this:

mass (kg) = force (N)/acceleration (m/s²)

$$m = F/a$$

For example, if a caravan (see Figure 2.4) required a steady force of 800 N to make it accelerate at 2 m/s², then its mass would be

Figure 2.4

$$m = F/a$$

$$m = \frac{800 \text{ N}}{2 \text{ m/s}^2} = \underline{400 \text{ kg}}$$

The **weight** of an object is caused by gravity. You can feel the weight of a heavy hammer when you pick it up. The weight is caused by the attraction between the hammer and the Earth. This attractive force due to gravity is what we measure if we support the hammer on a weighing machine. If our local gravitational field strength, g, is about 10 N/kg then a 2 kg hammer weights about 20 N. A 60 kg person weighs about 600 N (weight $= m \times g$).

On the **Moon** our 2 kg hammer will be just as good at hammering nails. It will be just as hard to accelerate when forced and it will have the same number of atoms within it. Its mass will be the same. This is no surprise as it is, after all, the same hammer. It will, however, be easier to pick up as it will weigh less. With gravity on the Moon being about 1.6 N/kg, our 2 kg hammer will weigh not 20 N but 3.2 N.

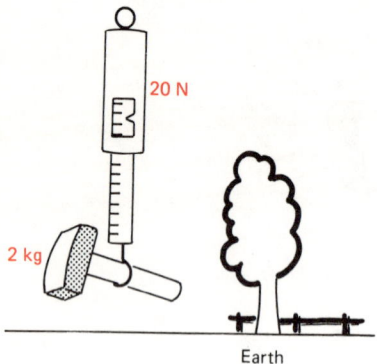

Figure 2.5 The weight of an object on Earth

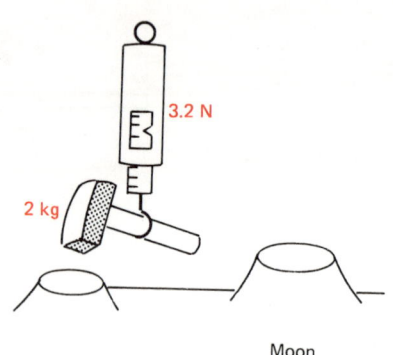

Figure 2.6 The weight of the same object is much less on the Moon

2.4 Falling with gravity

Galileo found that objects of different masses were accelerated equally by gravity. This might seem to defy common sense as objects which weigh more are being pulled downwards with a greater force. To understand the effect of gravity on falling objects it is important to make measurements. An experiment designed to measure the acceleration due to gravity is outlined in Figure 2.7.

An object is released and allowed to fall through a measured distance, s. The time taken for the fall needs to be noted, t.

The exact details of such an experiment will depend on the particular apparatus available.

To improve the accuracy of your result it might be possible to measure the time of fall electrically.

Repeating the experiment helps to average out any human errors.

Background

Assuming constant acceleration, the speed/time graph for a falling body will be

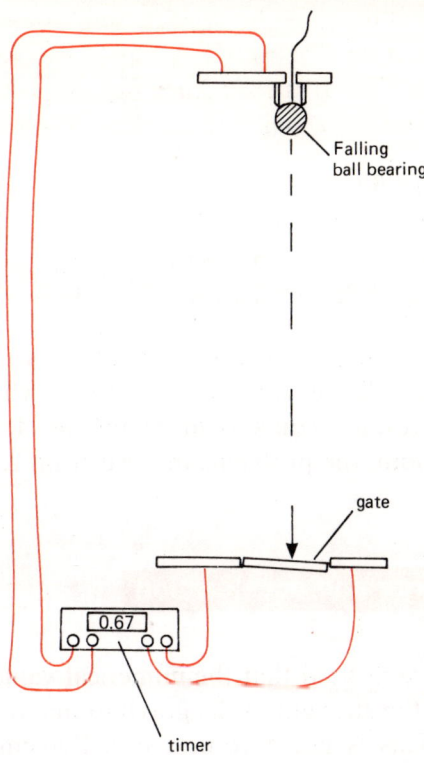

Figure 2.7 Finding a value for *g*

as shown in Figure 2.8. The rate of change of speed, the acceleration, is the slope. So

$$a = v/t \quad \text{or} \quad v = at$$

The distance fallen is given by the shaded area (see Unit 1). So

$$\text{distance fallen, } s = \frac{1}{2} \times at \times t$$

$$= \frac{1}{2}at^2$$

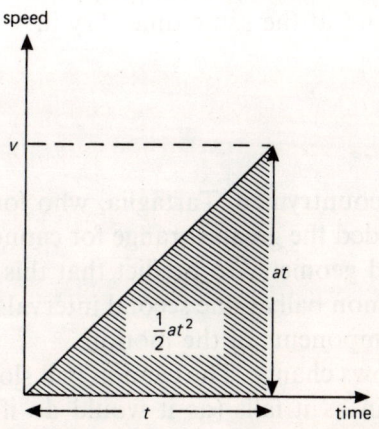

Figure 2.8

and rearranging

$$a = \frac{2s}{t^2}$$

Typical results and calculation
Free-fall distance = 2.16 m. Average time taken = 0.67 s

$$a = \frac{2s}{t^2} = \frac{2 \times 2.16}{(0.67)^2} = \underline{9.6 \text{ m/s}^2}$$

Repeated accurate measurements show that **9.81 m/s²** is the acceleration of free fall in the British Isles. There are several reasons why a college experiment might give inaccurate results. You should be able to identify one or two. Think about the air in the room, the problems in measuring 2.16 metres, the accuracy of the timer.

2.5 Gravitational force and acceleration

You will no doubt have noticed that the numerical value for the acceleration of free fall is the same as the strength of the gravitational pull on a 1 kg mass. They are both about 9.8. This is not a coincidence. Remembering the relationship between force, mass and acceleration it becomes clear that if gravity forces a 1 kg mass with a 9.8 N force, the acceleration will be 9.8 m/s².

$$\text{acceleration} = \frac{\text{force}}{\text{mass}} = \frac{9.8 \text{ N}}{1 \text{ kg}} = \underline{9.8 \text{ m/s}^2 = g}$$

also, for a 4 kg mass weighing 39.2 N:

$$\text{acceleration} = \frac{\text{force}}{\text{mass}} = \frac{39.2 \text{ N}}{4 \text{ kg}} = \underline{9.8 \text{ m/s}^2 = g}$$

So although greater masses weigh more, their acceleration due to gravity will always be 9.8 m/s² (about 10 m/s²). Two unequal masses, released at the same time, should hit the ground at the same time. Try it.

2.6 Ballistics

It was one of Galileo's countrymen, Tartaglia, who found that an initial firing angle of 45 degrees provided the greatest range for cannon balls. Galileo used his knowledge of gravity and geometry to predict that this would be the case.

Figure 2.9 shows a cannon ball at one second intervals during its motion. Lines help to show the two components of the motion.

The **vertical motion** shows change. The cannon ball slows down as it gets higher and then speeds up again as it falls (as it would do if it were fired vertically). Gravity is responsible for this vertical acceleration of 9.8 m/s².

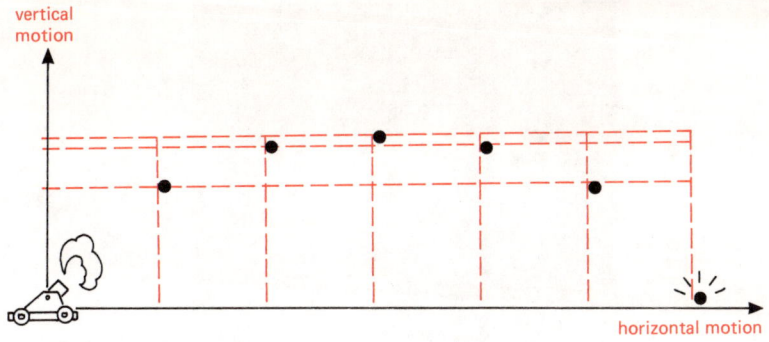

Figure 2.9 Gravity affects only the vertical motion

The **horizontal motion** is constant. Gravity does not act horizontally. The cannon ball moves equal horizontal distances each second. Its horizontal velocity is constant.

2.7 Resistance to motion, air resistance

Unfortunately the real world is not as simple as we would like. Real objects, especially lightweight ones, never go as far as we might predict. A falling feather will not accelerate at 9.8 m/s^2. Does this mean that gravity is selective and only works on heavy objects? Not at all. Feathers and cannon balls move through air. The air gets in the way and provides a resistive force which always acts against the direction of motion. Some examples of this resistance, often called air resistance, are shown in Figure 2.10.

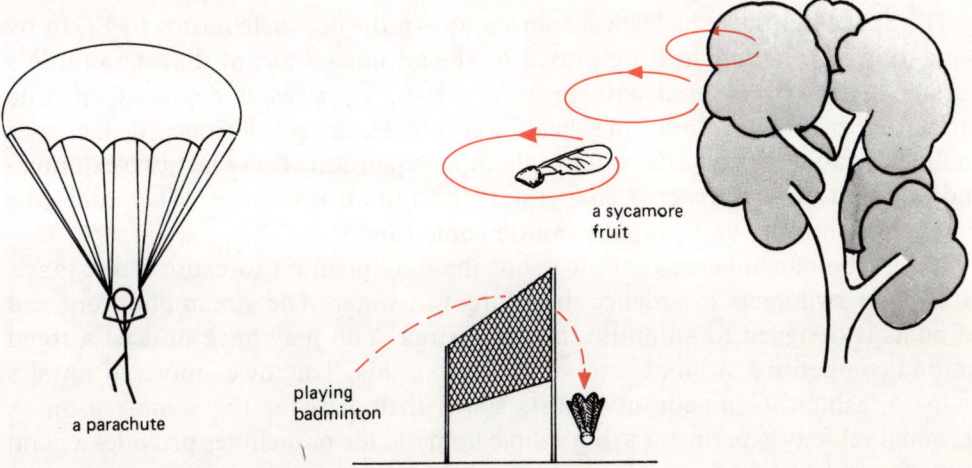

Figure 2.10 Everyday examples of terminal velocity

The resistance caused by air does have its uses. A parachute is designed to deliberately slow down a falling sky-diver to a steady speed, called his **terminal**

Figure 2.11 The 'Space Shuttle' had to be protected from the heating effect of wind resistance

velocity. The shape of a parachute determines how much air resistance there will be and how slow the terminal velocity will be.

The Space Shuttle vehicles were slowed down during their return to Earth by wind drag. The intense heating caused by the air impact meant that the shuttle's surface had to be covered with protective tiles. To a lesser degree, Concorde aircraft experience wind resistance heating effects. The length of Concorde increases in flight by about 30 cm as a result of thermal expansion. These last two examples indicate that there are energy changes involved in air resistance. Where does the energy which heats up the space shuttle come from?

It must be remembered that air is not the only medium to cause a resistance. Boats and swimmers experience drag forces in water. The streamline front end of boats is designed to minimise the water drag. You may have noticed a trend among competitive swimmers to shave their heads. This owes more to physics than to fashion. Competition cyclists shave their legs for the same reason. A terminal velocity experiment using simple home-made parachutes provides a good topic for an investigation.

2.8 Velocity—time graphs and free fall

The motions of objects in free fall, objects thrown upwards and objects experiencing resistance to motion can all be displayed on velocity/time graphs.

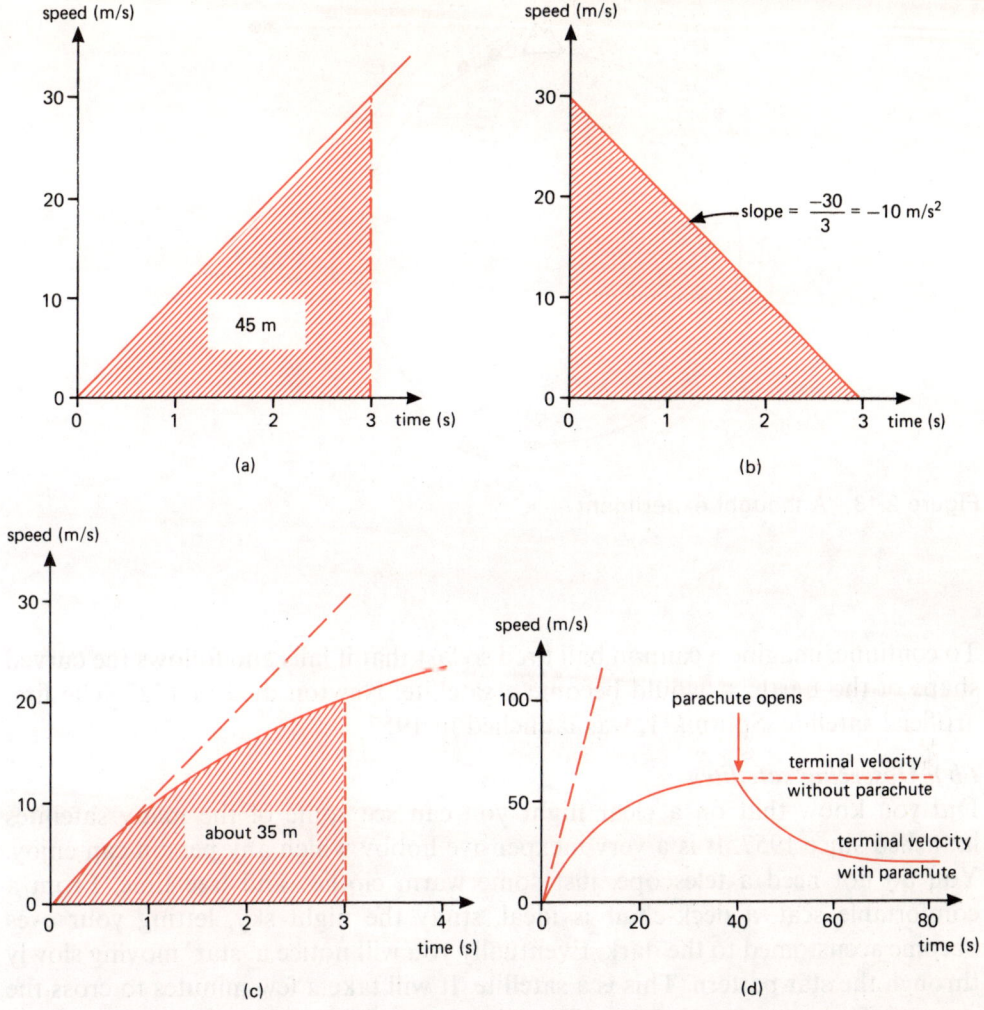

Figure 2.12 (a) A smooth stone falling from a high clifftop (ignoring air resistance). (b) A smooth stone thrown upwards into the air (ignoring air resistance). (c) A stone falling through the air. (d) A free-fall parachute sky-diver

These graphs were introduced in Unit 1. As an exercise, study each of the situations in Figure 2.12 and write down or explain to a friend exactly what stories the graphs tell. (Think about balanced and unbalanced forces, accelerations and imagine what is actually happening in each case.)

2.9 Related reading: Satellites

(a) Thinking about satellites

Imagine a cannon ball fired from a hilltop. The path it takes, a parabola, is caused by the acceleration due to gravity. A faster cannon ball travels further but is still accelerated by gravity. This 'thought experiment' was first reported by Newton.

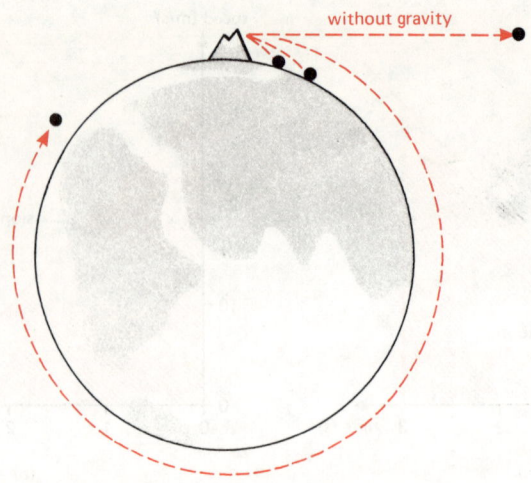

Figure 2.13 A thought experiment

To continue, imagine a cannon ball fired so fast that it falls and follows the curved shape of the Earth. It would become a satellite. Newton died in 1727. The first artificial satellite, Sputnik 1, was launched in 1957.

(b) Observing satellites

Did you know that on a clear night you can see some of the many satellites launched since 1957. It is a very inexpensive hobby which any person can enjoy. You do not need a telescope, just some warm clothes and free time. From a comfortable seat, a deck-chair is ideal, study the night sky, letting your eyes become accustomed to the dark. Eventually you will notice a 'star' moving slowly through the star pattern. This is a satellite. It will take a few minutes to cross the sky and if you are patient you will see it return after an orbit in about an hour.

Details of particular satellites can sometimes be found in the weather section of newspapers.

(c) Forces and satellites

Most of us have seen films of astronauts in their 'weightless' environments. A common misunderstanding which results from these experiences is to think that the astronauts are weightless because there is no gravity in space. This could not be further from the truth.

Referring back to the thought experiment, the very reason that satellites keep orbiting the Earth is because gravity is attracting them and forcing them towards the Earth. Without gravity the satellites would move in a straight line. We say that gravity provides the necessary **centripetal** force needed to pull the satellite towards the Earth.

The weightless experience is the effect of the astronauts and their vehicle freely falling towards the Earth. It would be the same effect as in a freely falling lift. In fact, to train astronauts they are taken to great heights in planes which then freely fall to Earth in order to create a spacelike environment.

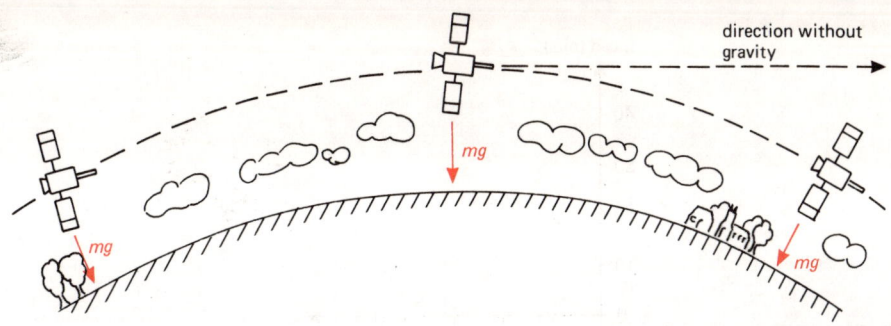

Figure 2.14 Satellites are constantly accelerating towards the centre of the Earth

2.10 Summary

- *Gravitational forces are weak attractive forces and exist between all masses.*
- *The forces increase with greater masses and smaller separations.*
- *The gravitational field strength at the Earth's surface, g, is 9.8 N/kg ($g \simeq 10$ N/kg).*
- *The force due to gravity gives any mass its* **weight**:

$$Weight = m \times g$$

- *The acceleration due to gravity at the Earth's surface is 9.8 m/s^2 ($g \simeq 10$ m/s^2). It is the same for all masses.*
- *Air resistance to motion causes bodies to reach their* **terminal velocity.**

2.11 Progress questions

(take $g = 10$ N/kg on the surface of the Earth)

1. How much will a 9 kg bag of shopping weigh
   (a) on the Moon, (b) on Earth, (c) on Jupiter?
2. (a) If you dropped a 1 kg bag of sugar, what would its acceleration be?
   (b) Sketch a velocity/time graph to show the motion of the bag of sugar in the first second of its fall.
   (c) Would these answers change if you were shopping on the Moon?
3. Outline the features of an experiment you would carry out to find an accurate value for the acceleration due to gravity. Where would you expect most error to arise? How could you improve on the method?

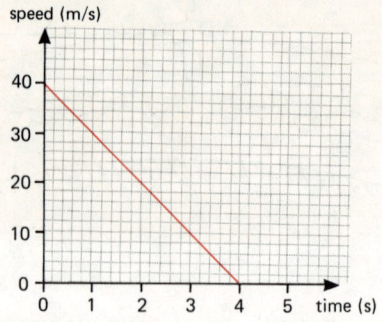

Figure 2.15

4. Figure 2.15 shows a speed/time graph of an object, mass 3 kg, which was thrown vertically upwards. Say what you can about the motion of the object. How far did it go? Did it accelerate? What forces were acting on it?
5. Calculations using the height of rainclouds show that a typical raindrop should reach the ground with a speed of about 60 m/s. If this were the case then we would suffer considerable headaches when it rains. Can you explain why it is safe to go out when it rains?
6. Take a friend out one evening to see a satellite. Try to explain to your friend, or to yourself, why the satellite goes round in an orbit.

ATOMS, MOLECULES AND MODELS

3

3.1 Questions and answers

People interested in science are forever asking questions. Some questions like 'what is the maximum weight which a rope can hold?' have straightforward answers. A simple experiment will provide the answer. 'How long does it take an object to fall 23 metres?' is another question which is easily answered by calculation or by an experiment. What about a question like 'why is a lead pipe so much heavier than a copper pipe?' or 'Why does water form drops?'

The answers to these questions cannot be discovered by experimenting. In fact, the answers are not discovered but are invented. Whenever scientists are faced with problems which cannot be solved by experimenting they often create their own answers by thinking up **theories**. There are theories about the Universe which help to answer questions about space. On the very small scale there are theories about things which are too small to be seen. The **particle theory of matter** is a theory which this unit will deal with.

3.2 Thinking about particles

From a distance a sandy beach looks smooth and solid. A closer inspection reveals millions of tiny grains of sand. If we could look more closely at one grain of sand would we see that one grain itself is made of millions of particles?

It is said that a Greek called Democritus first considered this problem over 2000 years ago. He imagined what would happen if things were divided in half, then half again, and again, and so on. To avoid his **'thought experiment'** going on

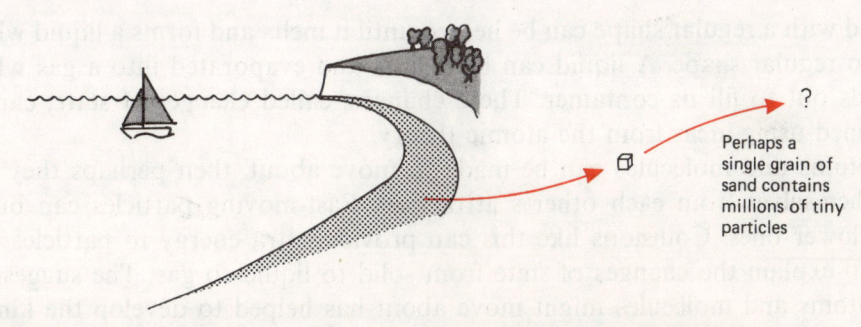

Figure 3.1 Smaller and smaller. Just what is smaller than a grain of sand?

Perhaps a single grain of sand contains millions of tiny particles forever, Democritus suggested that there would be a stage when the smallest indivisible particle would be reached. He called this an **atom**.

For Democritus the idea of atoms being the smallest particles helped to answer important questions about what things were made of. By the end of the 18th century the **atomic theory** was being used in physics and chemistry to explain why substances behaved as they did. To this day the atomic theory, involving atoms and groups of atoms called **molecules**, is one of the most important theories in science.

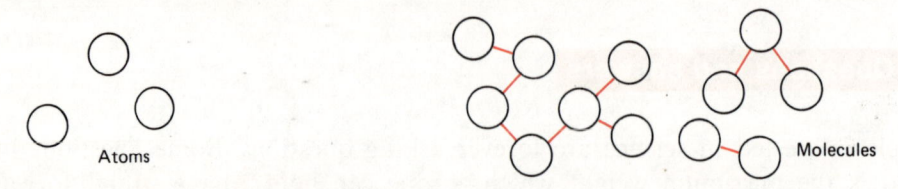

Figure 3.2 Simple models of atoms and molecules

3.3 Models of atoms and molecules

In any supermarket or greengrocer's shop you will see the ways in which lots of small items, apples, oranges or tomatoes, for example, can be piled together. The patterns they make can be recreated in the laboratory using expanded polystyrene spheres or soap bubbles. These natural arrangements provide us with a **model** of how atoms might arrange themselves in solids.

One success of atomic theory is its ability to explain the regular shapes of crystals. If all particles in a solid attract each other, then the flat sides and geometric shapes of crystals can be explained by the regular arrangements of atoms which attract each other to form a solid. Crystals can be easily **cleaved** in certain directions. The atomic theory suggests that the regular rows of atoms in crystals are the cause of this.

3.4 Molecules in liquids and gases

A solid with a regular shape can be heated until it melts and forms a liquid which has no regular shape. A liquid can be heated and evaporated into a gas which spreads out to fill its container. These changes, called **changes of state**, can be explained using ideas from the atomic theory.

If atoms and molecules can be made to move about, then perhaps they can free themselves from each other's attraction. Fast-moving particles can bump into slower ones. Collisions like this can provide extra energy to particles and help to explain the changes of state from solid to liquid to gas. The suggestion that atoms and molecules might move about has helped to develop the **kinetic theory** of matter (kinetic means moving).

'Cleaving' a crystal — explained using a model

(a)

(b)

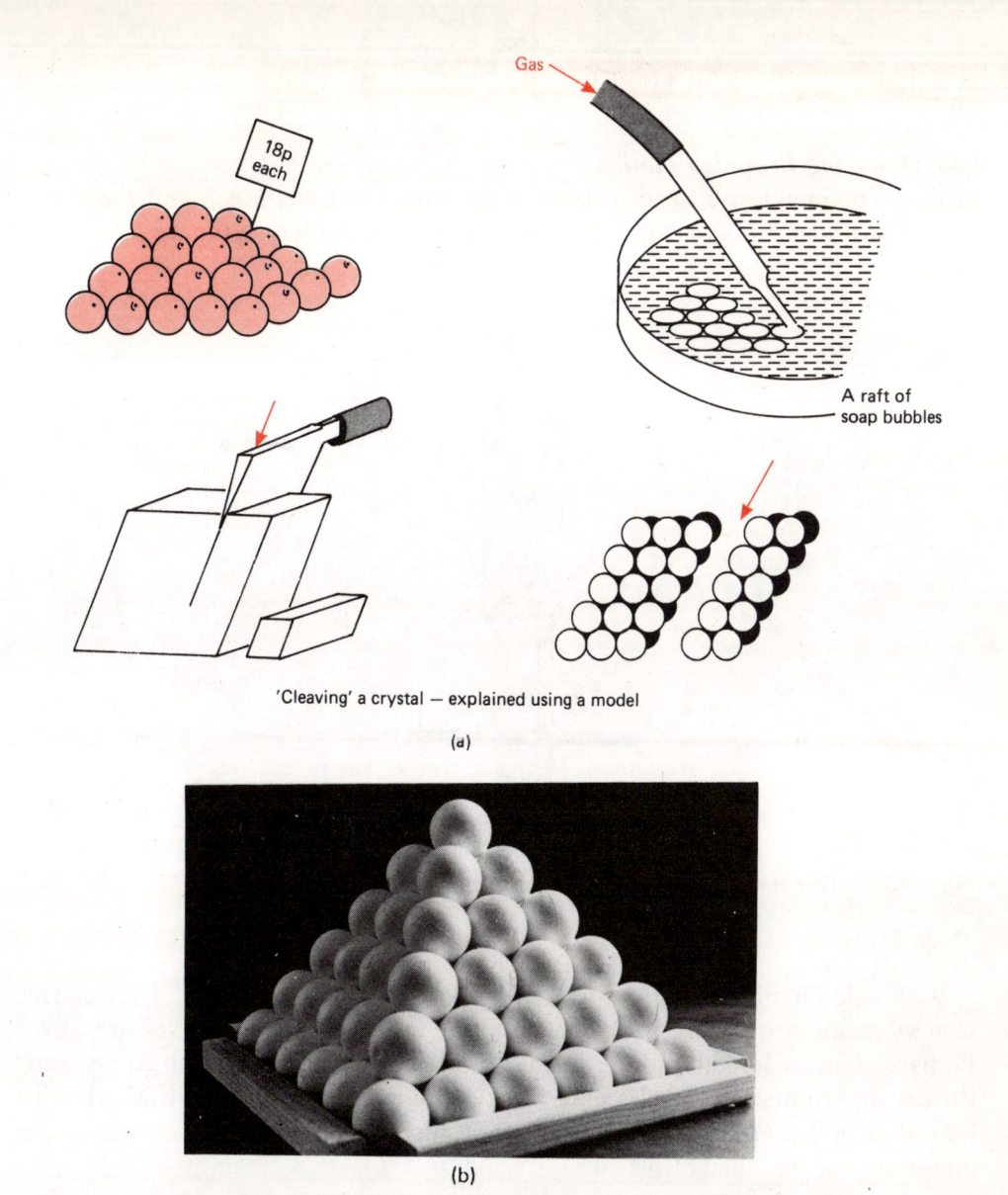

Figure 3.3 Identical particles form simple shapes

Molecules in a solid

Molecules in a liquid

Molecules in a gas

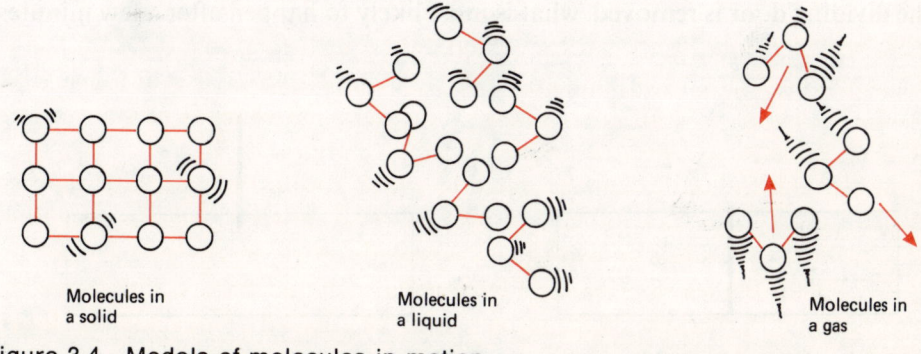

Figure 3.4 Models of molecules in motion

3.5 Some experiments to support the kinetic theory

(a) Observing Brownian motion

In this experiment you need to trap some smoke in a glass cell and look at it magnified under a microscope. The main stages are shown in Figure 3.5.

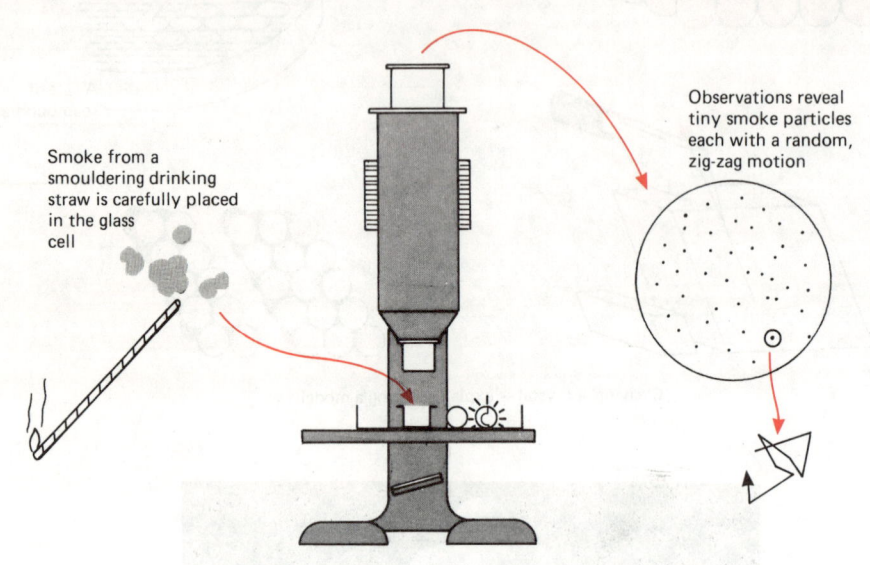

Figure 3.5 Observing Brownian motion in the laboratory

With side illumination, the tiny smoke particles look like stars. They can be seen vibrating around in an irregular way. Perhaps smoke particles are alive? Perhaps there is something else in the smoke cell, things too small to be seen? Robert Brown first recorded seeing this type of **random motion** in 1827 when he looked at pollen grains in water through a microscope. Why is this observation important for the kinetic theory?

(b) An experiment for your thoughts

Imagine a box containing two halves. A different type of gas occupies each half. If the dividing door is removed, what is most likely to happen after a few minutes?

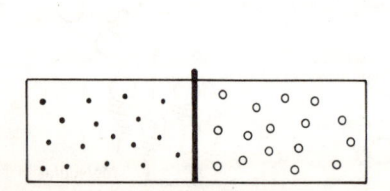

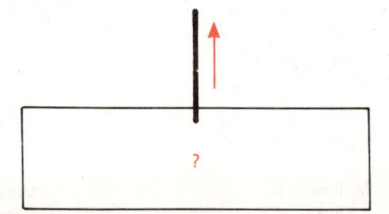

Figure 3.6 A thought experiment

(c) The size of a molecule

Oil floats on water. Oil consists of long molecules, each with one end which is attracted to water. As a result, oil spreads out over a clean water surface to form an oil slick which is only one molecule thick. A small drop of oil on the tip of a wire can spread into a large slick.

Estimate the volume of oil in your drop

wire

Spread the oil over a clean water surface. Measure the area of spread

oil drop

AREA

ruler

Volume of oil drop = Volume of oil slick
Volume = Area × Thickness
Volume = Area × L
$$\frac{Volume}{Area} = L$$

L is about the length of an oil molecule

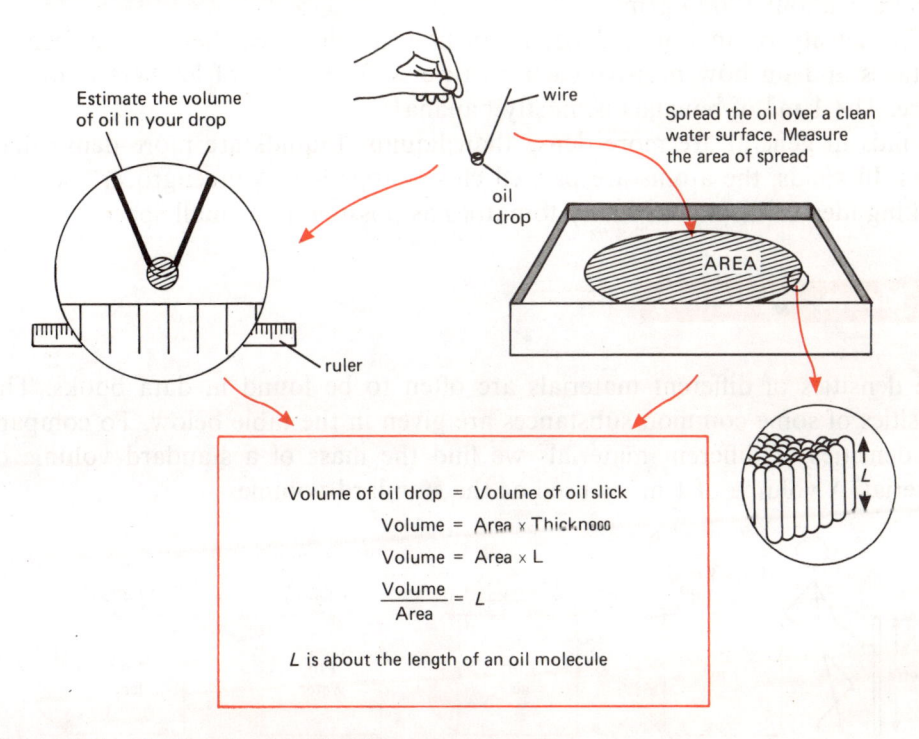

Figure 3.7   Finding the length of an oil molecule

3.6 Particles and density

Which weighs more: 1 kg of bananas or 1 kg of feathers? The answer to this very old question is that they weigh the same. Their weights, $m \times g$, are both about 10 newtons. They have the same **mass** and would balance each other on a see-saw

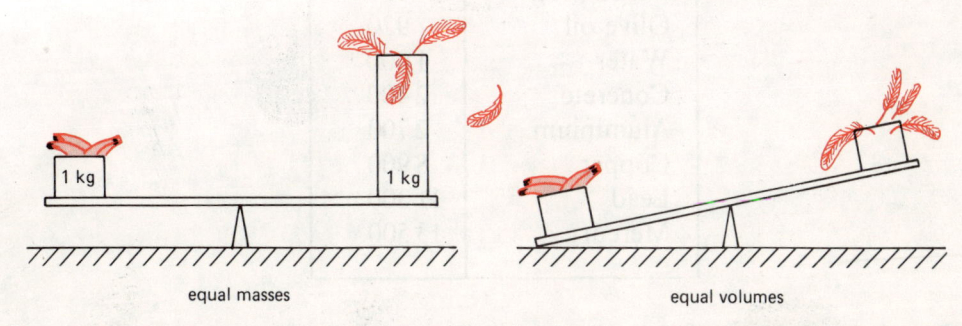

1 kg   1 kg

equal masses   equal volumes

Figure 3.8   Bananas are more dense than feathers

balance. The difference between 1 kg of bananas and 1 kg of feathers is in the volume that they occupy. 1 kg of feathers occupies a much larger **volume** than 1 kg of bananas. This is because bananas are more **dense** than feathers.

Now if we considered equal volumes, say 1 m³ of each, then the bananas would have a mass of about 1000 kg and the feathers about 10 kg. The **density** of a banana is about 1000 kg/m³.

The density of an object depends on how much space there is between its particles and on how massive each particle is. The 1 m³ of feathers is mostly space. The 1 m³ of bananas is mostly banana!

Solids in general are more dense than liquids. Liquids are more dense than gases. In solids, the atoms are packed closely together. A greengrocer uses this packing idea to display as many tomatoes as possible in a small space.

3.7 Measuring density

The densities of different materials are often to be found in data books. The densities of some common substances are given in the table below. To compare the densities of different materials we find the mass of a standard volume of material. A volume of 1 m³ is used as the standard volume.

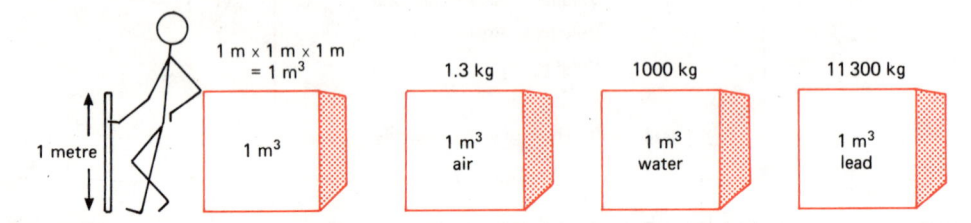

Figure 3.9 Comparing densities

Material	Density (kg/m³)
Helium	0.18
Air	1.3
Wood (oak)	650
Olive oil	920
Water	1 000
Concrete	2 400
Aluminium	2 700
Copper	8 900
Lead	11 300
Mercury	13 500

The density of an object can be calculated once measurements have been made of the object's mass and volume. Density is related to mass and volume by the relationship:

$$\text{density (kg/m}^3\text{)} = \frac{\text{mass (kg)}}{\text{volume (m}^3\text{)}}$$

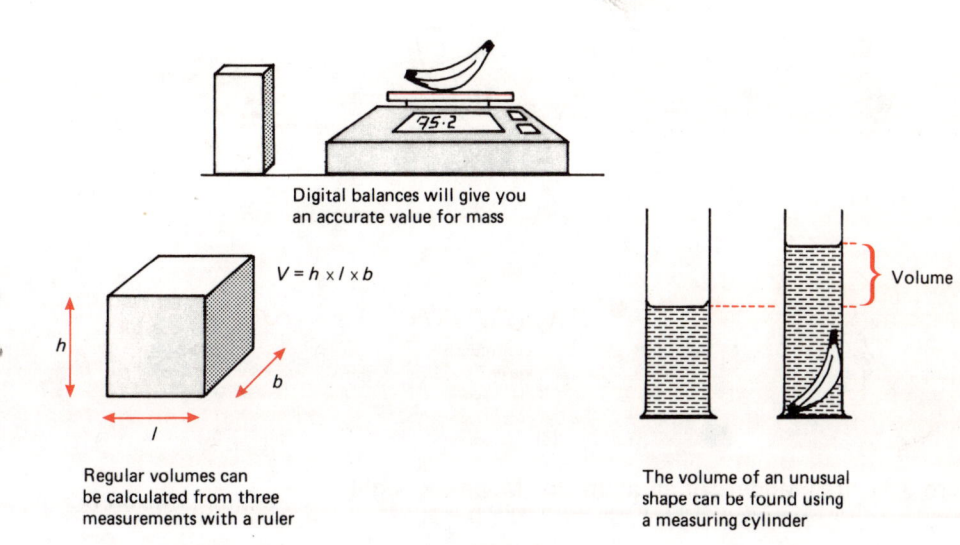

Digital balances will give you an accurate value for mass

$V = h \times l \times b$

Volume

Regular volumes can be calculated from three measurements with a ruler

The volume of an unusual shape can be found using a measuring cylinder

Figure 3.10 Finding densities in the laboratory

If you take measurements using grams and centimetres you will need to convert to kilograms and metres. Some useful conversions are:

$$1 \text{ cm} = 0.01 \text{ m}$$
$$1 \text{ g} = 0.001 \text{ kg}$$
$$1 \text{ cm}^3 = 0.000\,001 \text{ m}^3$$
$$1 \text{ g/cm}^3 = 1000 \text{ kg/m}^3$$

3.8 Related reading: Worlds within worlds—more models

The simple atomic theory of atoms as hard spheres has served science well for over 2000 years. In the last 100 years the advanced technologies of vacuum techniques, particle accelerators and computer-controlled experiments have directed attention to particles which are smaller than atoms. A whole new world of sub-atomic particles has emerged with new results requiring new models.

(a) The changing face of an atom

Professor J. J. Thomson helped to revive ideas about atoms in 1909 when he proposed a model of an atom consisting of charged particles, He called the negative charges **electrons**. Ernest Rutherford introduced the idea of a positively charged central **nucleus** in about 1910, and in 1932 James Chadwick proposed the existence of neutral particles called **neutrons**. While all this was happening, Niels Bohr in 1910 was suggesting that electrons arrange themselves in orbits around the nucleus, and other workers were trying to think of electrons as waves. The start of this century was a time of great change in ideas about atoms.

(a)

particles   continuous wave   photons

(b)

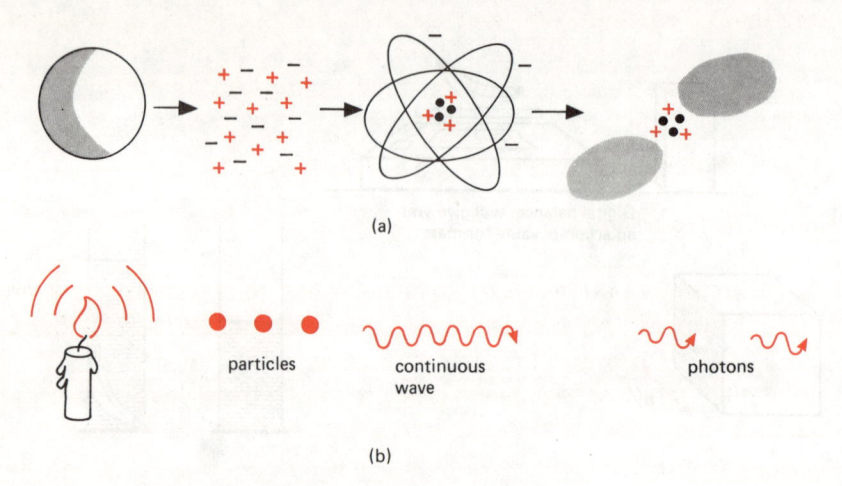

Figure 3.11 (a) Models of an atom. (b) Models of light

Figure 3.12 Evidence for new particles is found in the tracks made by high-speed collisions

(b) Particles or waves?

Isaac Newton suggested that light consisted of a stream of 'corpuscles'. In 1905 Albert Einstein used the idea that light was 'lumpy' to explain the fact that light could knock electrons out of some metals. This was the photoelectric effect. The lumps of light were called **photons**. At about the same time Max Planck was proposing that all energies could be regarded at the smallest level as lumps called **quanta**. To understand the **quantum theory**, we have to be prepared to think about particles acting like waves and waves acting like particles. Even sound waves can be thought of as particles called phonons! Modern physicists have to be able to think about wave-like particles!

(c) High-energy physics

In laboratories throughout the world, particles are being fired through particle **accelerators** at targets to see what happens when particles collide. Fragments smaller than protons have been discovered, some lasting less than a second. These **elementary particles** are encouraging physicists to try out new models for the atom based on a family of fundamental particles called **quarks**. The story goes on.

3.9 Summary

- *All things are thought to be made up of tiny particles called atoms and molecules.*
- *Atoms and molecules naturally arrange themselves into simple patterns. Models can show these arrangements.*
- *Changes of state, crystals and density can be explained simply using models of molecules.*
- *Brownian motion can be explained using ideas from the kinetic theory.*
- *The density of a substance is found by measuring mass and volume:*

$$density = \frac{mass}{volume}$$

3.10 Progress questions

1. Draw diagrams to show how particles are arranged in
   (a) a crystal
   (b) a drop of water
   (c) air in a bicycle tyre.
2. Arrange the following materials in order of increasing density (lowest density first):

   water, olive oil, aluminium, lead, hydrogen

3. You can see right through air. Air appears to be nothing. How could you explain to a friend that air is more than nothing?
4. In a restaurant the smell of fish and chips finds its way naturally from the kitchen to the dining area. How do you think this happens?

5. Wood floats on water. Warm air floats on top of cold air. What is the connection between these two facts?
6. The dimensions of a block of aluminium are given below. The block is placed in a measuring cylinder containing water.
   (a) What is the volume of the block in cm^3?
   (b) What would be the level of the water in the second measuring cylinder diagram of Figure 3.13?

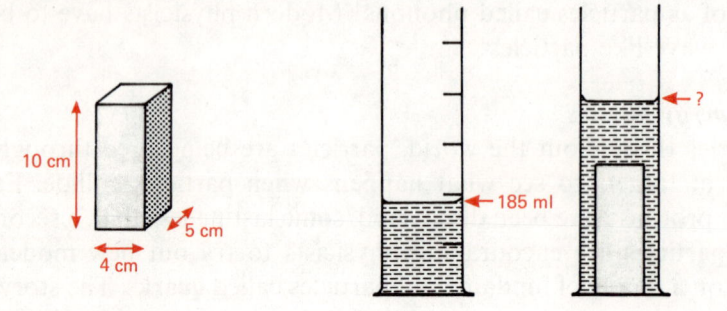

Figure 3.13

(c) The block was found to have a mass of 540 g. What do these results give as the density of aluminium?

4 STRETCHING SOLID MATERIALS

4.1 A material fit for the job

Rubber is a useful material but it would be no good for making knives and forks. Cutlery needs to be **stiff** with a **hard** cutting edge. Steel is used for cutlery but a car with steel tyres would give a bumpy ride and damage the road. Tyres need to be **flexible** and **tough**. Hardness, stiffness, toughness and flexibility are physical properties of materials. No material has all these properties. It is the task of the design engineer to select a material which has properties suited to a particular job. This Unit is about how you can test materials in the laboratory and what the results of your tests might mean. A number of new terms will be introduced. You will find a list of terms and meanings in Unit 5 (Section 5.5).

4.2 Stretching springs

Springs are cheap and have a variety of uses ranging from keeping a garden gate closed to storing energy in a clockwork toy. Springs used in a motor car suspension are very stiff. The spring which makes an ammeter needle return to zero is not stiff at all. In the laboratory, masses can be carefully added to a spring to see the effects of stretching. Before you start to stretch a spring remember:

i. Measure the original length of the unstretched spring before you start.
ii. Each 100 g mass will force the spring with a force of about one newton.
iii. 1 mm is the same as 0.001 m.

The slope or gradient of the graph can be measured. This tells you how stiff the spring is. The stiffness, k, is known as the **spring constant**. For Figure 4.1 the spring constant, k, is:

$$k = \frac{\text{force}}{\text{extension}} = \frac{10 \text{ N}}{20 \text{ cm}} = \frac{10 \text{ N}}{0.2 \text{ m}} = 50 \text{ N/m}$$

It was the scientist Robert Hooke who in 1678 realised that the force on a spring was proportional to the spring's extension. The relationship **force** = k × **extension** is known as **Hooke's Law**.

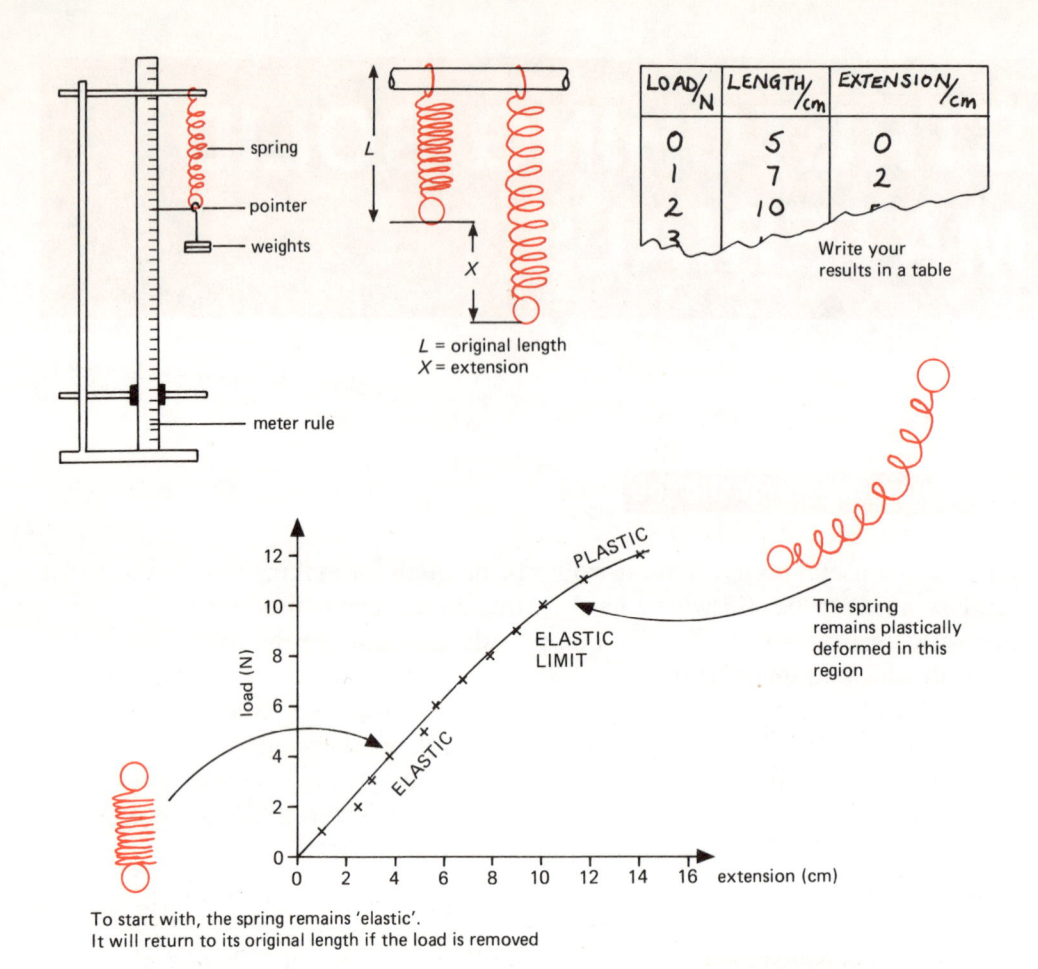

Figure 4.1 Stretching springs in the laboratory

LOAD/N	LENGTH/cm	EXTENSION/cm
0	5	0
1	7	2
2	10	
3		

Write your results in a table

L = original length
X = extension

To start with, the spring remains 'elastic'. It will return to its original length if the load is removed

The spring remains plastically deformed in this region

4.3 Stretching two springs

Two springs can be joined together in different ways. The results for stretching a two spring combination show that two springs connected in '**series**' are much easier to stretch than two springs in '**parallel**'.

Some springs are designed to be compressed as well as stretched. Most car bodies are suspended on wheels by four compression springs, one at each roadwheel. You may have a car or perhaps your friends, parents or teacher have one. Why not find the stiffness of a car spring? You need to know the weights of the passengers and the distance moved by the car body when they all climb inside.

You will notice that when people get out of a car, the level of the car rises again as the springs return to their original shape. We call this behaviour **elastic**. You will probably have noticed that all springs have this elastic property. There is a limit to how far you can stretch any spring and still expect it to return to its original length. When a spring is stretched beyond its elastic limit it becomes permanently deformed. This is called **plastic** behaviour.

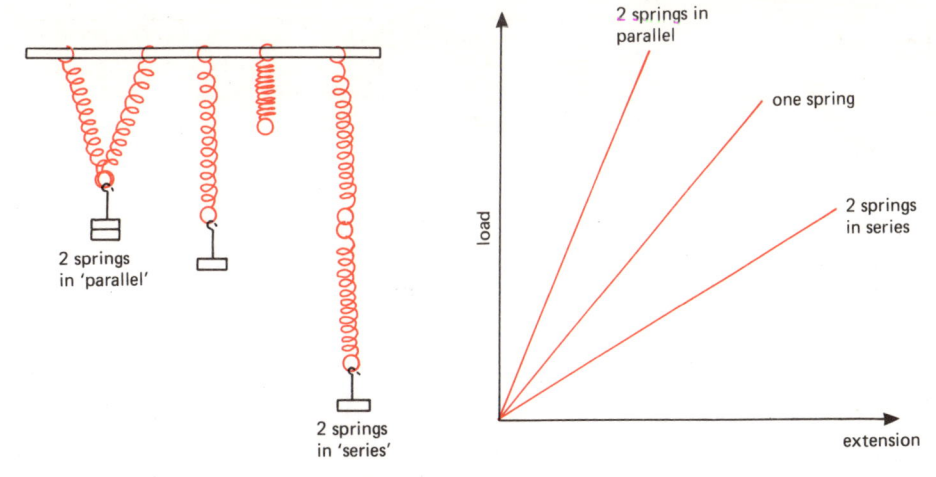

Figure 4.2 Springs in series and in parallel

Figure 4.3 Finding the stiffness of a car's suspension

4.4 Stretching a metal wire

The metal wire of a guitar string is being stretched constantly. We say that the wire is in a state of **tension**. Other examples of wires in tension are the wires holding up a lift in a department store and the steel wire of a crane on a building site. In the laboratory, a copper wire can be stretched and its extensions measured. One way to do this is shown in Figure 4.4. Students should wear goggles to protect themselves from the wire in case it breaks. A soft foam pad placed underneath the masses will protect them from impact with the floor.

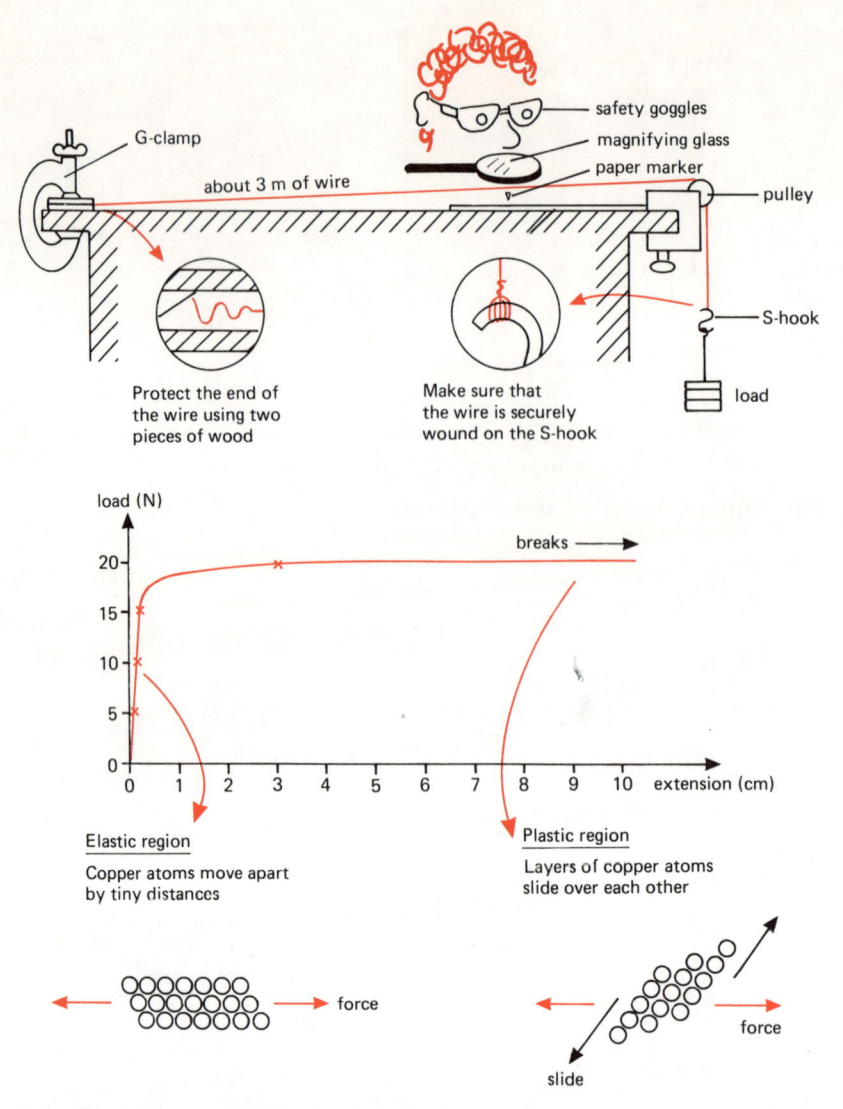

Figure 4.4 Stretching a metal wire in the laboratory

4.5 Stretching rubber bands

Modern 'rubber' bands are not made of rubber but from a number of man-made materials which behave like natural rubber. These man-made materials are called **polymers** and consist of very long molecules which can be tangled up or straightened out. Each polymer molecule may have over a thousand atoms making up a chain.

Hang your rubber band from a clampstand and measure the extensions produced by adding extra masses. Figure 4.5 shows how a rubber band might behave as it is stretched.

You will notice that a rubber band can extend to many times its original length before becoming very stiff. This change can be explained by thinking of the

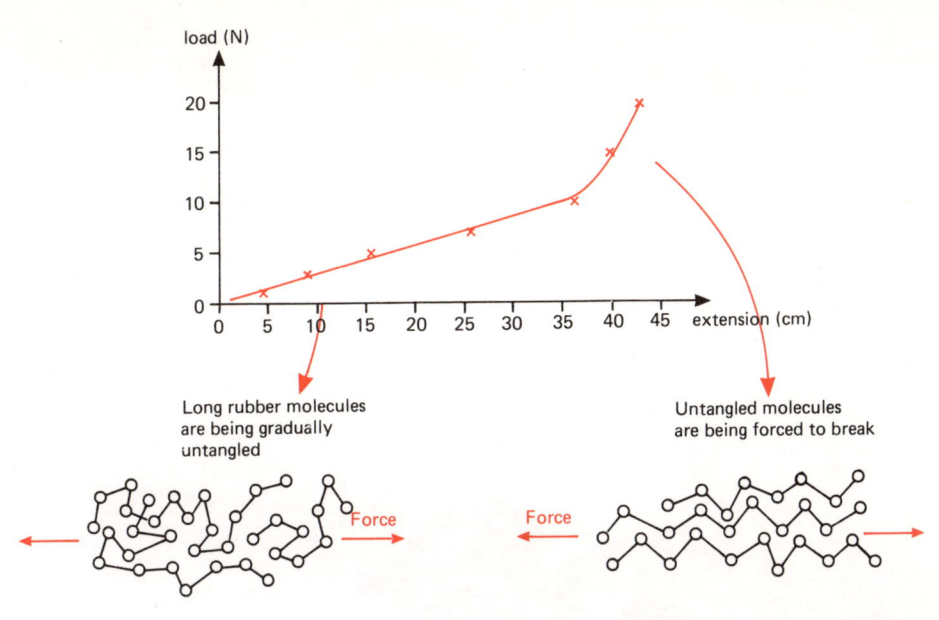

Figure 4.5 Polymer molecules help to explain the stretching of a rubber band

long-chain polymer molecules. In their relaxed state these molecules are tangled up in a random way. They easily untangle themselves as the rubber stretches. Fully untangled polymer molecules are difficult to separate because of the very large forces between the individual atoms in the molecule.

4.6 Glass and concrete. Ceramic materials

Metals and polymers are two families of materials. Glass and concrete belong to the family of materials called ceramics. The molecules in a ceramic material are arranged neither in long chains nor in regular crystalline planes. Ceramic materials consist of small molecules which are joined in an irregular way and are bound together by strong forces.

Ceramic materials are very stiff. It is very difficult to rearrange the molecules in glass or concrete. Ceramic materials do have one major weakness, cracks. Once a crack appears on the surface of a ceramic material a small tension force will make the crack spread right across the entire specimen. Glass-cutters and tile-cutters work on this principle. We use the word **brittle** to describe a material which cracks easily and breaks without deforming.

Because of the weakness caused by cracks, ceramic materials are rarely used in tension. The real strength of ceramics is in their ability to withstand large **compressive** forces. The compressive strength of concrete is used to support most modern buildings. Concrete foundations are laid down before any bricks can be arranged and walls built. The architects of the ancient Greek temples and of the world's cathedrals have all used the compressive strength of stone.

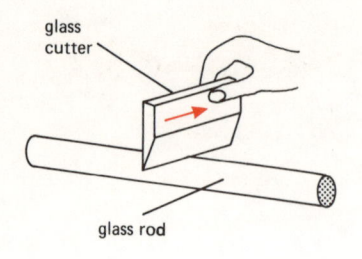

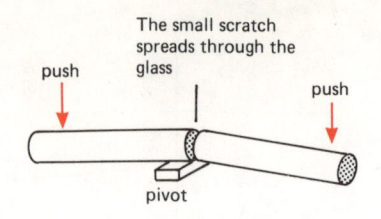

Figure 4.6 (a) Using a glass cutter. (b) Crushing a concrete block (notice the crack starting at the bottom)

4.7 Bending beams

A stretched wire is in tension. A squeezed concrete block is under compression. What forces act when a beam is forced to bend? How is the bending force related to the beam's deflection? You can set up a beam bending experiment in the classroom. A metre rule, a fallen branch of a tree or a knitting needle provide ideas for suitable beams to bend. One end of the beam needs to be securely clamped. A force/deflection graph may be plotted for a beam like the one shown in Figure 4.7.

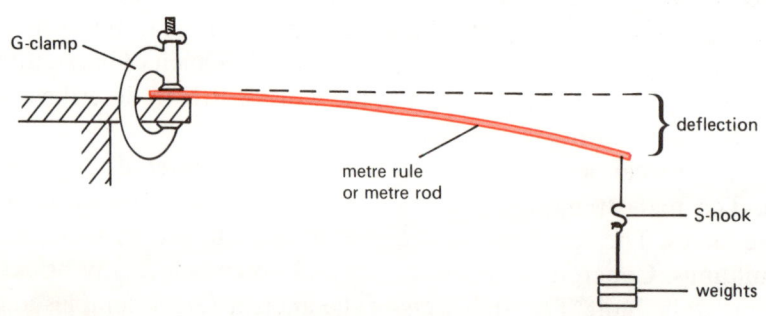

Figure 4.7 Bending a beam in the laboratory

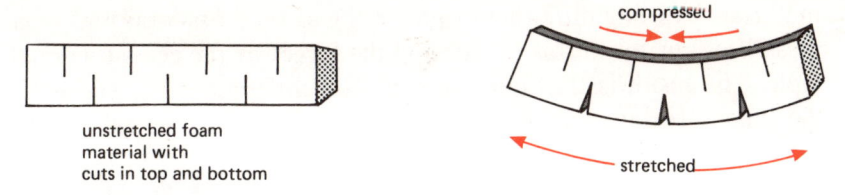

Figure 4.8 Bending results in two types of force

A piece of foam rubber helps to show how tension and compression forces act together on a bending beam. Any cracks in the beam will open up on the side under tension.

4.8 Shape, stiffness and strength

The physical behaviour of a piece of material depends on its shape. Thick samples are stiff and strong. They stretch less easily and hold more weight before breaking. To help scientists to take the shape of a sample of material into consideration the ideas of **stress** and **strain** are used.

(a) Stress

The graphs in Figure 4.9 show the effect that cross-sectional area has on the strength and stiffness of a material. It is possible to compare the stiffness of

$$\text{Stress} = \frac{\text{stretching force}}{\text{cross-sectional area}} \ (\text{N/m}^2)$$

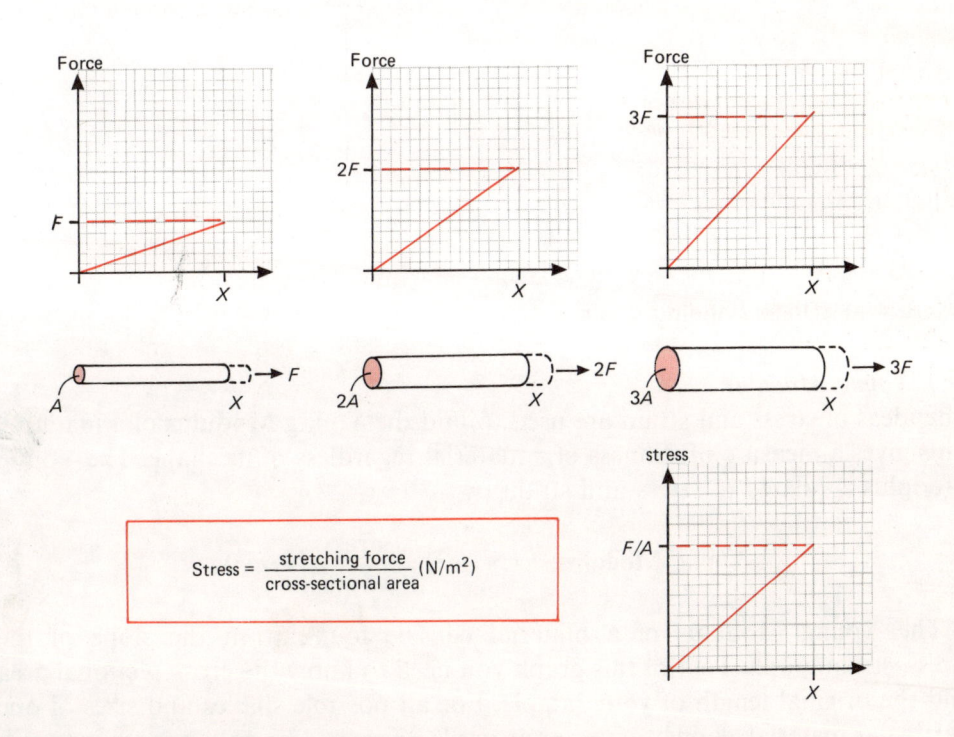

Figure 4.9 Understanding stress

different materials by imagining them to have the same cross-sectional area. The idea of stress allows us to do this by **dividing the forces by the cross-sectional area** of the sample. The result is that our samples with different cross-sectional areas all have the same stress/extension graph.

(b) Strain

Long samples of a material stretch more easily than short samples. The effects of different original lengths are shown in Figure 4.10. Strain is a way of regarding **extensions as a fraction of the original length**. The three examples in Figure 4.10 all have different extensions but have the same strain.

$$\text{strain} = \frac{\text{extension}}{\text{original length}} \quad \text{(no units)}$$

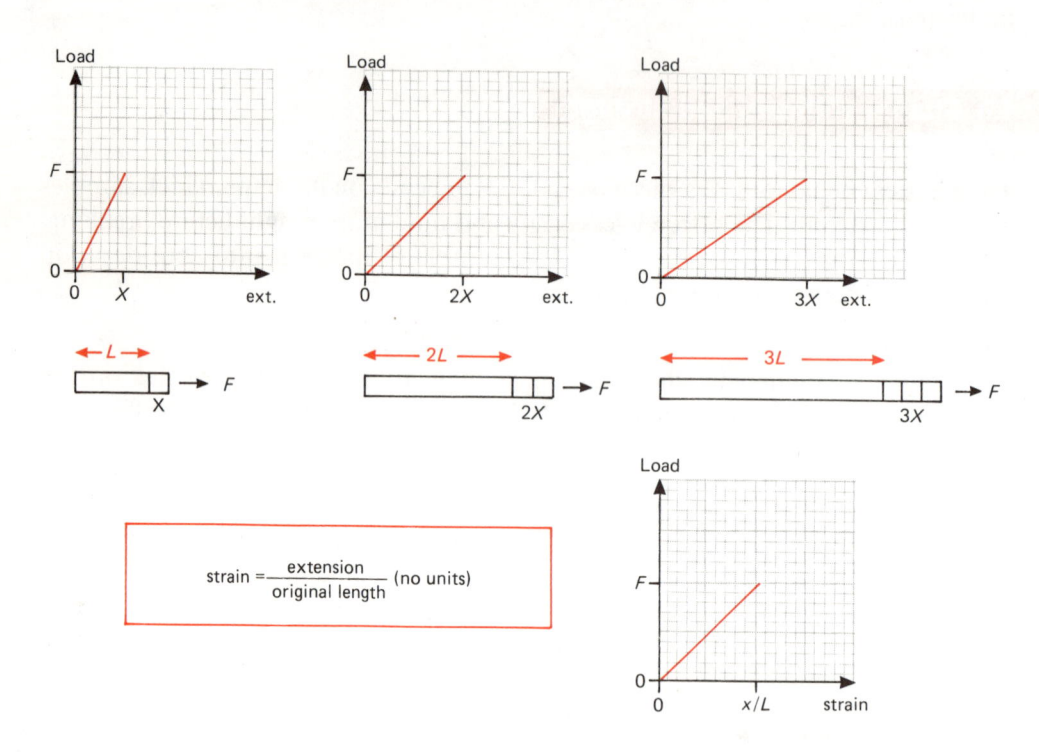

Figure 4.10 Understanding strain

(c) Young Modulus

The ideas of stress and strain are used to find the Young Modulus of a material. This gives a measure of stiffness of a material regardless of its shape. The Young Modulus is related to stress and strain by

$$\text{Young Modulus, } E(\text{N}/\text{m}^2) = \frac{\text{stress}}{\text{strain}} (\text{N}/\text{m}^2)$$

The Young Modulus of a material can be found from the slope of the stress/strain graph. To plot this graph you need to know the cross-sectional area and the original length of your sample. For all possible shapes and sizes of one particular material, copper wires for example, there will be only one stress/strain graph and only one value for the Young modulus for copper.

For copper:
$$E = \frac{\text{stress}}{\text{strain}} = \frac{10 \times 10^6}{1 \times 10^{-4}} = 1 \times 10^{11} \text{ N/m}^2$$

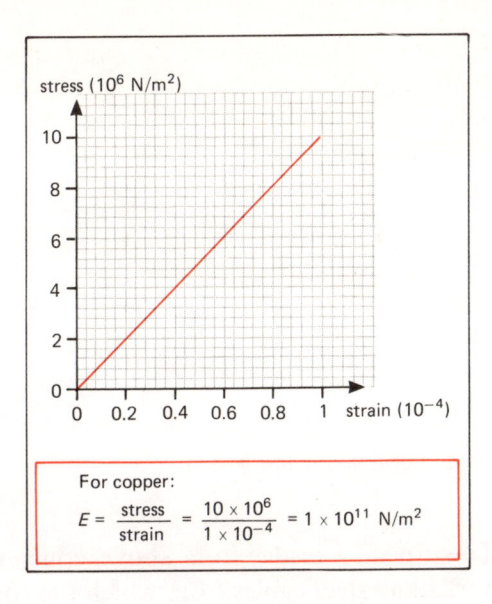

Figure 4.11 Understanding the Young Modulus

4.9 Related reading: Bridges under stress

From Richmond in Surrey to the Tower of London there are 25 bridges across the river Thames. Many have been standing for over 100 years and some are showing their age. Hammersmith bridge, built in 1887, was designed for horse-drawn transport. The heavy load of commuter traffic has caused severe damage over recent years.

The most simple kind of bridge design is the single beam. A single concrete beam is cheap and solid. However, tensile forces will soon start to open cracks underneath the beam when the bridge carries a load.

Figure 4.12 Cracks seriously weaken a single beam

To avoid this problem the concrete beam may be supported from below or suspended from above. A vertical pier, usually of concrete, can be placed under the beam. The concrete pier will be compressed by the load. Waterloo bridge, Hungerford train bridge and Putney train bridge are examples of Thames bridges

Concrete support pier in compression

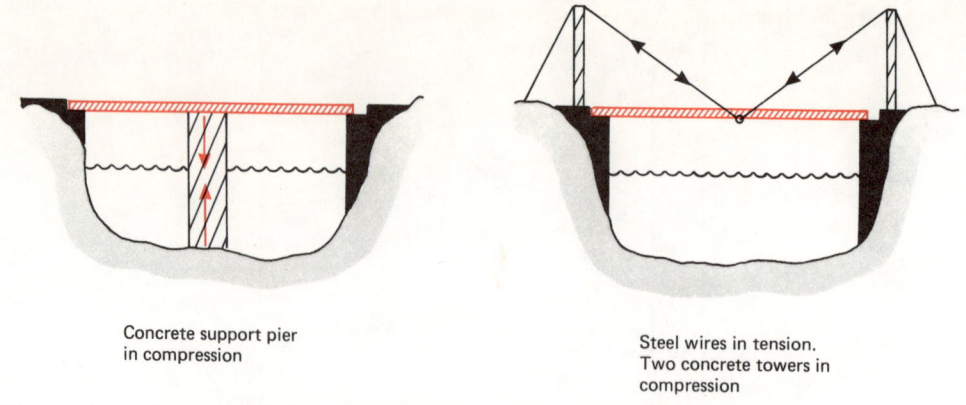

Steel wires in tension.
Two concrete towers in compression

Figure 4.13 Two ways of supporting the beam

with pier supports. To suspend a bridge from above, concrete or steel towers are used. Over these towers hang steel cables from which the roadway hangs. Tower bridge, Chelsea bridge and Hammersmith bridge are examples of suspension bridges. Steel in tension and concrete in compression remain the two main materials used in bridge building.

Figure 4.14 The Severn Bridge

4.10 Summary

- *For a spring stretched within its elastic limit, force is proportional to extension.*
- ***Elastic** behaviour is when a material returns to its original shape when released.*
  ***Plastic** behaviour is when a material remains permanently deformed.*

- *For a spring the stiffness is measured by the **spring constant**, k.*

$$k(N/m) = \frac{force\ (N)}{extension\ (m)}$$

- *The stretching of metals, polymers and ceramics can be related to changes in their molecular structure.*
- *When a material bends both compression and tension occur.*
- *Young's Modulus is given by:*

$$E(N/m^2) = \frac{stress}{strain}(N/m^2)$$

$$strain = \frac{extension\ (m)}{original\ length\ (m)}; \qquad stress = \frac{force\ (N)}{area\ (m^2)}$$

4.11 Progress questions

1. Figure 4.15 shows how the extension of a spring changed as it was stretched.

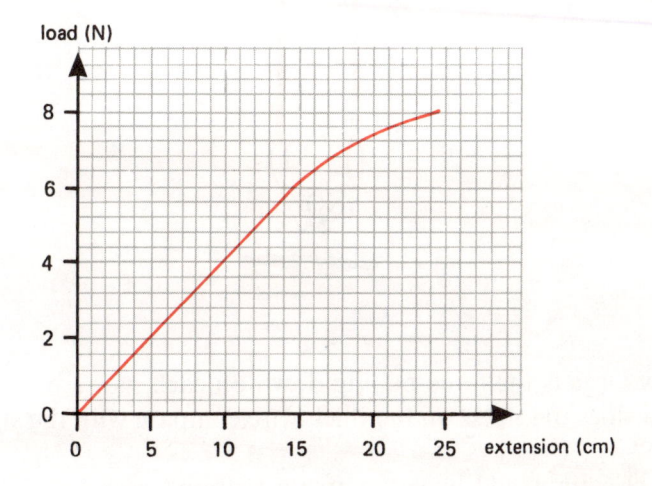

Figure 4.15

Use the graph to find:
(a) the extension for a 5 N load
(b) the extension of the spring at its elastic limit
(c) the slope of the straight line part of the graph
(d) the stiffness of the spring.

2. The table of results below are for a rubber band.

Force (N)	0.5	1.0	1.5	2.0	2.5	3.0	3.5	4.0	4.5
Extension (cm)	15	25	35	50	60	63	67	69	71

(a) Plot a graph of force against extension for the rubber band (plot force on the *y*-axis).
(b) Draw the curve of best fit through the points.
(c) Find the stiffness, *k*, of the band at the start of the stretching.
(d) If you were to connect three bands, identical to this one, in a parallel arrangement, what would the force/extension graph for this arrangement look like? Draw it using the same axes as used for part (a).

3. Use diagrams of molecules to explain why:
   (a) an aluminium wire can be permanently deformed by a large load
   (b) a rubber band can be stretched to many times its original length.
4. If a piece of rubber, 12 cm long, were stretched until it became 30 cm long:
   (a) what would its extension be?
   (b) what strain would have occurred?
5. A gymnast weighing 720 N is shown in Figure 4.16 hanging from two steel wires. The cross-sectional area of one wire is 1×10^{-5} m², the other is 2×10^{-5} m².

Figure 4.16

(a) How large is the force pulling down on each wire?
(b) How does the stress on the thick wire compare with the stress on the thin wire?
(c) Which wire would have the greatest strain?

MODERN MATERIALS 5

5.1 The new material demands of modern life

Designing a new bridge or a modern kitchen will involve an engineer in deciding which materials are best for the job. Heavier traffic, increased costs and higher safety standards have forced the development of cheap alternative materials. Advances in technology have given us plenty of new materials to choose from. Some new materials have been designed with particular properties for a particular job. Modern contact lenses may be made of clear soft plastic. The brake linings in modern cars have to be made from a new material other than asbestos. Space exploration has demanded materials of low density and which are resistant to extremes of temperature. This Unit will introduce you to some of the new materials now being used and to the language which describes them.

5.2 Plastics

These days we tend to take plastics for granted. Cheap pens, shirt buttons, calculator cases and disposable drinking cups are a part of our everyday life but they have not always been here. The first plastics appeared during the reign of Queen Victoria. Charles Goodyear developed the process of vulcanisation of rubber in 1840 and a Belgian scientist, Dr Bakeland, introduced 'Bakelite' in 1862. Polystyrene became available in 1930. Modern plastics are grouped into two categories: thermosetting materials and thermoplastic materials.

(a) Thermosetting
Some plastics undergo a chemical change when they are formed. After being heated, these plastics cool to a hard, rigid material which will not soften again when heated. For this reason, thermosetting plastics are used for fire-resistant fabrics, safety helmets and electrical sockets and plugs. Epoxy resins used in some glues and polyester resins used with glass fibres are examples of thermosetting plastics.

(b) Thermoplastic
These plastics soften when heated and harden again as they cool. In this way they can be remoulded into different shapes. Nylon, polythene, perspex and polyvinyl chloride (PVC) are thermoplastics.

The main difference between these two types of plastic is in the way in which the long polymer molecules are arranged. In a thermoplastic, the polymer chains are tangled but are free to move each other. In a thermosetting plastic, the polymer

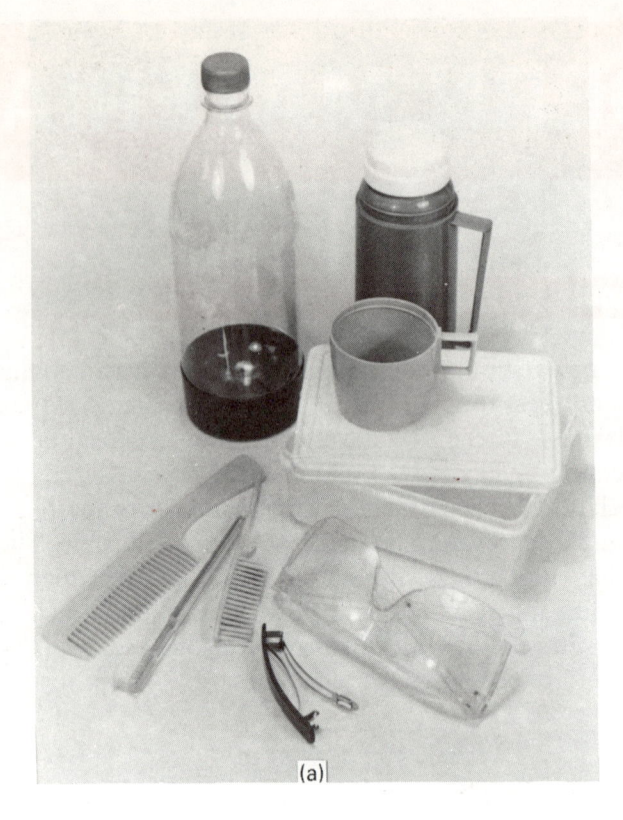

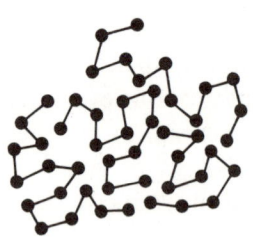

Polymer without cross-linking that is, a thermoplastic

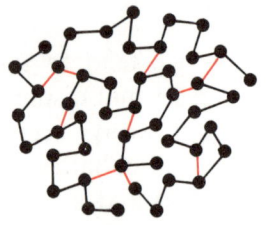

Cross-links will make this polymer less flexible, that is, a thermoset

(b)

Figure 5.1 (a) Some common uses of plastics. (b) Two types of polymer

chains are **cross-linked** to each other and so are prevented from rearranging their positions.

Plastics can be moulded or rolled into many shapes and can be dyed to bring a variety of colours to designs. This is particularly useful in electric circuits where wires can be colour-coded for safety and in fashion where colour-coordination is an important sales factor. Expanded plastics like polystyrene are used as low density packing material.

A feature of plastics is their resistance to chemical attack. This enables plastics to be used in buckets and pipes but it also poses a problem for disposal. Most plastics are not 'biodegradable'. They do not break down and rot naturally when buried although some biodegradable plastics are now available. There is also concern that toxic gases are given off when plastics are burned.

5.3 Metals

Metals are much older than plastics in the history of materials science. Many civilisations, the Babylonians, Inca, Indus and Chinese, had managed to use metals before about 1000 BC. The Bronze Age started at around this time. Bronze, an alloy of copper and tin, was fused in calculated proportions to make weapons and ornaments and so was perhaps one of the first designer-produced composite materials.

To understand how metals have been developed into a variety of useful materials we need to understand the microscopic structure of a metal. Metals are **polycrystalline**. A piece of copper, for example, contains millions of tiny crystal **grains**, less than a fraction of a millimetre across, in a random arrangement. In each grain the atoms of copper are regularly ordered in rows and planes just like a crystal. The polycrystalline nature of metals can be seen magnified on the insides of some cans of 'tinned' fruit and some 'galvanised' metal dustbins and wheelbarrows where grain sizes can be centimetres.

Figure 5.2 The bottom of a galvanised wheelbarrow showing large grains in a polycrystalline arrangement

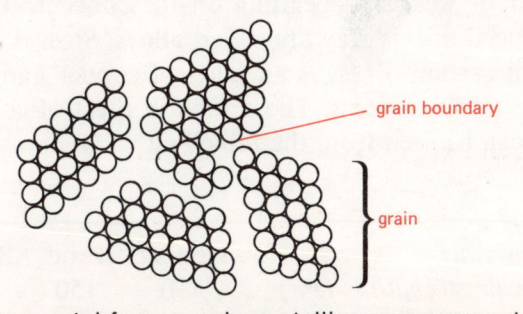

Figure 5.3 Atoms in a metal form a polycrystalline arrangement

The size of these grains determines how the metal will behave. Large grain size will result in a **tough** material which easily plastically deforms. This is because the long rows of atoms can easily slide over each other. Small grain size results in a much **stiffer**, **hard** and **brittle** material.

The properties of a material like steel can be changed by causing the grain structure to change. Two such processes are quenching and annealing. They are both heat treatments.

Quenching

A steel sample, a knitting needle for example, can be heated until it is red hot and then plunged into cold water or oil. This process will freeze into the crystal structure a disorder caused by a rearrangement of molecules in the hot metal. As a result the grains become smaller and more disorganised. The effect is to produce a hard, brittle sample.

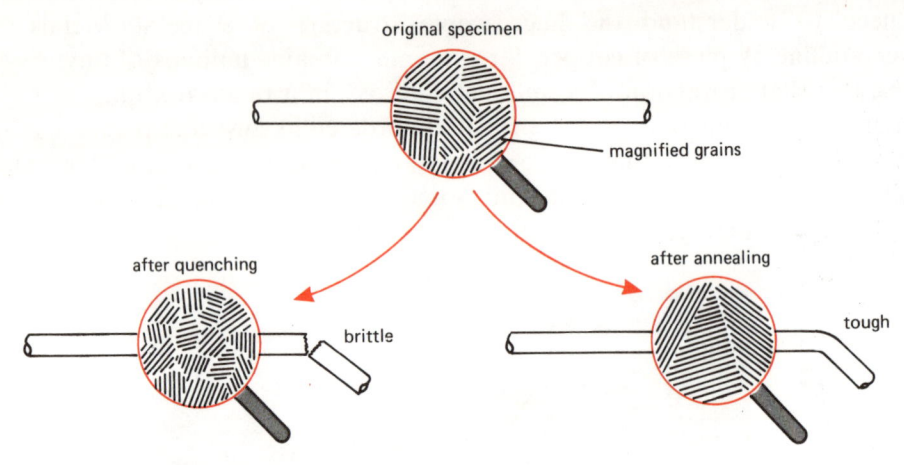

Figure 5.4   Heat treating a metal will change the grain structure

Annealing

A steel sample can be heated until it is red hot and then allowed to cool down very slowly. This will give the atoms time to reform in a larger grain structure which makes the sample much softer and tougher.

The physical properties of metals can be changed by the addition of impurity atoms. These atoms can disturb the regular polycrystalline structure and make the metal stronger or weaker depending on the concentration of the impurity. New metals produced in this way are called **alloys**. Steel is an alloy of iron and small quantities of carbon. Brass is an alloy of copper and zinc in the ratio of about 70 per cent to 30 per cent. The dramatic effect of combining two metals to form an alloy can be seen from the table below.

Material	Copper	Zinc	Brass
Tensile strength (MPa)	150	150	550

Modern alloys used for their great strength and stiffness are aluminium alloys and titanium alloys. Titanium, being about ten times more expensive than aluminium, is used when small items like bolts are required. Metals and metal alloys do have their disadvantages. They are subject to corrosion and so have a limited life. They are dense and so are unsuitable for uses requiring rapid motion or low fuel consumption and they are expensive. A new breed of materials has emerged to challenge the supremacy of metals and replace them in many applications, the composites.

5.4 Composite materials

For some jobs there is no single material which is suitable. Perhaps a metal is too dense, a plastic is too weak or a ceramic is too brittle. A solution is to combine the properties of two or more different materials to form a composite. Here are some examples of modern composites.

(a) Steel reinforced concrete

Concrete is weak in tension. It will crack where it is being stretched most. By adding steel rods to the concrete as it is mixed, they can be arranged so that they take most of the tension forces. With **pre-stressed concrete**, stretched steel rods are allowed to relax as the concrete sets around them. This creates a compression in the concrete to enable it to withstand a small degree of tension when in use.

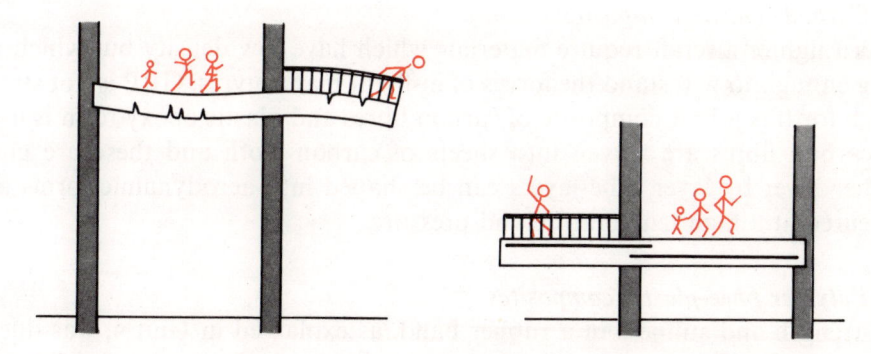

Figure 5.5   Steel is used to reinforce concrete floors and balconies

(b) Plywood and chip-board

Wood is perhaps the oldest building material. It is often used for the beauty of its 'grain' (this grain is not the same as the grain in a metal crystal structure). The grain pattern in a piece of wood runs in one direction only. This reveals the weakness of wood. When forced along the grain direction, wood is strong. When forced across the grain, wood is weak. Wooden planks often split as their grains are forced apart. Woodcutters know that chopping firewood is much easier if the grains are forced to split.

To produce a wood which is strong in all directions, thin sheets of wood can be glued together. If alternate sheets are arranged with their grain directions at right angles, a much more rigid and strong **plywood** material results.

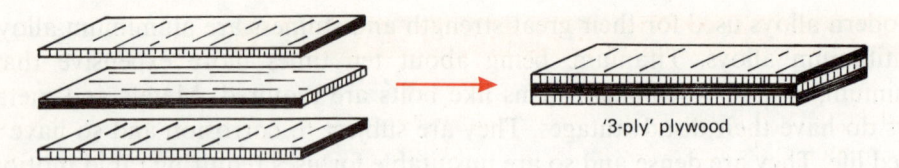

Figure 5.6 Plywood—a wood composite

The sawdust and wood chips produced each day by a saw-mill can be re-cycled to produce a composite called chip board. The leftover chips are held together by a glue 'matrix'. The result is a cheap sheet material which can be used for self-assembly kitchen cupboards and wardrobes. Although **chipboard** is cheap, it does tend to bend and crack more than natural wood.

(c) Glass-Reinforced Plastic, GRP
This material uses the most desirable properties of glass and plastic. Glass is very strong but cracks make glass brittle. Plastic, on the other hand, is not very strong but is tough and does not crack easily. GRP is made by placing a network of glass fibres in a matrix of plastic. The plastic is a thermoset which protects the glass from the effects of impact. GRP has been used to make car, boat and aeroplane bodies. It is cheap, of low density and strong, and can be moulded to aerodynamic shapes.

(d) Carbon–plastic composite
Modern fighter aircraft require materials which have low density but which are strong enough to withstand the forces of in-flight manoeuvres. GRP is not strong enough for this job. A composite of carbon fibres and plastic epoxy resin is used. The carbon fibres are woven into sheets of carbon cloth and these are glued together layer by layer. The layers can be shaped into aerodynamic forms and then **cured** at a high temperature and pressure.

(e) Polymer fibre-plastic composites
The strength and stiffness of a rubber band, as explained in Unit 4, was due to the stretched polymer molecules. The strength of stretched polymer molecules has recently been used to make a composite which is stronger than steel, GRP and carbon fibres. The stretched polymer molecules are held in a tough plastic matrix. One such material is Kevlar. Kevlar has been used to reinforce the brake linings of high-performance cars and to reinforce alpine overhead electric power lines. Another example is Spectra 1000. This is used to reinforce the sails of racing yachts and claims to be the strongest man-made fibre ever!

(f) Ceramic composites
One of the most modern composites uses a ceramic material as a matrix into which short fibres are embedded. Borosilicate glass reinforced with silicon carbide fibres retains its strength to 1000°C. It is used in high-temperature environments such as jet engines.

5.5 Concorde—a case study for modern materials

The designers of a supersonic passenger aircraft like Concorde make the most of modern materials. Just some of the materials currently used in Concorde are shown in Figure 5.7.

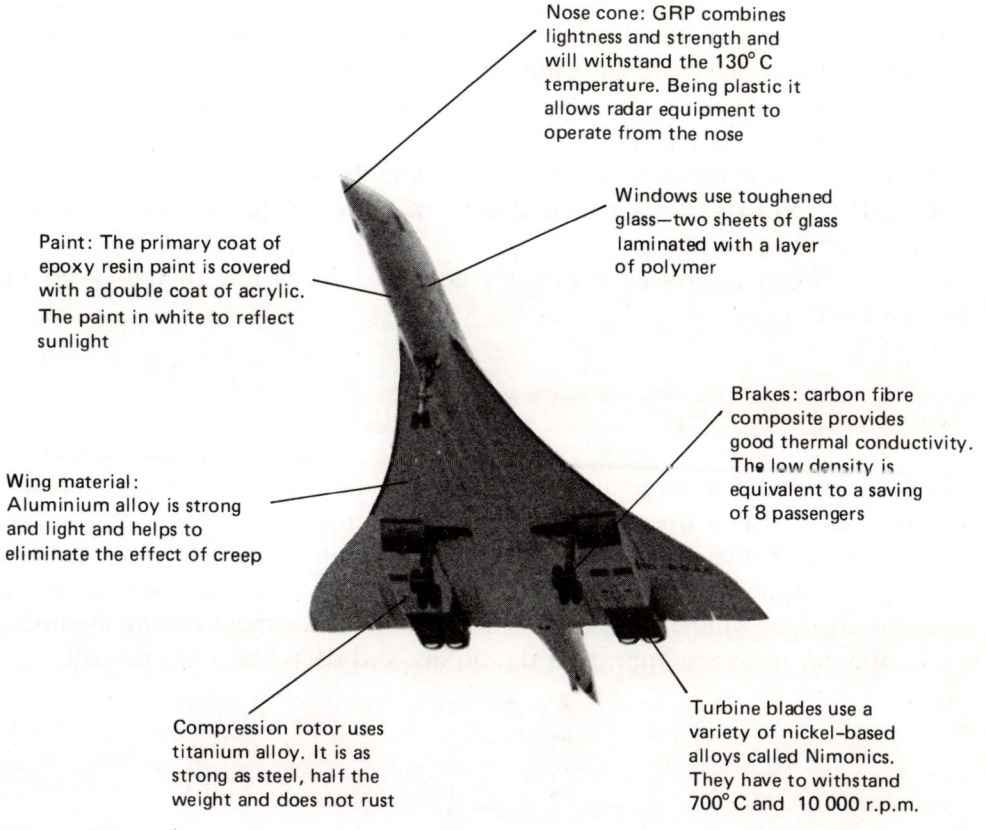

Nose cone: GRP combines lightness and strength and will withstand the 130°C temperature. Being plastic it allows radar equipment to operate from the nose

Windows use toughened glass—two sheets of glass laminated with a layer of polymer

Paint: The primary coat of epoxy resin paint is covered with a double coat of acrylic. The paint in white to reflect sunlight

Brakes: carbon fibre composite provides good thermal conductivity. The low density is equivalent to a saving of 8 passengers

Wing material: Aluminium alloy is strong and light and helps to eliminate the effect of creep

Compression rotor uses titanium alloy. It is as strong as steel, half the weight and does not rust

Turbine blades use a variety of nickel-based alloys called Nimonics. They have to withstand 700°C and 10 000 r.p.m.

Figure 5.7

5.6 The language of materials. Words and meanings

Many of these words have been used in the last two Units. You sould try to become familiar with most of them. Try also to think of a material which is described by each word. You will find that many words can be paired with their opposites.

ELASTIC/PLASTIC — An **elastic** material will return to its original shape or length after a load is removed. When a material remains permanently deformed after stretching it is described as **plastic**.
STRONG/WEAK — A material which can take a large load before breaking is **strong**. **Weak** materials break easily when stretched.

TOUGH/BRITTLE — A material which will deform rather than crack is described as **tough**. A **brittle** material will crack easily without deforming.
STIFF/FLEXIBLE — A **stiff** material is difficult to stretch or bend. **Flexible** materials bend easily.
HARD/SOFT — A material which does not easily scratch or dent is a **hard** material. **Soft** materials have surfaces which easily become scratched.
DUCTILE — A material which can be drawn out to make a wire.
MALLEABLE — A material which can be hammered into a permanent shape.
ALLOY — A metallic material made from two or more other metals.
COMPOSITE — When a new material is formed which uses the properties of two or more other materials.
POLYMER — A material made of long chain molecules.
POLYCRYSTALLINE — A material, like a metal, which has a grainy structure of many tiny crystals.
CREEP — When a stressed material gradually extends due to the effects of temperature change.

5.7 Related reading: The strength of cement

Cement is produced in large quantities to make concrete. It has the advantage over plastics in that it does not burn, dissolve or rot. It also has a reasonable compressive strength and can be made simply by adding water. However, cement is severely weakened by cracks. The theory of cracks predicts that the smaller the crack the stronger will be the cement. Using traditional cement mixing methods, cracks about 1 mm long appear on the surface and deep inside the cement.

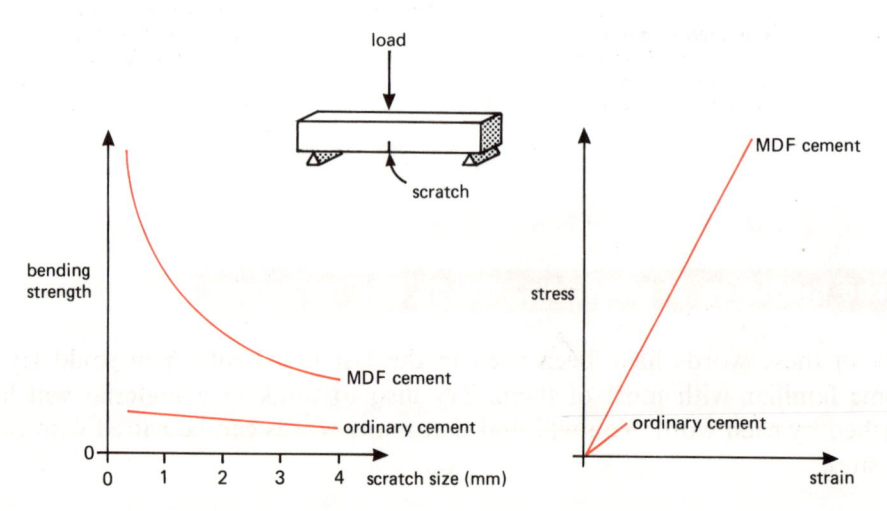

Figure 5.8 Comparing MDF cement with ordinary cement

Cement research has produced cement with cracks no larger than 1/500 mm. This new cement is known as **Macro Defect Free** cement, **MDF**, and is much stronger than traditional cement. A 3 mm thick sheet of MDF cement cannot be

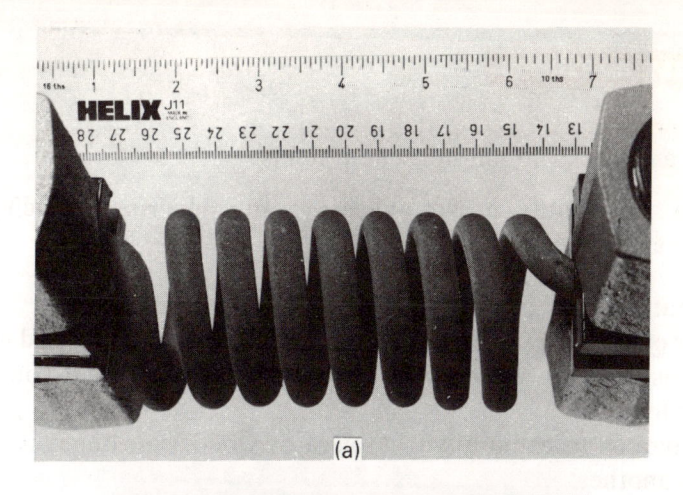

Figure 5.9 New uses for cement: (a) springs, (b) bottle caps

broken by hand or damaged when thrown on the floor. The new cement is almost as elastic as aluminium and can be used in place of metal in cladding pipes and buildings. MDF cement springs and bottle tops have been made.

5.8 Summary

- *A thermosetting plastic is usually rigid and will not soften when heated. Cross-linking causes this.*
- *A thermoplastic can be heated, softened and reshaped before cooling.*
- *Fibrous materials like wood have one strong direction along the fibres.*
- *A composite material combines the desirable properties of two or more materials.*
- *Many composite materials are designed with a strong material embedded in a tough matrix.*
- *A ceramic material is severely weakened by a crack.*
- *Metals are polycrystalline. Their properties depend on the arrangement of molecules.*
- *The grain structure of steel can be changed by quenching and annealing. This will change the physical properties of steel.*

5.9 Progress questions

1. Here is a list of common household items:

    frying pan, bottle opener, cheese grater, doormat, reading spectacles, door-key, light switch

    (a) What material is each of these made of in your home?
    (b) For one item in the list say why you think the material used is appropriate.
2. Childrens' toys are usually made of plastic or wood. Can you suggest some reasons for this?
3. Use diagrams to explain why a piece of wood is stronger in one direction than in another.
4. If a small crack appears on the surface of a sheet of glass it severely weakens the glass. If a small crack appears on the surface of a sheet of GRP it has almost no weakening effect. Can you explain why?
5. Reinforced concrete beams are often used across the top of a window.

    Figure 5.10

    (a) Why does the concrete need to be reinforced?
    (b) Draw a diagram to show where you think the steel reinforcement should be placed.

WORK, ENERGY, POWER

6.1 Doing work

The term 'work' is an everyday word which most people understand. In physics, 'work' has a special meaning. It is used when we want to describe the job done when a machine forces something to move.

The early steam engines were designed by James Watt in about 1780. In 1830 George Stephenson's 'Rocket' became the first passenger steam train. This period was one of revolution, an industrial revolution. Machines of all kinds were being designed to do jobs which were impossible for human machines to do, or which could be done automatically and much faster than by human machines. This was a time of doing work.

The work done by any machine, human or otherwise, can be calculated by knowing the forces involved and the distances they move. The amount of work done is given by

Work done = average force × distance moved by the force

or more simply

Work (J) = force (N) × distance (m)

The unit of work is the joule, J, and is named after an English experimenter James Prescott Joule (1818–1889).

Here are some examples of how this equation can be used.

(a) How much work is done when a train pulling with a force of 3000 N pulls a carriage from Stockton to Barton, a distance of 22 km?

work done = 3000 N × 22 000 m

= <u>66 000 000 J</u>

(b) An engineering student weighs 560 N. How much work does she do against gravity when she climbs to the top of a ladder 3 m high?

work done = 560 N × 3 m

= <u>1660 J</u>

6.2 Work and energy

All machines which do **work** must be supplied with a store of **energy**. As work is done a machine **transforms** (changes) energy from one form to another. The more work that is done the more energy is transformed. To help you get a feel for the idea of energy, study the energy changes shown in Figure 6.1. (An understanding of the concept of energy will come after you have used the idea in a number of different situations.)

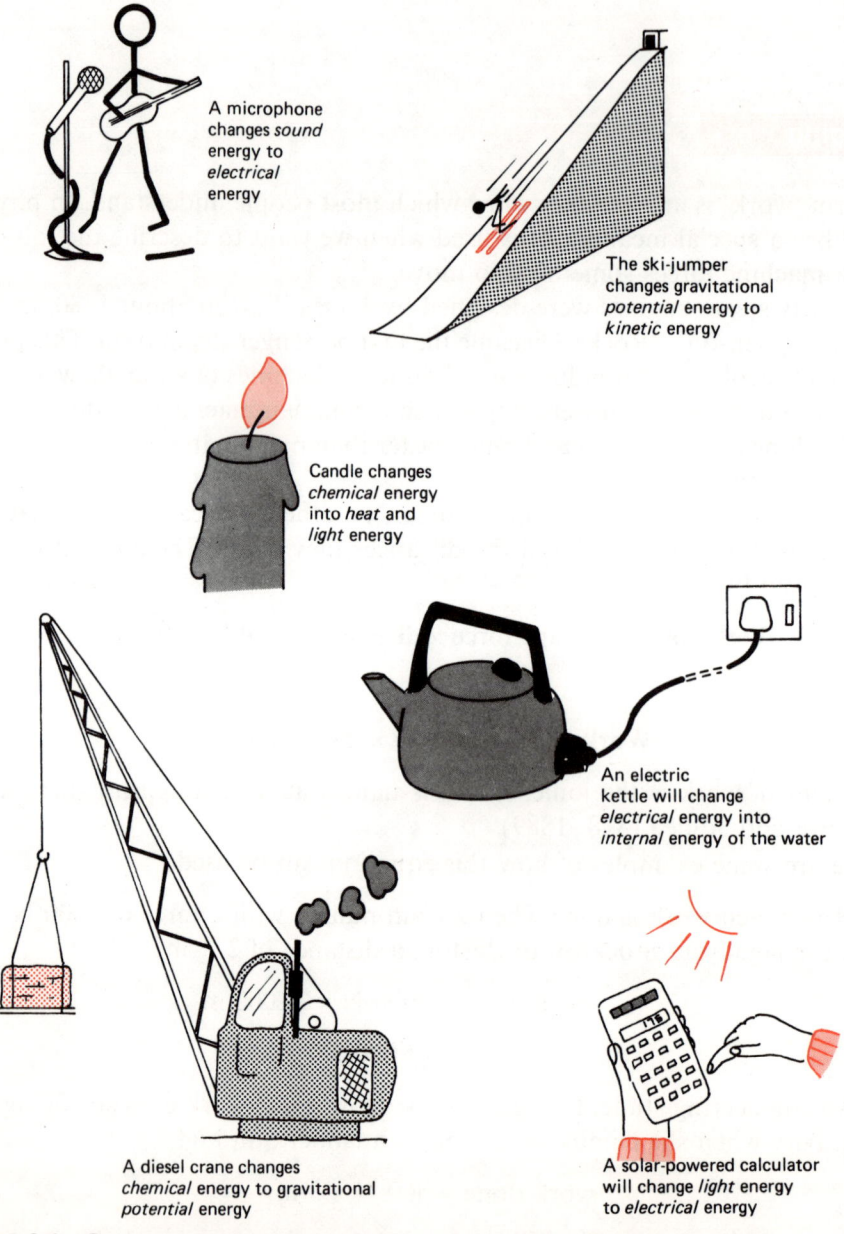

A microphone changes *sound* energy to *electrical* energy

The ski-jumper changes gravitational *potential* energy to *kinetic* energy

Candle changes *chemical* energy into *heat* and *light* energy

An electric kettle will change *electrical* energy into *internal* energy of the water

A diesel crane changes *chemical* energy to gravitational *potential* energy

A solar-powered calculator will change *light* energy to *electrical* energy

Figure 6.1 Some examples of energy transformations in everyday life

As a steam train pulls its load steadily along a track it changes **chemical energy** stored in the coal to **internal energy** of the tracks and the atmosphere, as friction heats up the tracks and wheels and waste steam warms up the atmosphere.

As the engineering student climbs a ladder, she transforms the **chemical energy** stored in the food she ate for breakfast into gravitational **potential energy**.

The amount of energy transformed is equal to the amount of work done.

Doing work and changing energy

Figure 6.2   Doing work transforming energy

6.3 Kinetic energy and gravitational potential energy

Two of the most common forms of energy changes are when an object moves faster (or slower) and when an object moves vertically upwards (or downwards). It is possible to calculate the exact amount of energy involved in these changes by using some simple equations.

(a) Kinetic energy

Work has to be done to get things moving. Think about the forces involved when you are asked to help push a car or when you throw a stone. We say that the moving object has 'kinetic energy'. The amount of kinetic energy depends on the mass and speed of the moving object. The equation which relates these quantities is

$$\text{Kinetic energy} = \frac{1}{2} \times \text{mass (kg)} \times \text{speed}^2 \text{ (m/s)}^2$$

$$KE = \frac{1}{2} mv^2$$

Here are two worked examples:
(a)   How much kinetic energy does a 6 kg cat have if it runs with a speed of 2 m/s?

$$KE = \frac{1}{2} mv^2$$
$$= \frac{1}{2} \times 6 \text{ kg} \times (2 \text{ m/s})^2$$
$$= \underline{12 \text{ J}}$$

(b) How much work must be done by a catapult to fire a 0.4 kg stone at a speed of 30 m/s?

$$\text{Work done} = \text{gain in KE}$$

$$= \frac{1}{2} mv^2$$

$$= \frac{1}{2} \times 0.4 \text{ kg} \times (30 \text{ m/s})^2$$

$$= \underline{180 \text{ J}}$$

(b) Gravitational potential energy

Lifting things up means doing work. You have to overcome the pull of gravity by pulling upwards with a force at least as great as the weight of the object to be lifted. The work you do becomes the gravitational potential energy of the object. The amount of gravitational potential energy gained depends on the weight of the object, the local gravitational field strength, g, and the vertical height raised. These quantities are related by

$$\text{Gravitational potential energy} = \text{weight} \times \text{vertical height}$$

$$\text{PE} = mg \times h$$

$$\text{PE} = mgh$$

For example: (a) How much work must be done to lift an 18 kg bag of shopping a distance of 4 m up a flight of steps?

$$\text{work done} = \text{gain in PE}$$

$$= mgh$$

$$= 18 \text{ kg} \times 10 \text{ N/kg} \times 4 \text{ m}$$

$$= \underline{720 \text{ J}}$$

(b) An object, mass 5 kg, is thrown upwards with an initial speed of 4 m/s. How high does it get?

$$\text{Decrease in kinetic energy} = \text{increase in gravitational potential energy}$$

$$\frac{1}{2} mv^2 = mgh$$

$$\frac{1}{2} \times 5 \text{ kg} \times (4 \text{ m/s})^2 = 5 \text{ kg} \times 10 \text{ N/kg} \times h$$

$$\frac{1/2 \times 5 \times 4^2}{5 \times 10} = h$$

$$\underline{h = 0.8 \text{ m}}$$

This last example illustrates the use of a most important principle in science—

the law of conservation of energy. This states that energy can neither be created from nowhere nor can it be lost and unaccounted for. It follows that if you start out with, as shown in Figure 6.3, 40 J of kinetic energy, you will transform this into 40 J of gravitational potential energy (ignoring air resistance).

mgh = 40J (gravitational potential energy)

$\frac{1}{2}mv^2$ = 40J (kinetic energy)

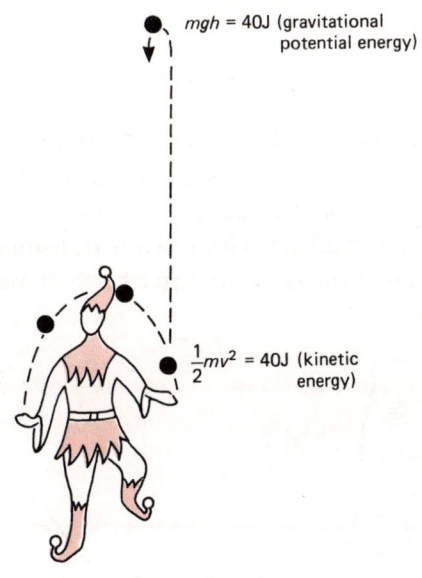

Figure 6.3 Kinetic into potential, none is 'lost'

6.4 Efficiency

The law of conservation of energy appears to suggest that there is no need to be concerned about the world's energy resources. After all, the energy on Earth today will be here forever as we cannot destroy energy. This is quite true. The problem is that most energy transformations result in heating up the surroundings, often through friction. When this happens, the energy becomes spread out among billions of air molecules and is impossible to control. This waste of useful energy has led to the design of more **efficient** machines which have less friction and few heating effects.

The efficiency of a machine is measured by comparing the useful energy output with the original energy input.

$$\text{Efficiency} = \frac{\text{useful energy output}}{\text{energy input}}$$

The efficiency fraction is sometimes expressed as a percentage, for example

$$\frac{1 \text{ joule out}}{4 \text{ joules in}} = 1/4 = 25 \text{ per cent efficient}$$

(The greatest possible efficiency for a machine is 100 per cent. Can you explain why?)

The huge cooling towers which you see next to power stations are used to get rid of hot steam from the boilers. Unfortunately power stations must produce hot steam in order to turn their turbines. Power stations therefore have to be inefficient in order to do work! You just cannot win.

6.5 Power

People use the word 'power' in different ways. Perhaps you have heard of 'power to the people', 'more power to your elbow', a 'power struggle', or even a 'power station'. In physics the word 'power' has a special meaning. It is a way of describing a machine. **The power of a machine is how fast it transforms energy.** Most electric appliances will have a label on them to describe their working power.

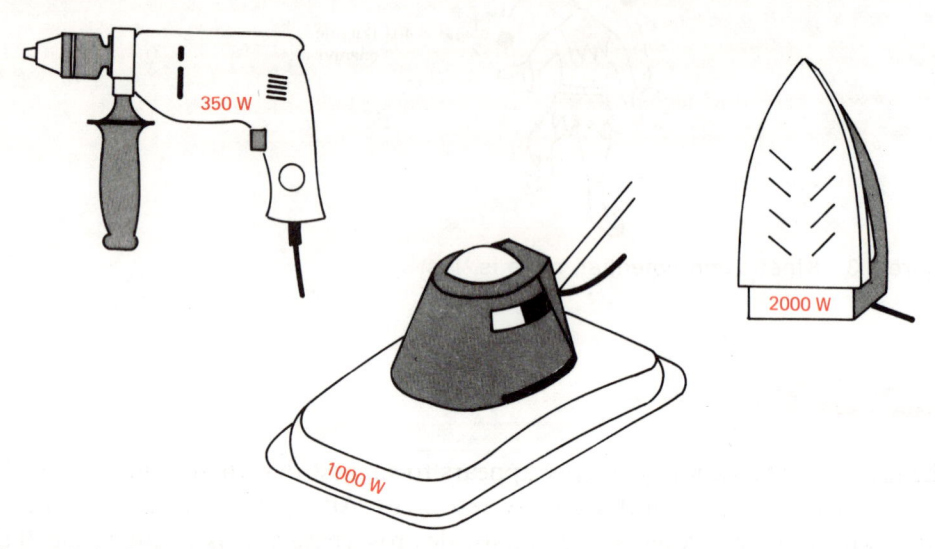

Figure 6.4 Machines are labelled with their power

The unit for measuring power is the watt (W), named after the Scot, James Watt. A machine with a power of one watt will be able to transform energy at the rate of one joule per second.

1 watt = 1 joule/1 second

A relationship which defines what we mean by the term power is:

power = energy transformed/time taken

or

power (W) = work done (J)/time taken (s)

Here are two worked examples which use this relationship:

(a) An electric iron was labelled 2000 W. How much energy would it transform in one minute?

$$\text{energy transformed} = \text{power} \times \text{time}$$
$$= 2000 \text{ W} \times 60 \text{ s}$$
$$= \underline{120\,000 \text{ J}}$$

(b) An electric motor raised a 300 g mass through a vertical distance of 4 m in a time of 6 seconds.
  (i) How much work was done?
  (ii) How powerful was the motor?

  (i) **work done = average force × distance**
  $$= mg \times h$$
  $$= 0.3 \text{ kg} \times 10 \text{ N/kg} \times 4 \text{ m}$$
  $$= \underline{12 \text{ J}}$$

  (ii) **power = work done/time taken**
  $$= 12 \text{ J}/6 \text{ s}$$
  $$= \underline{2 \text{ J/s}} \text{ or } \underline{2 \text{ W}}$$

6.6 Related reading: Your body as a machine

Most people have one main meal each day. Some people have more. Why do we eat? Apart from enjoying the taste of food, we eat because we have to. Food for us is like petrol for a car. It is our fuel.

Figure 6.5 A re-fuelling stop for cars and passengers

How much food does a person need? This depends on the amount of work the person does and on the amount of energy stored in food. Let us study the energy input and output of an average student during a normal working day.

It is obvious that we take in much more energy each day than we need for the work we do. Why do we do this? Is it just that humans eat more than they need to? Some people probably do eat more than they need to, but the energy which we take in does much more than just keep our mechanical body working.

Cycling to college and back:
Work done = force × distance
≃ 100 N × 3000 m
≃ 300 000 J

Walking upstairs to lessons:
Work done = force × distance
= 600 N × 4 m
= 2400 J
5 times during the day
= 2400 J × 5
= 12 000 J

Walking about:
Work done = force × distance
= 50 N × 8000 m
= 40 000 J

An average meal contains about 4 000 000 J

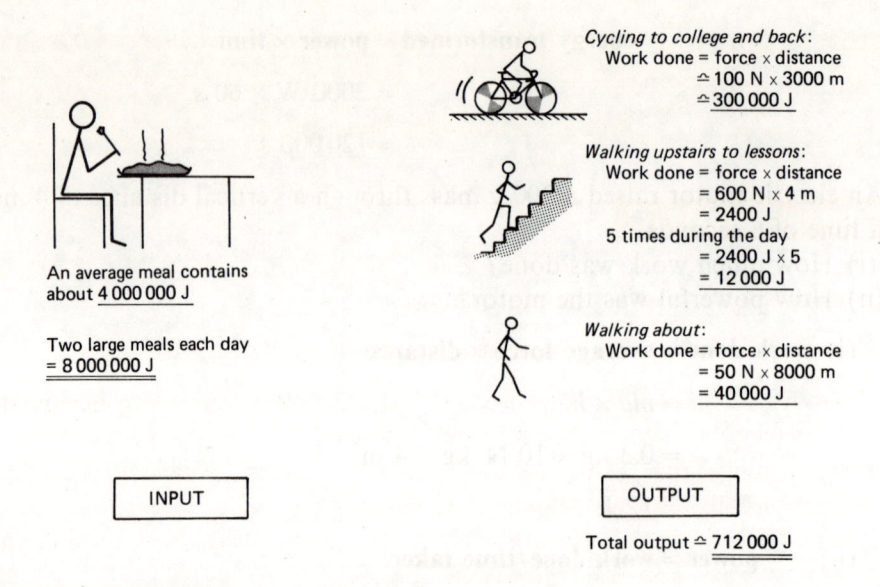

Two large meals each day = 8 000 000 J

INPUT

OUTPUT
Total output ≃ 712 000 J

Figure 6.6   The student—an inefficient machine?

With a body temperature of 37°C and an average surrounding temperature of about 10°C, we are constantly losing energy to the outside world through conduction, convection and radiation. In fact we lose energy in this way at a rate of about 100 W even with our clothes on. In a day then, roughly 86 400 s, we use 8 640 000 J of energy in just keeping at a temperature of 37°C. Humans are extremely inefficient machines.

6.7 Summary

- *Doing work means moving something by force. Work done can be calculated by*

$$\textit{Work done} = \textit{force} \times \textit{distance}$$

- *Energy is transformed when work is done. Energy and work are measured in joules (J).*
- *Energy can change between many forms but can never be created from nowhere nor be lost and unaccounted for.*
- *Kinetic and gravitational potential energies can be calculated using*

$$\textit{KE} = \frac{1}{2}\textit{mv}^2 \qquad \textit{GPE} = \textit{mgh}$$

- *All machines are inefficient. Efficiency can be defined as*

$$\textit{Efficiency} = \frac{\textit{useful energy output}}{\textit{energy input}}$$

- *Power is measured in watts (W). It is the rate at which a machine can transform energy.*

   Power = work done/time taken

6.8 Progress questions

1. What are the units used for measuring:

   (a) work, (b) energy, (c) power, (d) efficiency?

2. Shops offer a choice of lawnmower. You can buy a traditional roller mower or an electric air cushion 'hover' rotary mower.
   (a) How much work is done when a gardener pushes a roller mower with a force of 250 N for a distance of 12 m?
   (b) A hover mower requires a force of only 120 N. Why do you think that cutting grass is 'less bover with a hover'?

3. A force is required to stretch a spring. The force needs to increase as the extension increases. Figure 6.7 shows how the force needed to stretch a spring changes with the spring's extension.

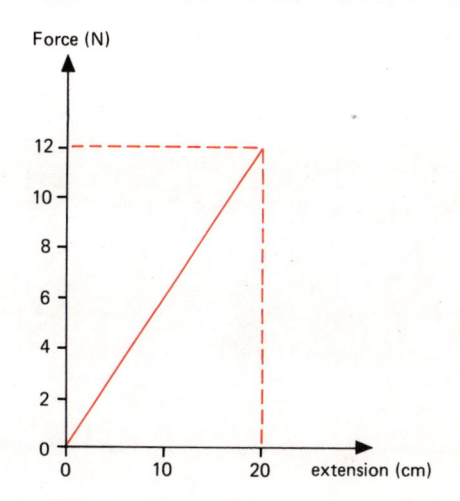

Figure 6.7

   (a) Is it true to say that work has to be done to stretch a spring?
   (b) What happens to the energy transformed as a spring is stretched?
   (c) The work done in stretching a spring is found from:

   Work done = **average** force × distance

   Can you show that the work done in stretching the spring to an extension of 18 cm is 1.08 J?   ½ × 10.8 × 0.18 = 0.972 J

4. A crane on a building site can raise a 1400 kg load of bricks to a height of 8 m in a time of 4 s.

(a) How much do 1400 kg of bricks weigh?
(b) How much work does the crane have to do?
(c) How powerful is the crane?
(d) The crane is powered by a petrol engine. What energy changes are occurring as the bricks are lifted?

5. Each plane on the London to Manchester shuttle flight carries on average 50 passengers. The average weight of a passenger is 650 N.
    (a) How much work is done to lift a load of passengers to the flight cruise height of 3000 m?
    (b) What energy changes take place during liftoff?
    (c) Give two reasons why the shuttle flight transforms more energy than calculated in part (a).
    (d) The cruising speed during the flight is 110 m/s. Use this information to compare the potential energy of a passenger with the kinetic energy of a passenger during the cruising part of the flight.

HEATING THINGS

7.1 Heat and heating

Have you ever said that a hot cup of tea contains more 'heat' than a cold cup of tea, or perhaps that when the cup of tea cools down it loses its 'heat'? Many people have used the word 'heat' in this way. The idea that 'heat' exists as a real substance goes back to at least the 18th century when it was believed that hot objects contained a fine fluid called 'caloric' (heat) and that as objects cooled the 'caloric' flowed out of them.

Today we try not to think of 'heat' as a substance. It is a misleading idea. Hot objects are hot because of the kinetic energy (movement) of their particles. This energy is called '**internal energy**' and can be increased by a process called '**heating**'.

Heating produces change. The changes which we shall consider will be changes in temperature (getting hotter), changes in shape (expanding), changes in state (freezing and boiling) and the movement of internal energy (conduction and convection).

7.2 Changes in temperature

Temperature is a measure of hotness. A temperature, such as 21°C, is just a hotness number on an invented scale. The same hotness might be described on another scale of numbers by 70°F or evern 294 K. The same temperature is often given in weather forecasts on both the celsius scale, °C (often called centigrade), and on the fahrenheit scale °F. You should try to get a feel for hotness measured on the celsius scale. For example, would you wear your overcoat if the temperature outside were 26°C? Would you be able to drink a cup of coffee if it were 78°C? All substances are capable of increasing their temperature when they are heated. Objects with a large mass take longer to warm up as their internal energy is shared out among many particles.

Materials respond to energy changes in different ways. Given equal amounts of internal energy, particles in some materials will move faster. The temperature changes in these materials will be greater. To compare how easy it is to increase the temperature of different materials we can measure how much energy needs to be supplied to do a specific warming up job. This job is to increase the temperature of **1 kg** of material by **1°C**. The energy needed to do this job is called the **specific heat capacity**, c, of the material. Figure 7.2 gives the specific heat capacities of some common materials. Note that the units for specific heat capacity are J/kg°C.

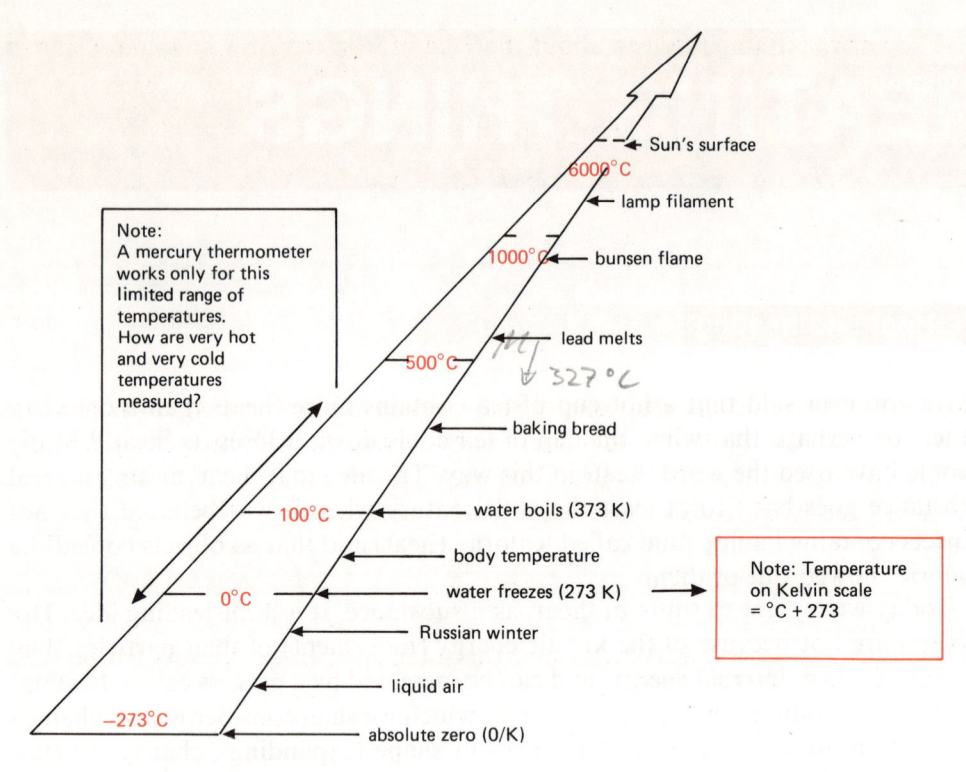

Figure 7.1 Temperatures on the celsius scale

Material	c (J/Kg °C)
Aluminium	913
Copper	385
Cast iron	500
Zinc	385
Lead	126

Material	c J/KG °C
Concrete	3350
Crown glass	670
Water	4200
Air	993
Olive oil	1970

Figure 7.2 Specific heat capacities of some common materials

From this figure you can see that a 1 kg block of iron requires 500 J to increase its temperature by 1°C. It follows that you would require 1000 J of energy to increase the temperature of 2 kg of iron by 1°C, or to increase the temperature of 1 kg of iron by 2°C. How much energy is required to increase the temperature of 2 kg of iron by 3°C? To enable you to calculate the answers to problems like this, you could use an equation:

change in energy = mass × specific heat capacity × temperature change

or

$$\Delta Q = m \times c \times \Delta \theta$$

or

$$\Delta Q = mc\Delta\theta$$

The answer to the question about the 2 kg of iron can now be found using an equation:

$$\Delta Q = mc\Delta\theta$$
$$\Delta Q = 2 \text{ kg} \times 500 \text{ J/kg }°C \times 3°C$$
$$\Delta Q = \underline{30\,000 \text{ J}}$$

7.3 Measuring specific heat capacity, c

Under most conditions the specific heat capacity, c, is a constant for any one type of material. To find c requires you to measure a quantity of energy, ΔQ, given to a mass, m, and a resulting temperature change $\Delta\theta$. The value for c can then be calculated from

$$c = \frac{\Delta Q}{m\Delta\theta}$$

An immersion heater, joulemeter and thermometer can be used to find a value for the specific heat capacity of a material in the laboratory.

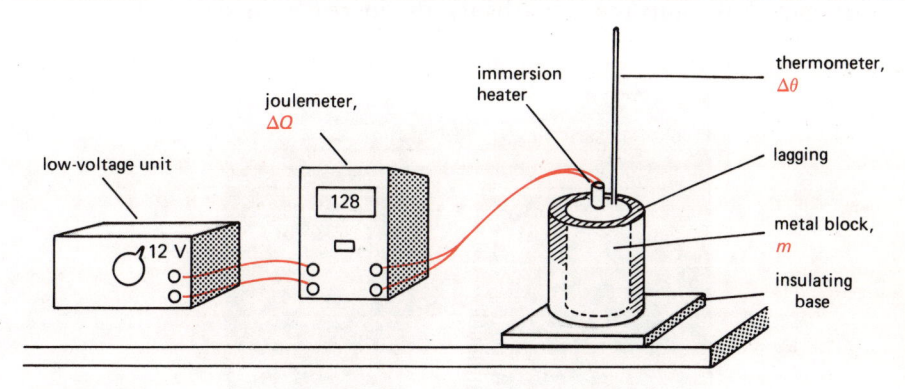

Figure 7.3 Finding the specific heat capacity of a metal

7.4 Changes in size. Thermal expansion

A mercury in glass thermometer clearly shows the effect of heating on the volume of a quantity of mercury. As the mercury expands it rises up the narrow capillary tube and this enables a temperature to be read. This thermal expansion of mercury is a desirable effect. The expansion of metals can be used as a temperature-sensitive switch. A **bimetallic strip** made of two different metals will bend when it is heated. This is because one metal expands more than the other. An electric iron might use this principle as a thermostat.

Large structures will give large expansions. The Eiffel Tower in Paris is capable of expanding vertically by up to 13 cm on a hot summer day. The London to

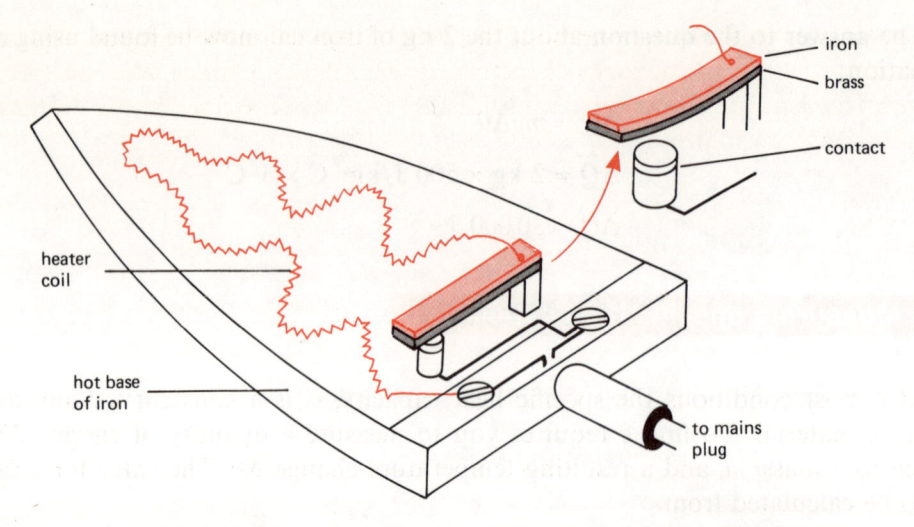

Figure 7.4 A bimetal strip can be used as a thermostat in an electric iron

Glasgow railway line expands by nine metres for each degree celsius increase in temperature! Perhaps this is why the train fares increase in the summer season.

To avoid problems caused by thermal expansion, large structures often have expansion gaps built into them to absorb the increases in size.

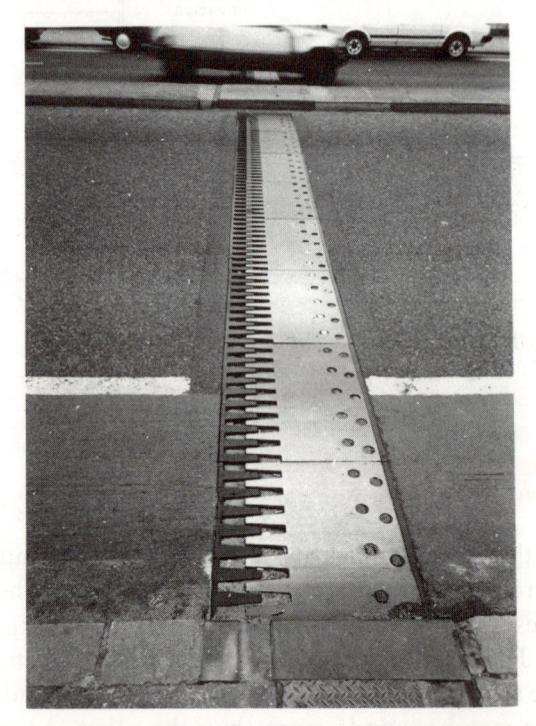

Figure 7.5 One of two expansion gaps in Waterloo Bridge, London

Why does heating cause expansion? To answer this question we must use the ideas of the 'kinetic theory' first introduced in Unit 3. As materials are heated their particles gain kinetic energy. The particles vibrate more energetically and the average separation of particles increases. The solid as a whole takes up a little more space because of the extra internal energy of its particles. This is the story behind thermal expansion.

more energetic vibrations need more space

Figure 7.6

7.5 Changes of state

Water from a drinking tap can be boiled to make tea or it can be frozen to make ice-cubes. In these three 'states' of matter, **solid**, **liquid** and **gas**, it is still water. The main difference between the three states is the internal energy of the water molecules. In steam, the water molecules move about freely with lots of kinetic energy. A typical average speed for a molecule in steam might be 500 m/s. In liquid tap water, the molecules move on average much more slowly. In ice, the molecules move hardly anwhere at all. They just vibrate.

(a) Freezing and melting (solid–liquid)

The attractive forces between molecules help to keep them grouped together. In a solid these forces allow molecules only enough freedom to vibrate. The average kinetic energy of molecules is small. As a solid is heated the average kinetic energy of molecules increases and the temperature rises (see Section 7.2 on specific heat capacity). There comes a point when the molecules have enough energy to break

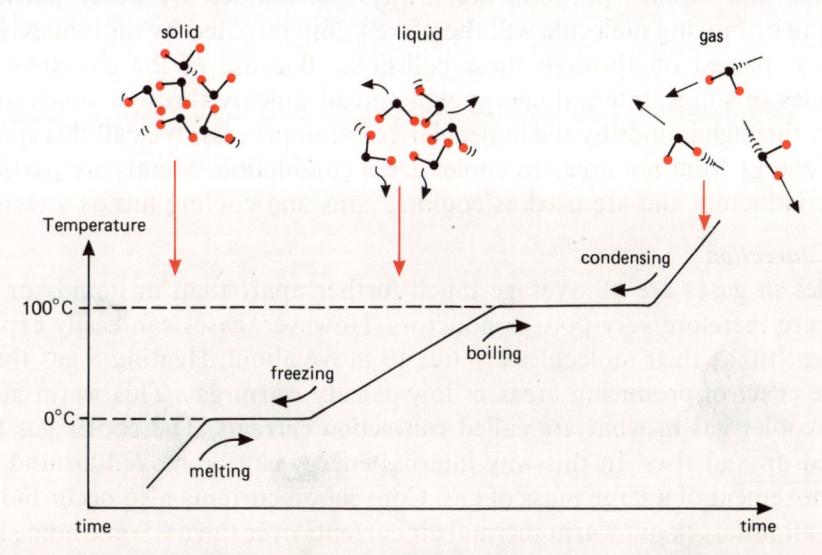

Figure 7.7 Heating up, cooling down and changing state

free from the forces which bind them. As this happens, the temperature of the solid remains constant. Any extra energy supplied to the solid is used to free a molecule from its neighbour. This extra energy needed to change the state from solid to liquid is called **latent heat energy**. When a liquid cools down the molecules move more slowly. As the liquid freezes the molecules combine together, reform their bonds and lose their latent heat energy to the surroundings.

(b) Boiling and condensing (liquid–gas)

Water in its liquid form exists usually from 0°C to 100°C. At room temperature the fastest molecules in a cup of water will break free from the liquid. This process is called **evaporation**. The rate of evaporation increases as the temperature of the water increases. As the water is heated the molecules continue to move about faster as the temperature increases. The most energetic molecules are fast enough to break free from their attractive forces. At 100°C any energy given to the water will help the water molecules to break free from the liquid and escape into the gas. This 'break free energy' is another example of **latent heat energy**. When a gas **condenses** it loses its latent heat energy to the surroundings as the molecules slow down and reform bonds together.

7.6 Conduction and convection

Once an object is hot it is very difficult to keep it hot. In cool surroundings hot things naturally cool down. Two ways in which internal energy can be lost from a hot object are conduction and convection. They both require the ideas of moving molecules to explain them.

(a) Conduction

In solids and liquids, particles are always surrounded by other particles. A vibrating or moving molecule will therefore bump into nearby molecules. Kinetic energy is passed on through these collisions. Because of the closeness of the molecules in solids, internal energy will spread quickly through solids and less quickly through liquids by the molecular collision process. We call this spreading out of energy from hot areas to cooler areas conduction. Metals are particularly good conductors and are used as cooking pans and cooling fins as a result.

(b) Convection

Particles in gases are on average much further apart than in liquids or solids. Gases are therefore very poor conductors. However, gases can easily expand as they heat up as their molecules are free to move about. Heating a gas therefore has the effect of producing areas of low-density warm gas. This warm gas rises above cooler gas in what are called **convection currents**. The cooler gas falls, is warmed up and rises. In this way internal energy can be moved around by the bulk movement of a large mass of gas. Convection currents also occur in liquids. Glider aircraft seek out warm thermal air currents over towns. Some home heaters use natural convection currents to spread energy around.

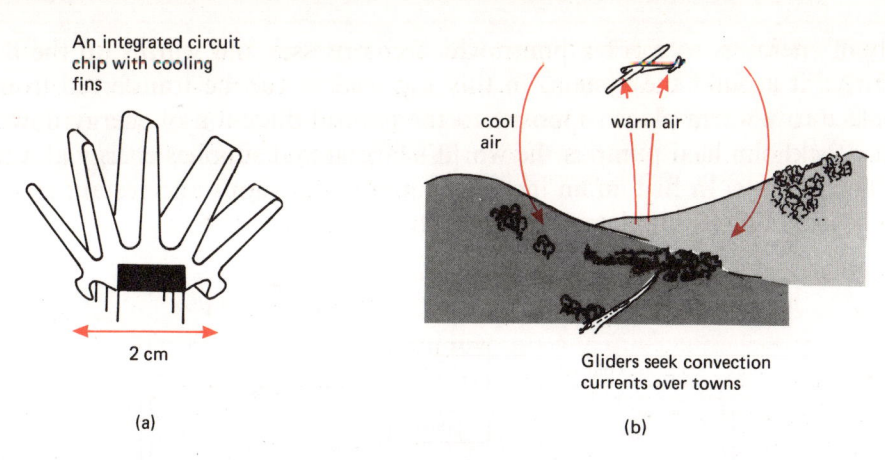

Figure 7.8 Making use of conduction and convection

7.7 Related reading: Refrigerators and heat pumps

A cold pack of butter will melt in a warm kitchen. Yet inside a refrigerator the cold butter keeps cold even though the fridge is itself in the warm kitchen! The sea around Stockholm in Sweden gets as cold as 2°C yet energy from this icy sea is being used to heat 100 000 homes in the city of Stockholm. Both of these situations work because of the use of '**heat pumps**'. To understand how 'heat pumps' work, let us look back at the ideas of 'latent heat energy'.

When a liquid evaporates, it takes in latent heat energy from the surroundings to break bonds between molecules. When a gas condenses, it gives latent heat energy to the surroundings as the bonds reform.

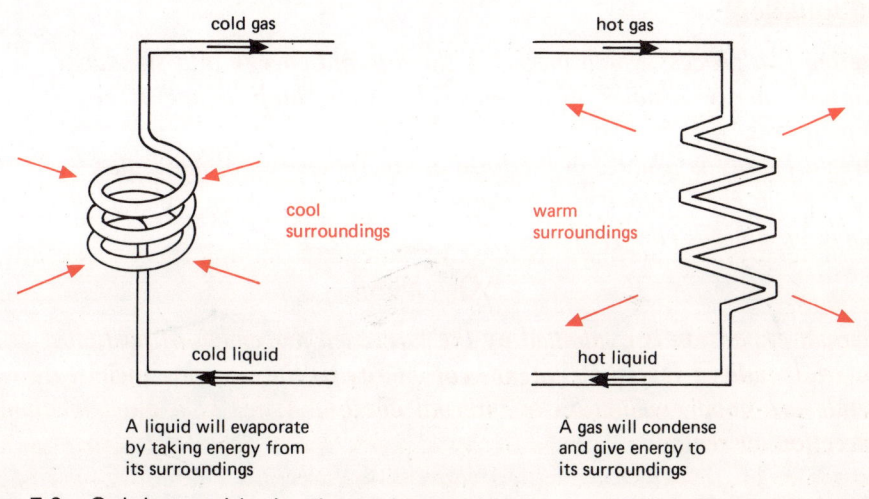

Figure 7.9 Gaining and losing latent heat energy

A heat pump combines these two processes into a cycle. A fluid passes around the system and repeatedly is evaporated and then condenses. The only extra supply of energy is to work a pump which compresses and warms up the fluid and forces it around the system. In this way energy can be transferred from a cool place to a warm place (opposite to the natural direction of energy flow!)

The Stockholm heat pump is the world's largest and supplies energy at a rate of 160 megawatts. In Britain an increasing number of shops and restaurants are using heat pumps to supplement their heating.

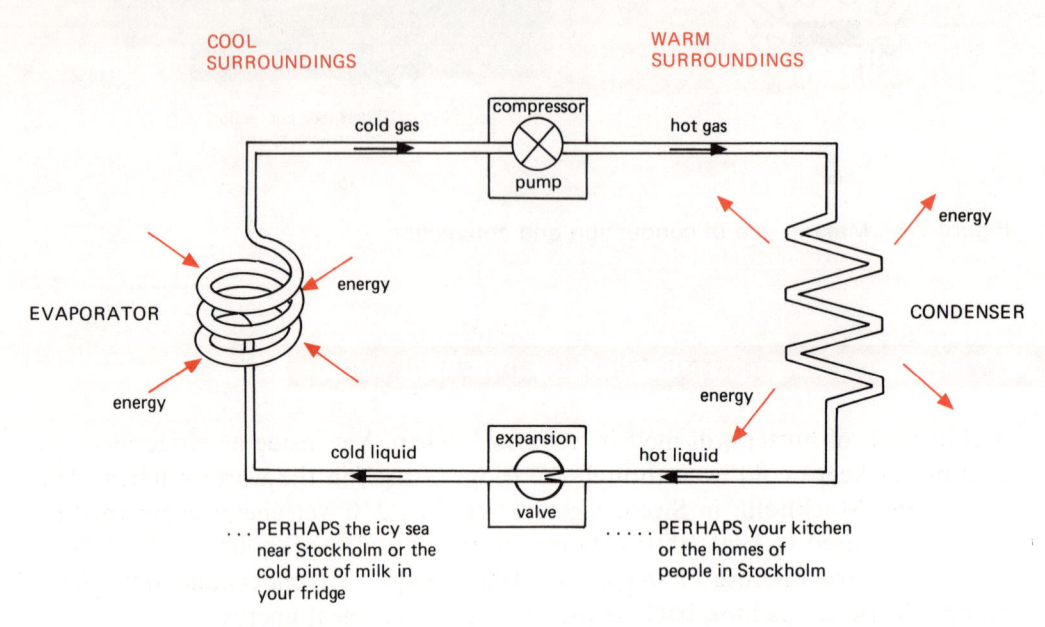

Figure 7.10 A heat pump takes energy from cool places to warmer places

7.8 Summary

- ***Heating*** *is a process which increases the **internal energy** of a substance.*
- *Internal energy usually flows naturally from high temperatures to lower temperatures.*
- *Internal energy is usually in the form of kinetic energy of molecules.*
- *The specific heat capacity of a material relates the temperature change to the change in internal energy:*

$$\Delta Q = mc\Delta\theta$$

- *Thermal expansion is explained by the increased movement of particles.*
- *Materials gain or lose their latent heat energy as they change their state.*
- *Metals are good conductors of internal energy. A gas is a good medium for convection currents.*

7.9 Progress questions

1. When a piece of metal is heated, a number of changes occur, both visible and invisible.

(a) Give three changes which might occur when a piece of brass is heated.
(b) Which of these can be measured?
(c) Explain briefly how you would measure this change.
2. Here are some temperatures together with their units.

$\quad\quad$ 4°C $\quad\quad$ 25°C $\quad\quad$ 300°C $\quad\quad$ 70°F $\quad\quad$ 0 K $\quad\quad$ 39°C

Which temperature from the list is most likely to be:
(a) the lowest possible temperature
(b) the temperature on a winter's day
(c) the temperature of a person with a fever?
3. The specific heat capacity of lead is 126 J/kg °C but that of nickel is 460 J/kg °C. If identical pieces of lead and nickel were heated electrically by the same heater, which would warm up faster?
4. The specific heat capacity of tin is 226 J/kg °C.
   (a) How much energy would it require to increase the temperature of 1 kg of tin by 3°C?
   (b) How much energy would you need to warm up a 0.45 kg piece of tin from 22°C to 34°C?
5. The specific heat capacity of water is 4200 J/kg °C.
   (a) How much energy would be required to increase the temperature of 2 kg of water by 2°C?
   (b) How much energy would you need to bring 2 kg of water at 20°C to the boil for a cup of tea?
   (c) In real life you must pay for more energy than this for the water for a cup of tea. Can you think of a reason why?
6. Expresso coffee is made by bubbling hot steam through cold milk to make the milk warm and frothy. What energy changes happen during this process?
7. Warm water needs energy for it to change into steam. Use this idea to explain why you feel cold when you first get out of a bath?
8. Some modern saucepans have wooden handles and copper bottoms. Why do you think they are designed like this?

PRESSURE

8.1 Pressure in solids, stress

The idea of 'stress' was introduced in Unit 4. (You might like to revise Unit 4 before continuing with Unit 8.) When a force is used to squash or compress a solid, the effect on the solid depends on its shape. A force spread over a large area will have less effect than the same force when concentrated on a small area. This effect called **stress** or **pressure** is calculated using the relationship

$$\text{pressure or stress} = \frac{\text{force}}{\text{area}}$$

The unit of stress and pressure is the pascal, Pa. One pascal is the pressure when a force of one newton forces on an area of one square metre. $1 \text{ Pa} = 1 \text{ N/m}^2$. Blaise Pascal, 1623 to 1662, was a French scientist who discovered that atmospheric pressure decreased with altitude.

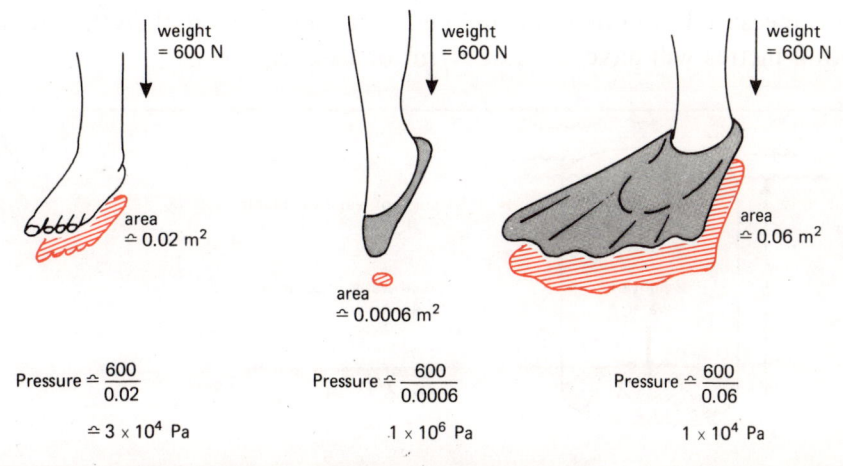

Figue 8.1 Calculating pressures using force and area

8.2 Pressure in liquids

The water in most reservoirs is held back by a dam. The design of the dam must take into account the pressure of the water contained in the reservoir. The bottom of the dam wall is made thicker than the top as the water pressure is greatest at the bottom of the reservoir. This is simply because of the weight of the water.

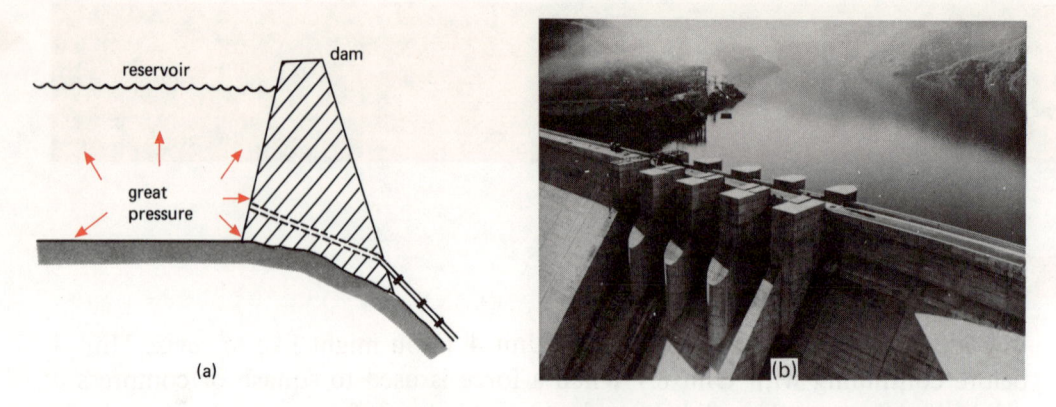

Figure 8.2 (a) Water pressure increases with depth. (b) The Antonivanovtzi dam in Bulgaria has been built to withstand the pressure

Deep sea diving suits and submarines have to be designed to withstand the considerable water pressure found at great depths. To help plan these designs it is possible to calculate using an equation how great the pressure will be at a certain depth.

The pressure at a depth h metres is given by:

$$\textbf{Pressure} = \boldsymbol{h\rho g}$$

where ρ is the density of the liquid and g is the gravitational field strength.

If ρ is measured in units of kg/m^3 and g has units N/kg, then the pressure at a depth h metres will have units of **N/m^2** or **pascals, Pa.**

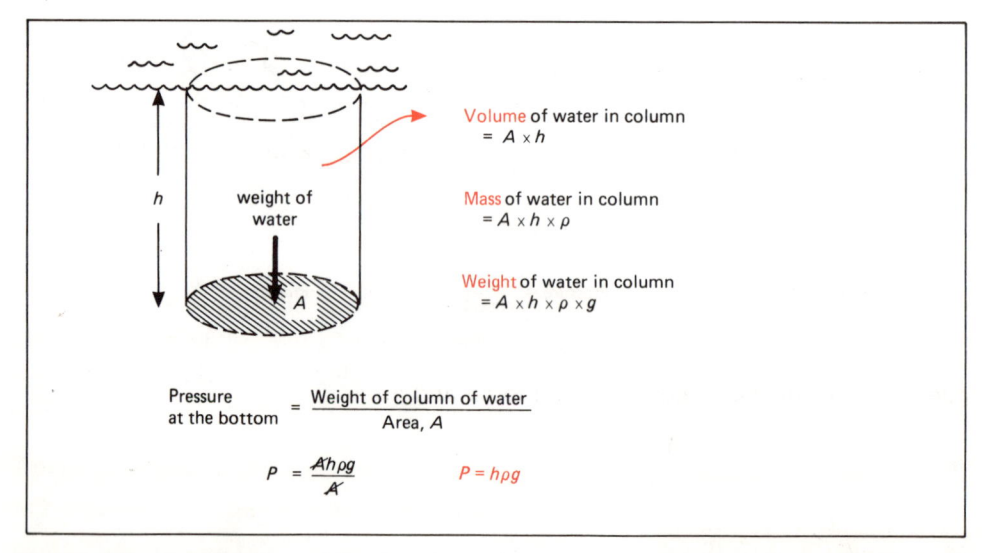

Figure 8.3 A derivation of the $h\rho g$ formula

The use of this equation is illustrated by the following examples:

(1) Calculate the water pressure at a tap due to the water in a water tower 7 m above the tap. (The density of water is 1000 kg/m^3. Take g as 10 m/s^2.)

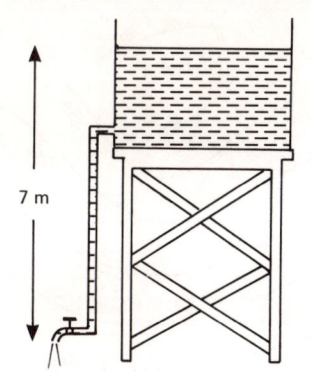

Figure 8.4

$$\text{pressure} = h\rho g$$

$$p = 7 \text{ m} \times 1000 \text{ kg/m}^3 \times 10 \text{ N/kg}$$

$$p = \underline{70\,000 \text{ Pa}}$$

(2) If a submarine can safely withstand a water pressure of 1.6×10^6 Pa, to what depth can it safely dive?

Starting with: $\quad\text{pressure} = h\rho g$

rearranging gives: $\quad h = p\rho g$

$$h = \frac{1.6 \times 10^6 \text{ Pa}}{1000 \text{ kg/m}^3 \times 10 \text{ N/kg}}$$

$$h = \underline{160 \text{ m}}$$

8.3 Pressure in gases

(a) Atmospheric pressure

The air which we breath is part of the atmosphere of air which surrounds the Earth. The weight of the air in the atmosphere pushing down on us gives the air at sea level a pressure. We call this pressure 'atmospheric pressure' and its value can be related to the average height and density of the atmosphere using the equation $p = h\rho g$ (see Section 8.2).

The size of the atmospheric pressure at sea level can vary a little because of winds and temperature changes, but on average it remains close to 100 000 Pa. This is sometimes called one **atmosphere** or one **bar**. In weather forecasts, lines are drawn linking places with the same pressure. These lines are called isobars and are labelled with pressure values in millibars (1 bar = 1000 millibars).

In Figure 8.5 the air pressure over Scotland is 980 millibars. This is 0.980 bar or 0.980 atmospheres (low pressure and perhaps rain). The air pressure over France is 1.004 atmospheres (high pressure and probably clear skies).

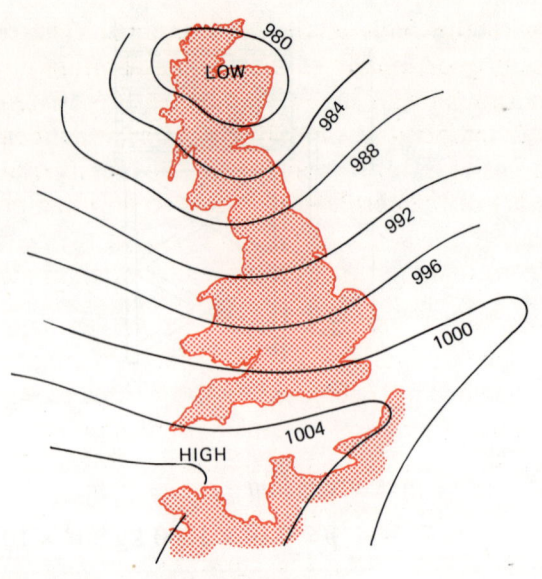

Figure 8.5 A pressure pattern over the Channel

(b) The pressure of a fixed mass of gas

In the laboratory, gases are usually found in containers like gas cylinders or glass tubes. These gases also have pressures. It is easier to understand the pressure of a **fixed mass** of gas if we think about the particles which make up the gas. The molecules in a gas are moving about freely, colliding with each other and with the walls of the gas container. These collisions cause an outward force on the walls of the gas container. The collisions give the gas its pressure. Can the pressure of a fixed mass of gas be changed? Yes, if either the temperatue or volume of the gas is changed because these changes affect the particles in the gas.

(i) *Changing the temperature.* The molecules in a hot gas move on average faster than in a cold gas. This results in each molecule colliding more frequently and

Pressure proportional to absolute temperatures
$P \propto T$

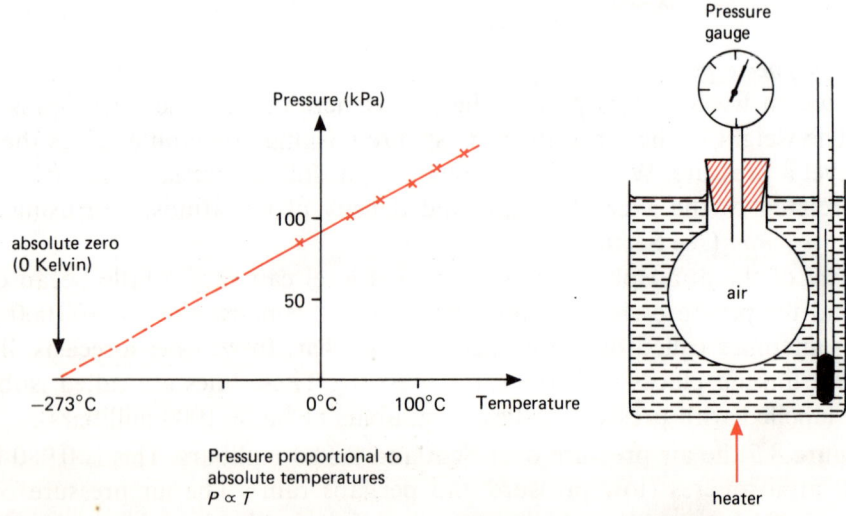

Figure 8.6 Temperatures and pressures for a fixed mass of gas

more forcefully with the walls of the gas container. The result is that the gas pressure increases proportionally as the gas temperature increases. Experiments have shown that this pattern holds for many gases. Extending the pattern of behaviour to lower temperatures leads to an interesting idea. At about $-273\,°C$ the pressure of a gas appears to reach zero. This temperature is called **absolute zero** and is the start of the **absolute** or **Kelvin** scale of temperature. Each degree on the Kelvin scale is the same size as a degree on the celsius scale. It appears that at absolute zero temperature, the molecules in a gas stop moving!

(ii) Changing the volume. When a gas is squeezed into a smaller space, the pressure increases. When a gas expands into a larger space, the pressure decreases. Robert Boyle, working in Oxford in 1650 noted that, provided the temperature and mass of a gas do not change, there was a simple relationship between the pressure and volume for many gases. This relationship, known as **Boyle's Law**, is summarised by

pressure × volume = constant   for a
$$P \times V = \text{constant}$$ fixed mass of
$$P = \frac{\text{constant}}{V}$$ gas at a constant temperature

This result means that as a gas is compressed into half its volume, the pressure of the gas will double. If all the molecules of a gas are forced to occupy a smaller space, they will collide more frequently with the walls of their container and so the pressure will increase.

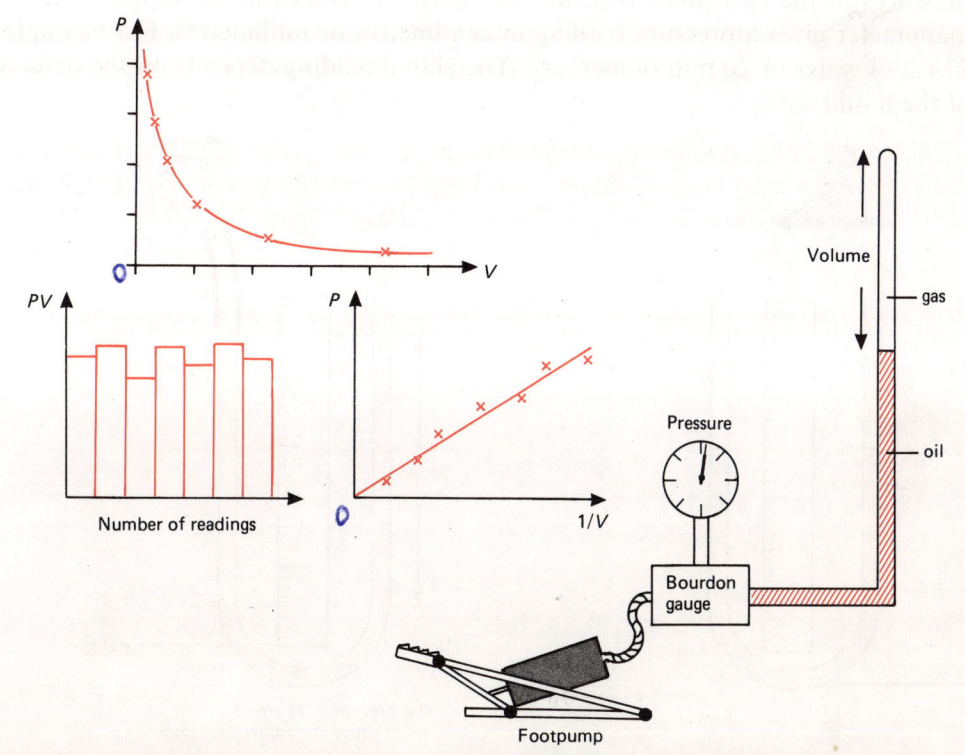

Figure 8.7 Pressures and volumes for a fixed mass of gas at constant temperature

8.4 Measuring pressures

The pressure or stress in a solid can only be measured directly by finding both the **force** acting (newtons) and the surface **area** (square metres) in question. A force meter and metre rule are needed to do this.

A number of instruments may be used to find the pressure in fluids (liquids or gases).

A **bourdon gauge** works by allowing the fluid to force a coiled tube to straighten out. A needle attached to the tube moves to show the pressure.

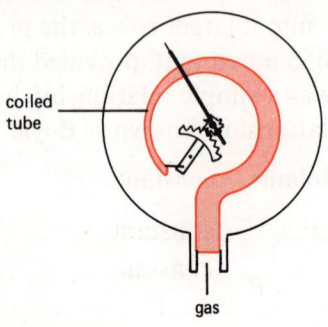

Figure 8.8 Inside a bourdon gauge

A **manometer** is a U-tube containing a liquid. With atmospheric pressure pushing on both sides of the tube the liquid levels are the same. When one end experiences a change in pressure the balance is disturbed. The difference in pressures in the two tubes is measured by the difference in the liquid levels. A manometer gives a pressure reading in centimetres or millimetres. For example: 27 cm of water or 20 mm of mercury. The actual reading depends on the density of the liquid used.

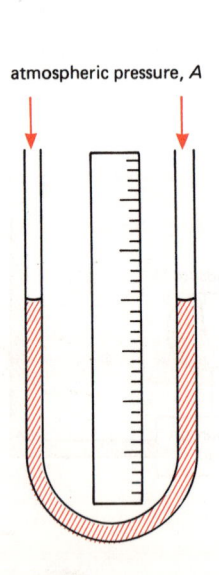

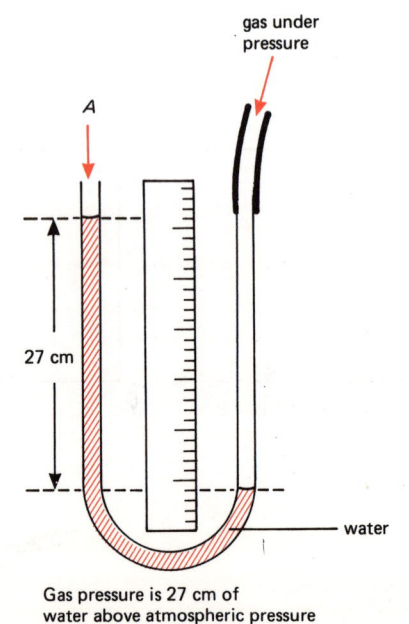

Figure 8.9 Using a manometer

A **barometer** measures air pressure. A mercury barometer uses the same idea as a manometer. The distance between two mercury levels in a tube gives a way of measuring the air pressure. At the top of the tube there is a vacuum. The only downward force is due to the weight of the mercury in the tube. On a fine day when the air pressure is high, the mercury column will be pushed higher. The air pressure on a normal day is about 760 mm of mercury.

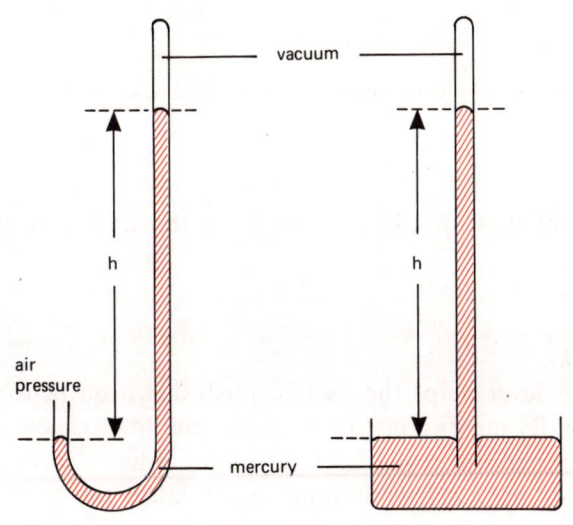

Figure 8.10   A mercury barometer measures atmospheric pressure in cm of mercury

A barometer can be designed which works on a different idea; one that does not require a liquid. The **aneroid barometer** measures the squashing effect which air has on an evacuated box. As the air pressure rises the box is squashed further and this is registered by a moving needle arrangement.

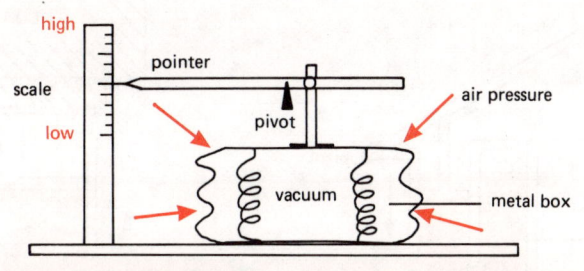

Figure 8.11   An aneroid barometer

As air pressure falls when you rise to greater heights in the atmosphere, you can use a barometer to tell you how far up you are. Aneroid barometers are used as altimeters in aeroplanes for this purpose.

8.5 Related reading: Hydraulic systems

Blaise Pascal is credited with realising that the pressure in a fluid will act in all directions.

The pressure is the same
at all places in the fluid

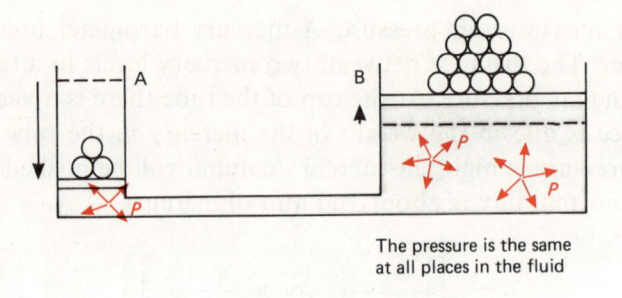

Figure 8.12 'Pressure acts throughout a fluid'—Pascal

Two examples of how this idea is used are the hydraulic jack and the car braking system.

The hydraulic jack

See Figure 8.13. A lever helps the user to push down on piston A which has a small surface area. By moving piston A several centimetres, oil is forced through a connecting valve and into cylinder B. Cylinder B has a large surface area and so piston B moves only a few millimetres. Because the pressure is the same throughout the oil, a small force on a small area becomes a large force on a large area. Before the next stroke, cylinder A is refilled from a reservoir.

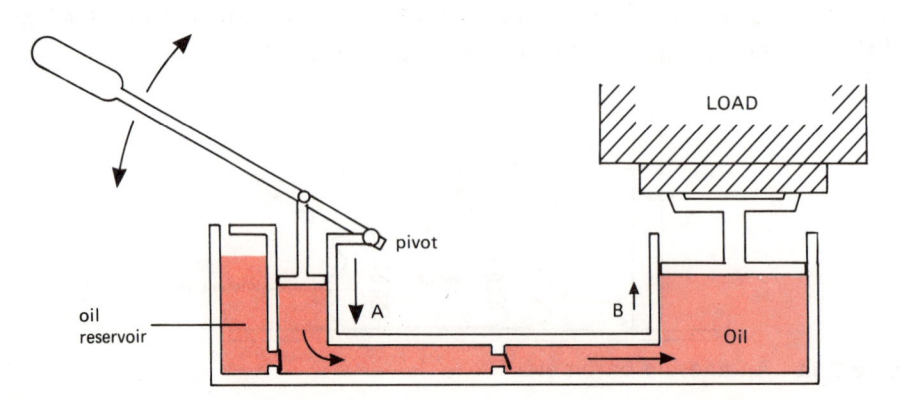

Figure 8.13 Inside a hydraulic jack

Car brakes

A large force is needed to stop a car. A large force is provided by pistons with large surface areas. When the brake pedal is depressed the small piston in the master cylinder moves and compresses all the brake fluid in the system. This extra pressure forces larger pistons, usually one at each wheel, to move a small distance on to the moving wheel. Friction then causes the wheels to slow down.

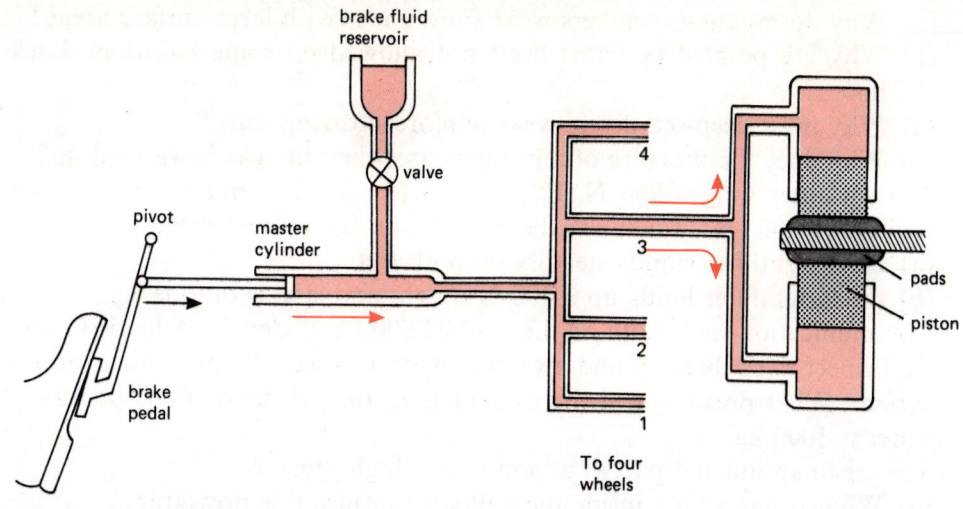

Figure 8.14 A car braking system

8.6 Summary

- *Stress and pressure can be related to forces by*

$$pressure = \frac{force}{area}$$

- *The unit for measuring pressure is the pascal, Pa.*

$$1\ Pa = 1\ N/m^2$$

- *The pressure in a liquid or gas increases with depth.*

$$p = h\rho g$$

- *The pressure of a fixed mass of gas is proportional to its temperature as measured on the absolute scale of temperatures.*

$$p \propto T$$

- *The pressure of a fixed mass of gas at a constant temperature increases as the gas is squeezed.*

$$P \times V = constant$$

- *A pressure applied to a fluid is spread everywhere in the fluid.*
- *Gas pressures may be measured in cm or mm of liquid if a manometer or barometer is used.*
- *Normal air pressure at sea level is about 76 cm height of mercury or about 1.0×10^5 Pa.*

8.7 Progress questions

1. Use ideas about pressure to explain the following:

(a) Why do mountain walkers wear snow shoes with large surface areas?
(b) Why are pointed (stiletto) heels not allowed on some ballroom dance floors?
(c) Why must deep-sea divers wear reinforced diving suits?
(d) Why does the pressure of a gas increase when the gas is warmed up?

2. A weightlifter weighs 960 N. Each of his feet has a contact area with the ground of 0.003 m². Calculate the pressure on the ground when
   (a) the weightlifter stands steadily on both feet
   (b) the weightlifter holds up a 400 N weight and stands on one leg.

3. Communication cables run on the sea bed 6000 m under the Atlantic Ocean. To inspect the cables an underwater camera is lowered from a boat on the surface. What pressure will the camera need to withstand? (The density of water is 1000 kg/m³).

4. The air in an inflated party balloon is at a high pressure.
   (a) What is happening inside the balloon to cause this pressure?
   (b) What happens to the pressure in a party balloon if the temperature of the air inside decreases? Explain your answer.

5. Figure 8.15 shows a syringe containing 200 cm³ of hydrogen gas at normal atmospheric pressure. Weights were slowly added to the syringe until the volume became 50 cm³.

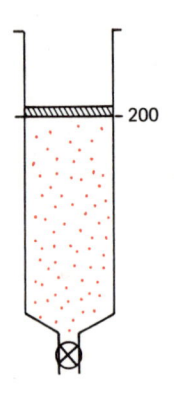

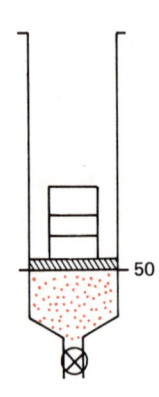

Figure 8.15

What has happened to:
(a) the volume of the gas in the syringe?
(b) the mass of gas in the syringe?
(c) the density of the gas in the syringe?
(d) the pressure of the gas in the syringe?

6. Figure 8.16 shows a simple barometer.
   (a) Use the diagram to find a value for the air pressure at the place where the barometer is being used.
   (b) What do you think would happen to the barometer measurements if the barometer were taken to the top of Ben Nevis, the highest peak in Scotland?

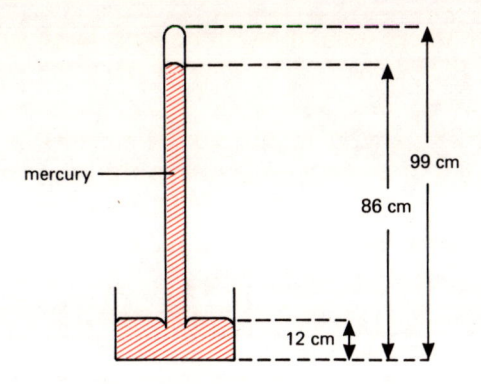

Figure 8.16

PRACTICAL WORK

9.1 Why do practical work?

A simple answer to this question is to realise that much of the knowledge and understanding which scientists have developed throughout history has been acquired by testing out ideas practically. Testing out ideas, investigating phenomena in controlled conditions and accurately making measurements are part of the everyday life of scientists. How can you be sure that an idea works unless you test it?

For science students there are other reasons for doing practical work. For a start, practical work can help you to understand ideas which you meet in theory lessons. You can read about Hooke's Law for example, but when you experiment with stretching springs you develop a 'feel' for what the Law says. Secondly, doing practical work brings you face to face with physics apparatus which you would not normally use at home. Knowing about the names and applications of items of equipment and using them will give you a chance to develop some **practical skills**. These skills may be tested in examinations and will also give you confidence when faced with new practical work in the future. Finally, practical work gives you the chance to work at your own pace, test your own ideas and enjoy your physics!

9.2 Safety in the laboratory

A feature of practical work is that it can be dangerous. All students should realise that danger can be avoided if everybody is aware of how to behave sensibly and safely. Here is some advice on being as safe as possible.

(a) Fire
Know what sound the fire alarm makes and find out the exit route from the room you work in. In the event of a fire, do not panic. Inform your teacher straight away.

(b) First aid
All laboratories will have a first-aid box or cupboard. All accidents must be reported.

(c) Eyes
Eye protection should be worn whenever there is a possibility that chemicals will splash. Goggles help to protect the eyes from glass fragments and stretched metal wires. There should be an eye-wash available in the laboratory. Plenty of running water should be used as soon as a chemical splash hits your eye. Special goggles

should be worn when using a laser. Never look into a laser beam. A 'danger laser' notice should be placed outside the lab.

(d) Electrical apparatus

Never use apparatus with worn leads or broken plugs. Report these to the lab technician. Switch off the apparatus before plugging into the mains supply. Check your circuit connections, preferably with your teacher, before starting work. Never 'experiment' with electricity or open up electric apparatus. If you think something is going wrong, **switch off** immediately.

(e) Radioactivity

The radioactive sources which you will be exposed to in school or college should be 'sealed' and of low activity. Nevertheless you should always handle sources with tongs and point them away from people. Store all sources in labelled lead-lined boxes.

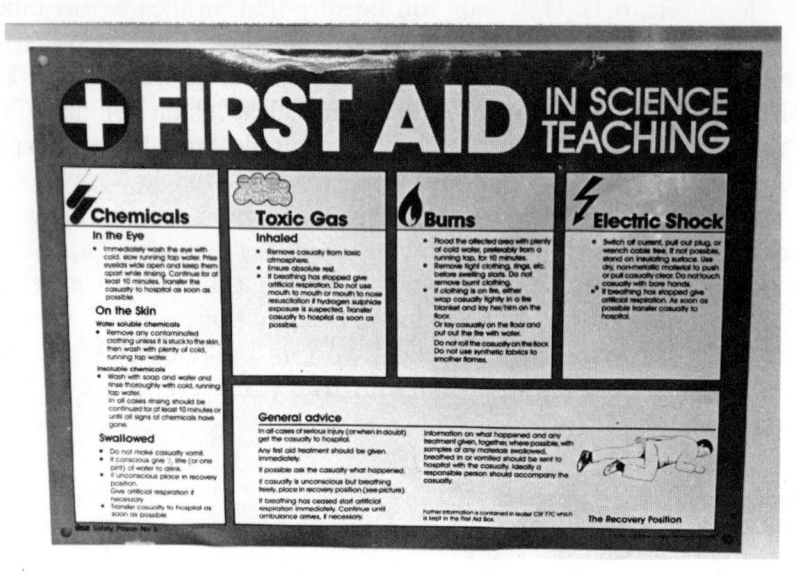

Figure 9.1 Be as safe as possible. Read the safety notices

(f) Chemicals

You are unlikely to meet many chemicals in your physics course. Listen carefully to your teacher's instructions whenever chemicals are used. You may need to wear eye protection. The main dangers are splashing and spillage. The laboratory technician or your teacher should be informed if, for example, a mercury thermometer breaks. If you decide to wear a lab-coat be aware of the sleeves as they tend to drag things around with them.

(g) General common sense

Being safe is being sensible. Practical work often involves moving around the laboratory. Do not leave your coats and bags in the way of others and always walk rather than run even when you are excited about a discovery. Do not be tempted to eat in a laboratory as contamination is likely to result. Perhaps most importantly you should think twice before doing anything. Ask yourself some simple questions, for example, have I checked the circuit, what are the possible dangers, is my thermometer going to roll off the bench?

9.3 Getting started

(a) Preparing

Before you start taking measurements it is a good idea to plan your work. Ask yourself a few questions.

- *Are there instructions? Do I understand them?*
- *Is this all the apparatus I need?*
- *How much time has been allowed?*
- *Where shall I write down the results?*
- *Is my note book ready? Should I work in best or in rough first?*
- *Have I organised the bench space effectively?*
- *What is the purpose of doing this practical?*

(b) Assembling apparatus

Quite often you will have to assemble pieces of apparatus together before taking measurements. If there is a diagram to follow, use it, especially if it is an electric circuit diagram. A few hints which you will find useful are:

- Check your circuit with the diagram by starting at the battery and working your way around the circuit. If there is a voltmeter in the circuit, leave it out at first. Connect it last of all.

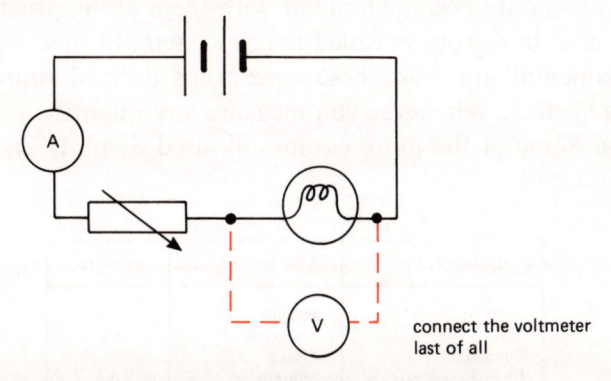

Figure 9.2 Circuit diagrams should be followed carefully

- If you need to use a clampstand, boss and clamp, check that the rod is firmly screwed into its base. Do not overtighten the boss and clamp. You may need to adjust their positions later. Ensure that the stand will not overbalance by making sure that the load is over the base of the stand.
- Clamping glassware needs some care. Do not overtighten clamps.
- If your are using heavy weights to stretch springs, for example, ensure that there is soft protection below the weights in case they fall. (This protects the weights and the floor!)

- When using dynamics trolleys and runways it is a good idea to tilt the runway a little before you start. This allows the trolleys to run freely along the runway without being slowed by friction. Remember to arrange to catch runaway trolleys before they fall off the end of the runway.

9.4 Making measurements

Practical skills, like planning your work and appreciating safety rules, rely greatly on your own common sense. The skills needed to make good measurements have to be learnt and practised.

(a) Observations

Before taking a measurement you need to decide what exactly is going to be measured and when to take your measurements. Only by observing closely will you know what is changing and how often to measure the change. Observation does not only mean looking. You can listen for changes, feel temperature changes and even smell changes. Use all your senses when observing. Write down notes about changes before you forget them. If nothing happens, then record that nothing happens. Realising that nothing changes can be a very useful result. A material that does not conduct electricity will make a useful insulator!

(b) Units, symbols and quantities

Most measurements you make will be of quantities. Your value will have a size and a unit. Some examples are: 2.3 cm, 16 volts, 10.5 N. Many units are used in physics and you will only become familiar with them all by practice. The agreed system of units used in Europe is called the *SI* system. In this system some units are called 'fundamental' and from these some other 'derived' units have emerged. Each unit has a symbol. Whenever you measure any quantity you must state its **size** and its **unit**. Some of the more commonly used SI units and their symbols are given in Figure 9.3.

QUANTITY	SI UNIT	SYMBOL
Time	second	s
Mass	kilogram	kg
Length	metre	m
Electric current	ampere	A
Force	newton	N
Work	joule	J
Pressure	pascal	Pa
Charge	coulomb	C
Power	watt	W
Frequency	hertz	Hz
Electrical resistance	ohm	Ω
Velocity or speed	metre/second	m/s

Figure 9.3 Common SI units and their symbols

(c) Reading scales

A measurement requires a scale to give it a size. Apart from reading the scale, a good physics student should be able to estimate a rough value for the quantity before making a measurement and needs also to know how to handle the measuring instrument. Figure 9.4 gives some examples for you to practise with.

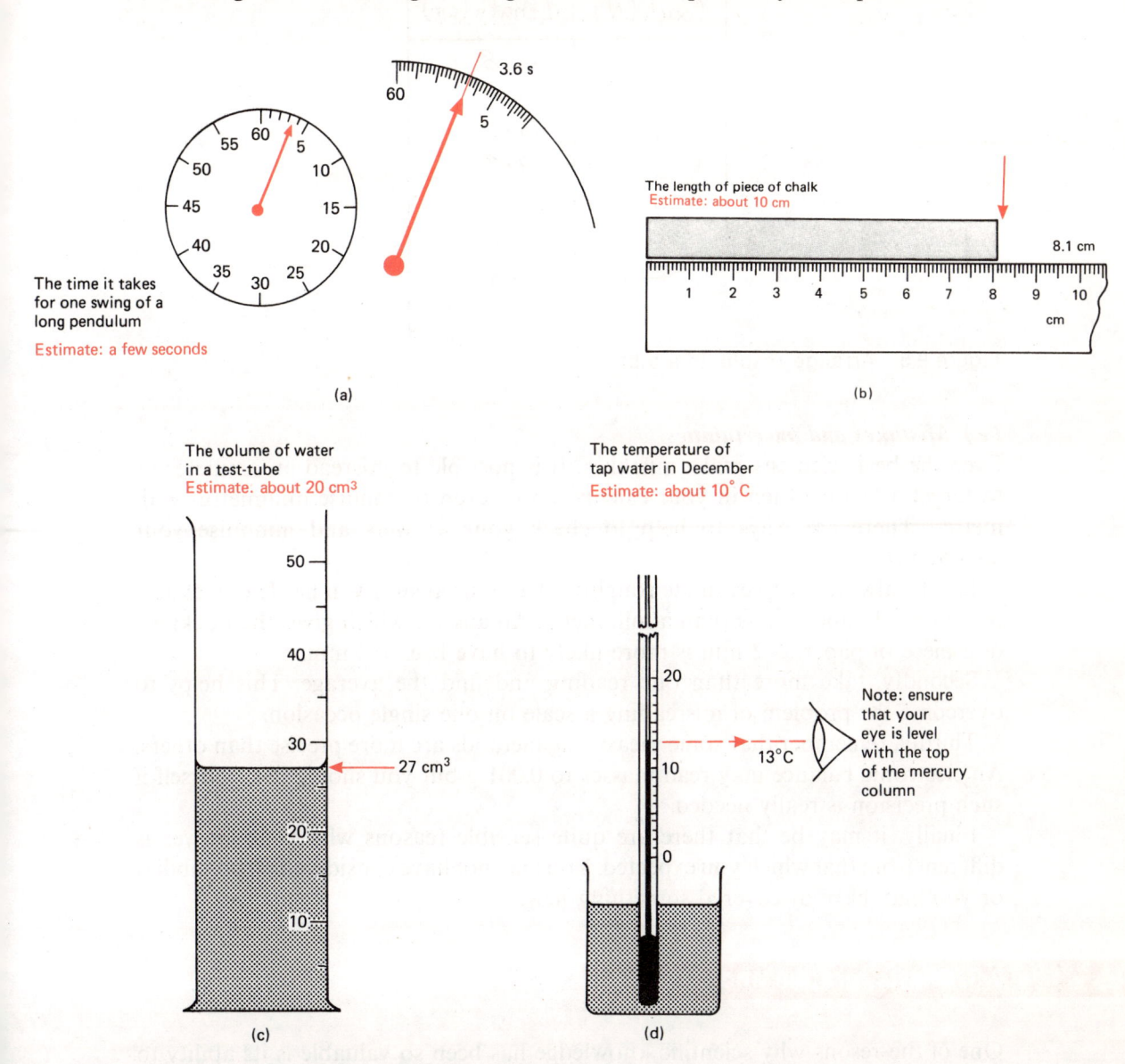

Figure 9.4 Estimating and measuring

(d) Recording results

A good way to record your results is to construct a table. The table should have a title and each result needs to be clearly labelled with its correct unit. You can save space by writing the unit at the top of the table. If you know the range of your results then you could plot the results directly on to a graph as you take them. (It is safer to record them in a table first.)

Stretching two springs in series	
Load (N)	Length (cm)
0	4.8
1	10.0
2	14.6
3	19.8
4	24.2
5	29.0
	34.3

Figure 9.5 Arrange results in a table

(e) Mistakes and uncertainties

Even the best scientists make mistakes. It is possible to misread an ammeter or to forget a factor of ten in your calculation or even to confuse millimetres with metres. There are ways to help to check your answers and minimise your uncertainty.

Firstly, always try to estimate roughly what your answer will be. The thickness of a sheet of paper is less than a millimetre. An answer which gives the thickness of a piece of paper as 2 mm is more likely to have been 0.2 mm.

Secondly, take more than one reading and find the average. This helps to overcome the problem of misreading a scale on one single occasion.

Thirdly, remember that some measuring methods are more precise than others. An electronic balance may read masses to 0.001 g but you should ask yourself if such precision is really needed.

Finally, it may be that there are quite sensible reasons why your answer is different from that which you expected. You may not have considered all possibilities or you may have discovered something new.

9.5 Charts, graphs and patterns

One of the resons why scientific knowledge has been so valuable is its ability to predict things. It does this by discovering patterns in nature. Scientists will look closely at their results to uncover simple patterns and then extend these patterns to new situations or look for reasons for the patterns. One way to see if your results reveal a pattern is to make a chart or a graph of them. Charts and graphs reveal shapes which are easier to recognise as patterns.

At the end of your practical lesson you may find that you have gained useful knowledge about how pieces of equipment work or perhaps you have measured a physical constant, a density or an acceleration perhaps. Occasionally you will have found out something that you previously did not understand or did not

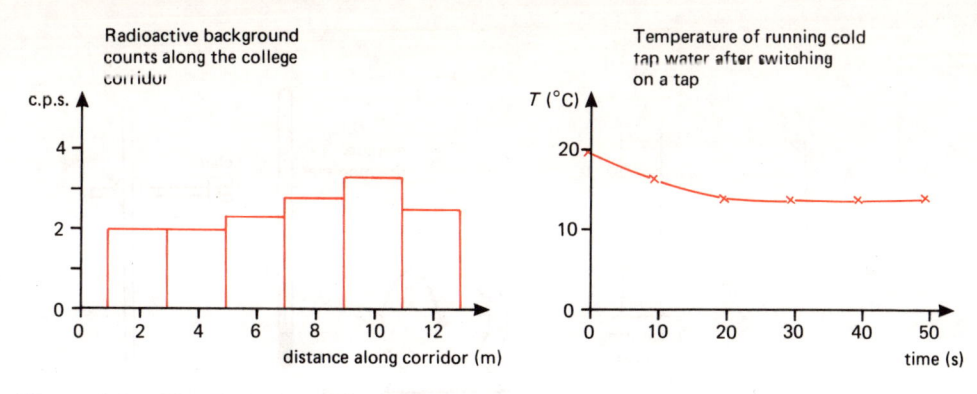

Figure 9.6 Charts and graphs help to make patterns clearer

expect. All these final end-points can be written down as a **conclusion** at the end of your experimental notes.

9.6 Physics apparatus

Listed in Figure 9.7 are items of special equipment that you will have met during your course. Some items you will have seen demonstrated and others you will have used yourself. Not every college or school has every item, so do not worry if there are some which you have not seen.

9.7 Summary

- *Practical work has many purposes. It can help you to understand some theoretical ideas. It can teach you practical skills and it can allow you to explore situations on your own.*
- *You must be aware of safety at all times.*
- *Plan your practical work and try to be organised.*
- *Taking measurements requires skills and techniques which need to be learned.*

9.8 Progress questions

1. What unit would you use to measure the following quantities?

   (a) energy, (b) potential difference, (c) force, (d) distance, (e) time, (f) velocity.

2. Write down the readings shown on the scales in Figure 9.8.
3. Below are some estimations of quantities:

   - about 20 mm
   - about 50 g
   - about 30 N
   - about 30 cm

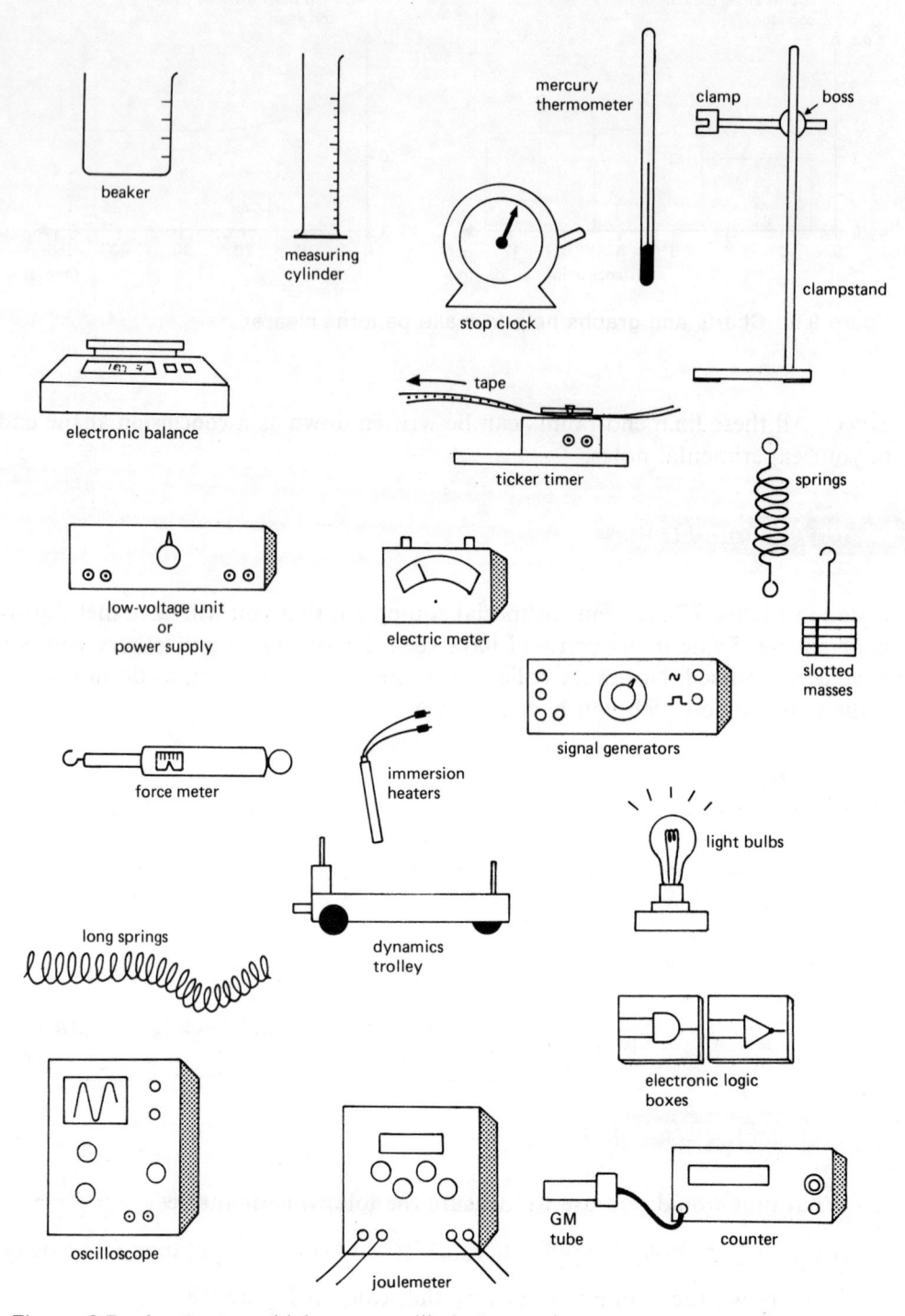

Figure 9.7 Apparatus which you are likely to use in your course

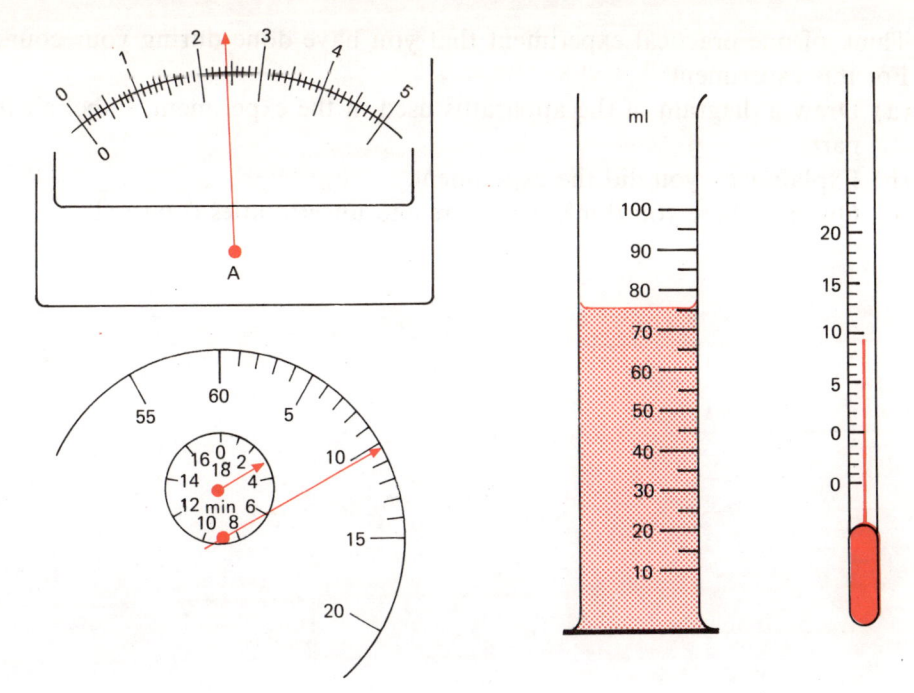

Figure 9.8

- about 1 kg
- about 2 m
- about 30 s
- about 100 W
- about 5 min
- about 0.1 N

Which estimation would be closest for:
(a) the mass of a litre of milk
(b) the time it takes to run 1600 m
(c) the height of a policeman
(d) the power of a lightbulb
(e) the thickness of your thumb.

4. Seven students were asked to measure the length of a piece of string. Here are the seven results:

    460 mm, 448 mm, 44.5 cm, 455 mm, 46.1 mm, 458 mm, 450 mm

    (a) One of these values is very different from the rest. Which one?
    (b) What is the average value for the length of the string?
    (c) Why do you think the seven values were all different?

5. What is the name of the piece of apparatus used for
    (a) measuring temperature?
    (b) measuring electric current?
    (c) measuring distances?
    (d) measuring liquid volumes?

6. Think of one practical experiment that you have done during your course. For this experiment:
   (a) Draw a diagram of the apparatus used in the experiment. Label all the parts.
   (b) Explain why you did the experiment.
   (c) Outline where you think the errors and uncertainties occurred.

MATHEMATICAL SKILLS

10.1 Physics and mathematics

Studying physics is about understanding ideas, the meanings of new words and how to apply these to solving problems. In the real world of engineering and practical science, words and ideas are not enough. The physics student needs to be able to perform calculations in order to test predictions accurately and to be able to process information gained from laboratory measurements.

A good physics student does not need to be a good mathematician but must at least know how to handle numbers confidently. This Unit cannot teach you how to do maths. It will outline the maths you need for a GCSE physics course. Perhaps a maths teacher will help to explain some of the ideas and techniques covered here.

10.2 Handling numbers

(a) Four operations ($+ - \times \div$)

The numbers you get from experiments are rarely simple. You will need to use a calculator to perform some operations for you. A cheap *'scientific'* calculator is a good investment. Learn how to use it early on in your course. Calculator instructions are not always clear. Perhaps a friend or your teacher can show you how all the functions work.

It is always useful to be able to do simple operations in your head or using rough paper. This will help you to check your calculator answer by having a rough idea of what it should be.

(b) Squares and square roots

You need to understand these two ideas, for example, 5^2 is 25 *(5 × 5)* and the square root of 16 is 4 *(16 = 4 × 4)*. Remember that 'squared' does **not** mean 'multiply by two'.

Many formulae in physics contain squares, for example, kinetic energy ($\frac{1}{2}mv^2$) and electrical power (I^2R). What effect does the 'square' have? Let us take an example of a 1000 kg bus moving at 4 m/s. What happens to the kinetic energy of the bus when it doubles its speed?

$$\begin{aligned}
\text{KE before} &= \tfrac{1}{2}mv^2 & \text{KE after} &= \tfrac{1}{2}mv^2 \\
&= \tfrac{1}{2} \times 1000 \times 4^2 & &= \tfrac{1}{2} \times 1000 \times 8^2 \\
&= \underline{8000 \text{ J}} & &= \underline{32000 \text{ J}}
\end{aligned}$$

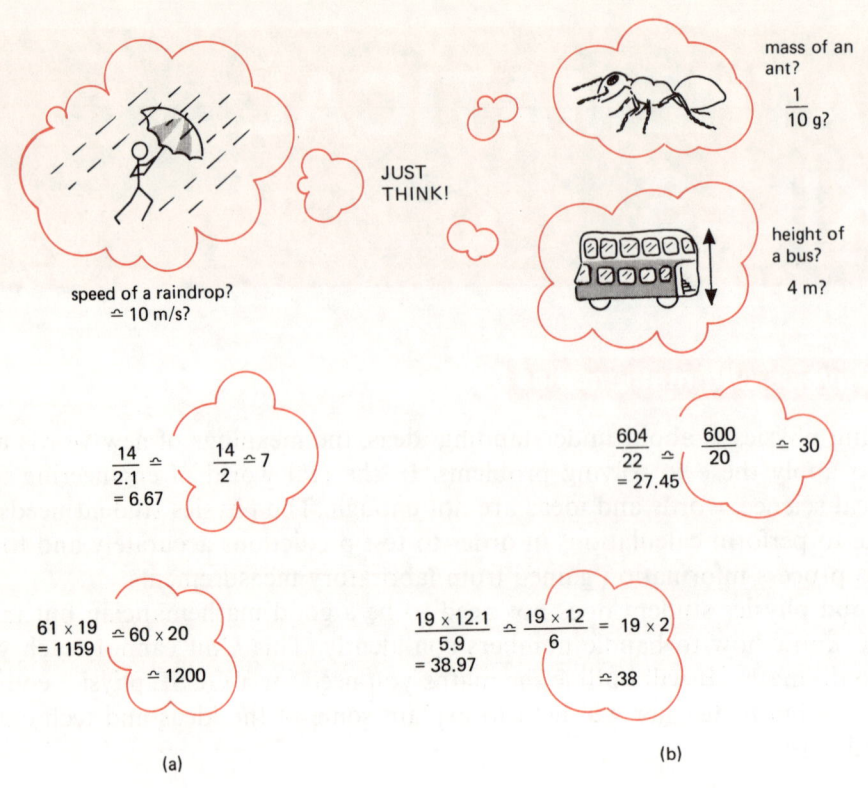

Figure 10.1 You should gain practice estimating physical quantities and answers to numerical problems

You will notice that by doubling the speed, the kinetic energy increased four times. This is the effect of the 'square'.

(c) Percentage, fractions and decimals

Are there any numbers between 0 and 1? Yes, but they are expressed only as fractions or decimals.

All fractions and decimals can be turned into percentages by multiplying by 100. They then become numbers between 0 and 100.

Here is an example where both fractions and decimals might be used.

A copper wire 200 cm long was extended by 40 cm before breaking. The extension as a **fraction** of the original length was $40/200 = 1.5$. As a **percentage** this is $1/5 \times 100 =$ **20 per cent**

(d) Significant figures

Let us suppose that you had the job of cutting up a length of string 22 m long to make seven equal length pendulums. Using a calculator, $22/7 =$ **3.142 857 1** m. This answer contains eight 'significant figures'. How important is each figure?

If you are measuring the length with a metre rule, the smallest division is a millimetre. This is as close as you can measure. This cuts your number down to four significant figures **3.143** m.

Now your scissors may not be sharp enough for you to judge closer than the

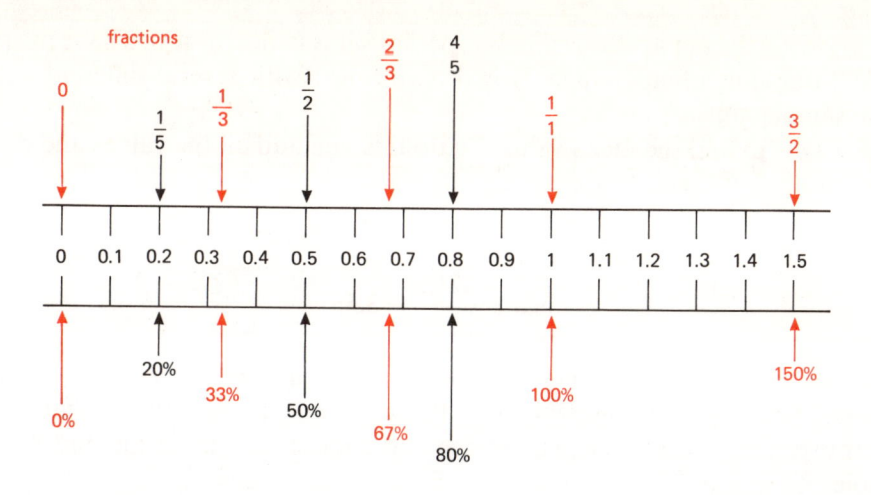

Figure 10.2 Between 0 and 1—fractions and decimals

nearest centimetre. The length you need to cut is then **3.14** m, three significant figures.

If the exact length is not important you may decide to make each pendulum about **3** m, one significant figure.

The important thing about significant figures is to realise that what is significant depends on the situation you find yourself in. If you are taking measurements from a scale to two significant figures, for example

$$\text{current} = 1.4 \text{ A, voltage} = 2.7 \text{ V}$$

then a calculation of resistance, V/I, should not be quoted as $2.7/1.4 =$ **1.928 571 4** ohms but as **1.9** ohms.

A point to remember is that your calculator is only as accurate as the numbers you enter. For GCSE you are unlikely to do many experiments which justify results to more than two significant figures.

(e) Standard form

You will sometimes have to deal with very small or very large numbers, for example, the size of a molecule might be about 0.000 000 004 m or the mass of a train about 60 000 kg. To save you the job of writing out all these zeros, it is possible to use what is called a standard form. Standard form uses a number between 1 and 10 and a power of ten.

$$
\begin{aligned}
0.000\,000\,004 \text{ m} &= 4 \times 0.000\,000\,01 = 4 \times 10^{-8} \text{ m} \\
60\,000 \text{ kg} &= 6 \times 10\,000 = 6 \times 10^{4} \text{ kg} \\
268\,000 \text{ m} &= 2.68 \times 10^{5} \text{ m} \\
0.085 \text{ kg} &= 8.5 \times 10^{-2} \text{ kg} \\
0.000\,000\,57 \text{ kg} &= 5.7 \times 10^{-7} \text{ g}
\end{aligned}
$$

Figure 10.3 Converting to standard form

(f) Averages

It is always good practice to repeat a reading when taking measurements. You never known if the apparatus is reliable, perhaps it is faulty, or if you have misread a scale. Situations often change. How do you deal with several different values for the same quantity?

One way is to find the **mean** value. To do this you add all the values and divide by the number of them. For example

values: 3.4, 3.6, 4.0, 3.2, 3.5, 3.6

$$\text{mean} = \frac{21.3}{6} = \mathbf{3.55}$$

Another way is to find the **median** value. This is particularly useful if you have one result which is very different from all the others. To find the median value, you arrange the values in increasing size and choose the one in the middle. For example

values: 3.4, 3.6, 78.1, 4.0, 3.2, 3.5, 3.6

arranged in order: 3.2, 3.4, 3.5, **3.6**, 3.6, 4.0, 78.1

median = **3.6**

Finally, if you find that most of your values are the same then you might choose the one which occurs most often. This is called the **mode**. For example

values: 3.4, **3.6**, **3.6**, 4.0, 3.2, **3.6**, **3.6**

mode = **3.6**

10.3 Length and shape

(a) Measuring distance
A ruler is perhaps the most simple and often used measuring instrument. You need to be familiar with the difference between a centimetre, a millimetre and a metre. Most rulers are marked with millimetres as their smallest division. There is a greater chance of an error when measuring small distances, say a few mm, with a ruler. Micrometers and vernier scales are used for small distances.

(b) Measuring angles
You need to know how to use a protractor to measure angles. Angles are measured in degrees. The corner of a square is 90 degrees and called a *'right angle'*.

(c) Calculating areas
The area of a rectangle is found by finding the length and the breadth and multiplying them. The units of area are the units of length × breadth. (Both length and breadth should have the same unit.) For example

$$2 \text{ mm} \times 4 \text{ mm} = 8 \text{ mm}^2$$

$$5 \text{ cm} \times 5 \text{ cm} = 25 \text{ cm}^2$$

$$1.2 \text{ m} \times 0.6 \text{ m} = 0.72 \text{ m}^2$$

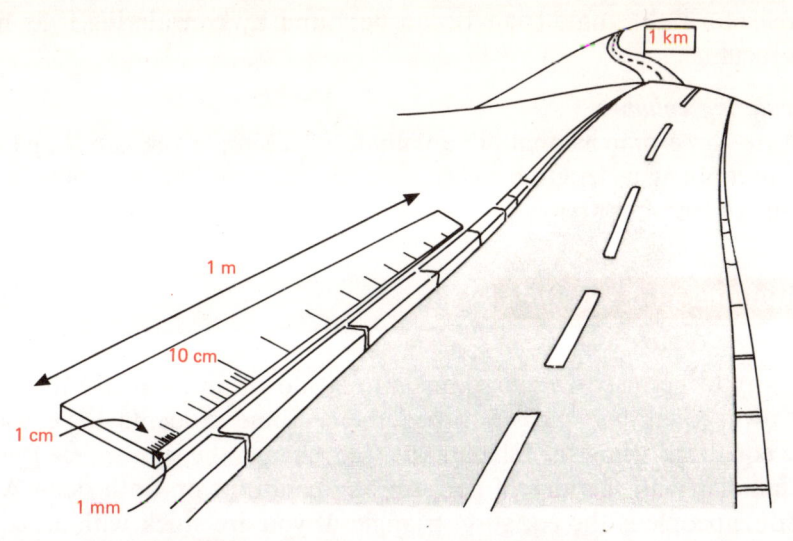

Figure 10.4 It is important to develop a sense of distance

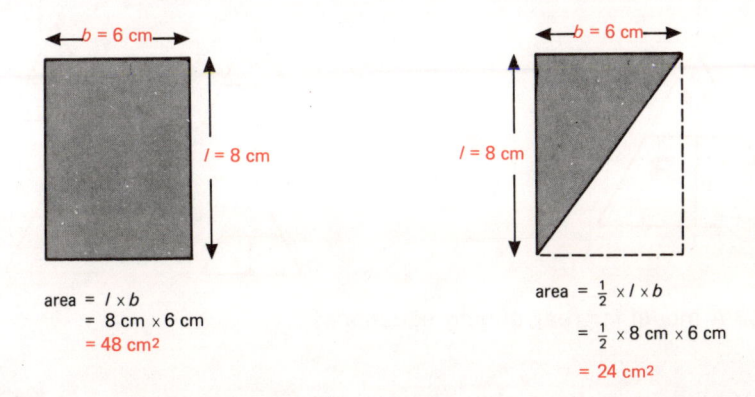

area = $l \times b$
     = 8 cm × 6 cm
     = 48 cm²

area = $\frac{1}{2} \times l \times b$
     = $\frac{1}{2}$ × 8 cm × 6 cm
     = 24 cm²

Figure 10.5 Calculating areas

volume = 6 cm × 15 cm²
       = 90 m³

length = 6 cm

cross-sectional area = 15 cm²

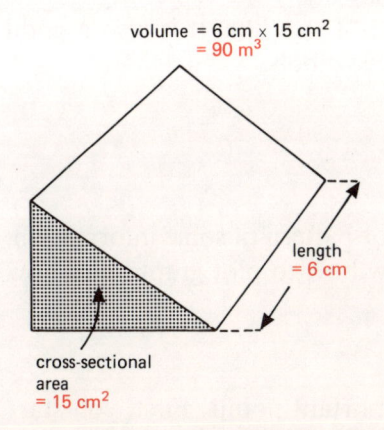

area = 4 cm²

12 cm

volume = 12 cm × 4 cm²
       = 48 m⁶

Figure 10.6 Calculating volumes

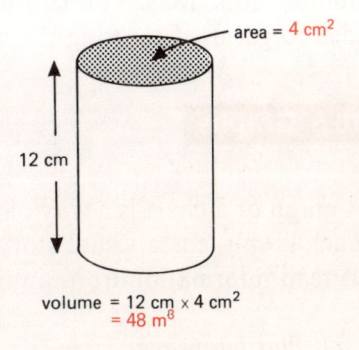

107

The area of a right angle triangle can be found by considering it as half the area of a rectangle.

(d) Calculating volumes

Volumes are three dimensional. The volume of a simple regular shape can be found by multiplying its length by its cross-sectional area. The units of volume will be the units of length × area.

10.4 Equations and symbols

The best way to get used to equations is to sit down and practise them. Make up your own equations and rearrange them. Some students have learnt to rearrange equations using the 'change the side, change the sign' rule. Others will be more familiar with the idea of performing operations on both sides. A useful tool for some people is the equation triangle. If you are stuck with an equation you might like to use a simple model to help solve your problem.

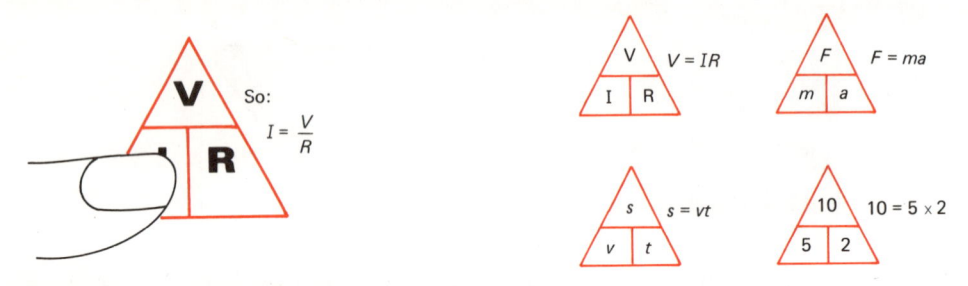

Figure 10.7 A model for rearranging equations

You must remember that to keep both sides of an equation equal, whatever is done to one side must also be done to the other.

Many equations in science start off with symbols in place of numbers, $V = I \times R$, and $F = m \times a$ for example. You can treat these in exactly the same ways as the number equations. You can use equation triangles if you like. It is also a good idea to get used to using the words as well as the symbols.

10.5 Graphs

A graph or a chart is a way of showing the shape or pattern of some information. Each graph tells a visual story. You need to know how to plot graphs and how to read information from a graph.

(a) Plotting graphs

Study the following example. It will cover the important points. First, you start off with some pairs of values, perhaps the results of an experiment.

force (N)	1	2	3	4	5	6	7
acceleration (m/s²)	0.5	0.9	1.5	2.0	2.4	3.0	3.5

- Plan your axes. They do not have to fill up the entire graph paper space. Choose a sensible scale (avoid 0, 3, 6, 9, etc.) Use a ruler. Label the axes with quantity and units.

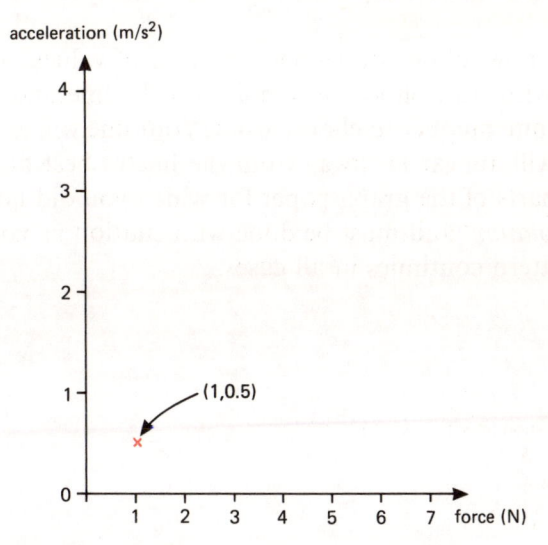

Figure 10.8 Starting a graph

- Select a pair of values, called coordinates, and plot a cross or dot legibly on the graph in the correct place.

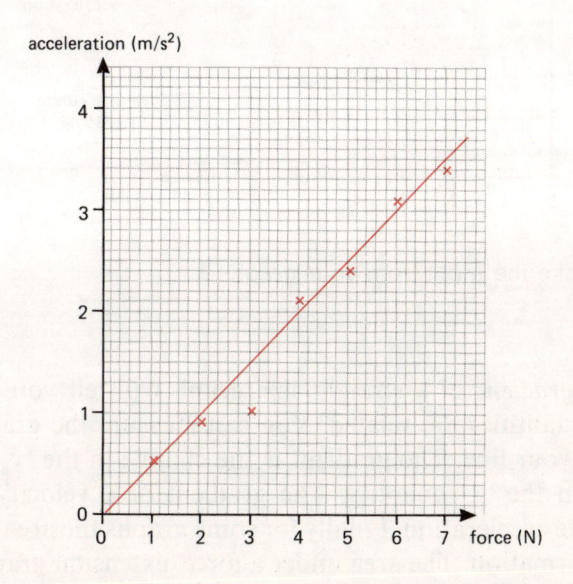

Figure 10.9 A line of best fit

109

- Decide whether the pattern is a line or a curve. If it looks like a line, then use a ruler to draw the *line of best fit*. This does not have to pass through any points, although it might. Avoid the temptation to join the first and last points. A curve of best fit can be drawn if the points lie in a curve.

(b) Information from your graph

The first thing a graph can show is whether there is a regular pattern. If there is, then it is likely that there is a physical relationship between the two quantities plotted—perhaps a relationship which can later be expressed by an equation (see Section 10.5).

Your line will now allow you to find any pair of values, not just those which you started off with. Just choose any point on the line and read off the values. You have an infinite number to choose from. Your line will expose any inaccurate readings. They will appear far away from the line of best fit. Your line can also be extended to parts of the graph paper for which you did not have results. This is called '*extrapolation*' and must be done with caution as you cannot always be sure that the pattern continues in all cases.

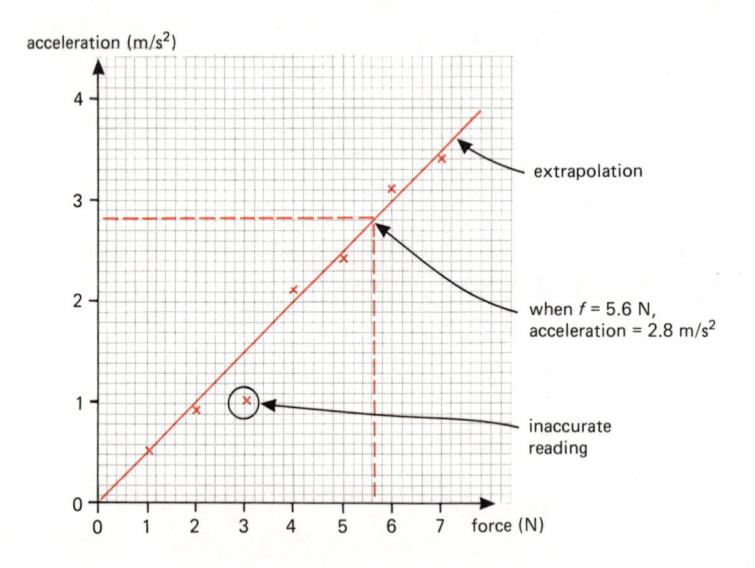

Figure 10.10 Make the most from your graph

The *slope* or *gradient* of a straight line graph will tell you something about how your two quantities are related. You can measure the gradient by drawing a triangle using your line. The gradient is the change in the 'y' quantity divided by the change in the 'x' quantity. The gradient of a velocity/time graph, for example, gives the acceleration. Finally for some graphs the area '*under*' the graph carries some information. The area under a force/extension graph gives the work done in stretching.

velocity (m/s)

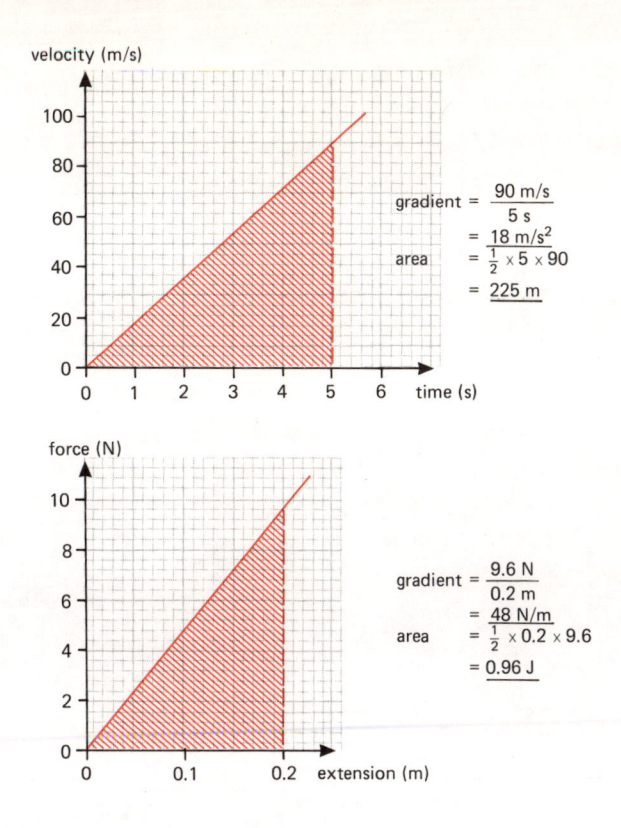

gradient = $\dfrac{90 \text{ m/s}}{5 \text{ s}}$
       = $\underline{18 \text{ m/s}^2}$
area = $\tfrac{1}{2} \times 5 \times 90$
    = $\underline{225 \text{ m}}$

force (N)

gradient = $\dfrac{9.6 \text{ N}}{0.2 \text{ m}}$
       = $\underline{48 \text{ N/m}}$
area = $\tfrac{1}{2} \times 0.2 \times 9.6$
    = $\underline{0.96 \text{ J}}$

Figure 10.11 Slopes and areas can have physical meaning

10.6 Relationships and proportion

A relationship describes the way in which one quantity depends on another. There is a relationship between the speed of a train and the time it takes for a journey. In your course you will meet a relationship between the temperature of a gas and the pressure of the gas, and many more besides. Three common types of relationships are explained below.

(a) Direct proportion
This relationship is shown by a straight line graph passing through the origin (0, 0). The load/extension graph for a spring shows that, within the elastic limit, there is a relationship between the load and the extension. If the load doubles then the extension will double. This is what is meant by direct proportion. An everyday example of direct proportion is the teacher to pupil ratio in a school. For each new class of students there needs to be another teacher. The ratio is about 1 to 17.

(b) Inverse proportion
Inverse proportion might be thought of as the opposite to direct proportion. An inverse relationship results in an increase in one quantity with a decrease in the

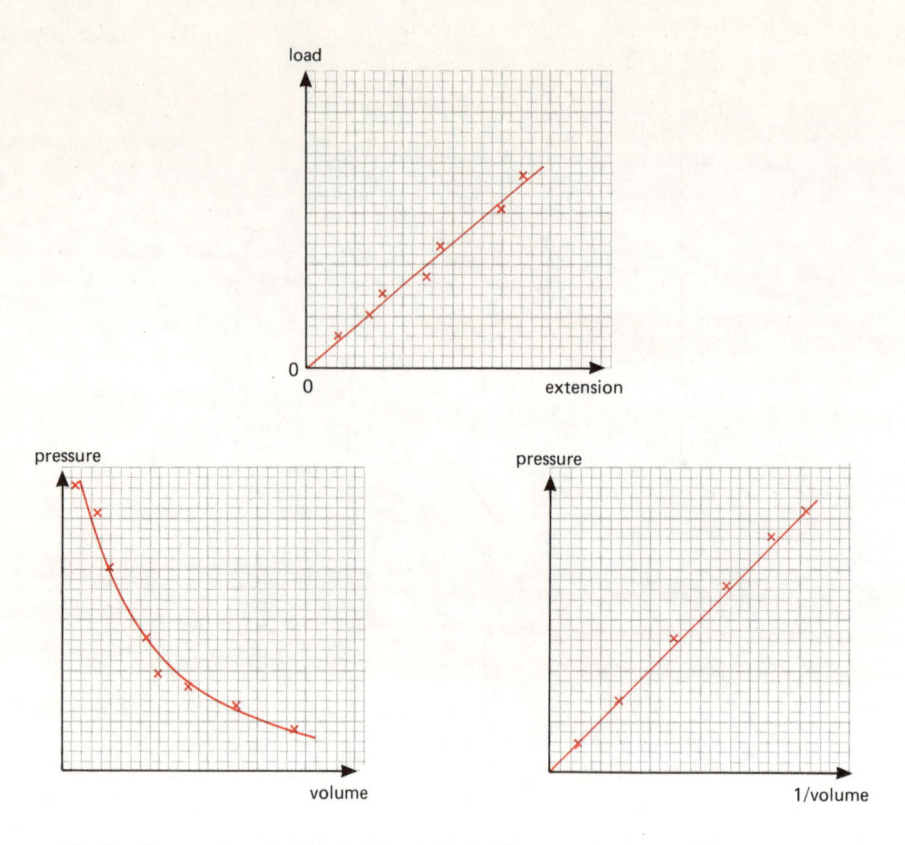

Figure 10.12 Proportion and inverse proportion

other. One gets greater as the other gets smaller. An example of an inverse proportionality is that between the pressure of a fixed mass of gas and its volume.

(c) 'Square' proportion
This is a common relationship which appears as a curve on a graph. An example

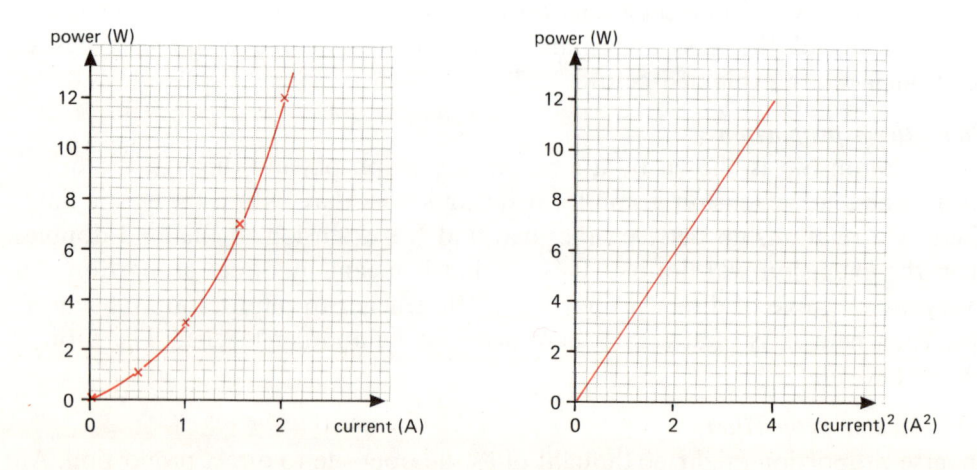

Figure 10.13 Graphs showing a 'square' relationship

is the relationship between the current through an electric heater and the energy transformed per second (power) of the heater.

We can say that the power increases as the square of the current. This means that as the current *doubles* the power increases by *four* times. (see 10.1b)

10.7 Summary and practice equations

1. Without using a calculator try to estimate a rough answer to the following:
   (a) 24.489/3.1, (b) 604 × 20.2, (c) $\dfrac{31 \times 22}{599}$.

2. Use a calculator to see how close you were to the answers in question 1.
3. The area of a square solar collecting panel is given by d^2 where d is the length of one side.
   (a) 'What would the area be for a panel with sides 2 m long?
   (b) What would the area be for a panel with sides 6 m long (three times as long as 2 m)?
   (c) Would the new panel collect three times as much energy?
4. A lightbulb which gives out a total of 60 J of energy each second is inefficient. Only 5 J of this energy is light. What percentage of the total energy is this?
5. Use a calculator to find the answers to the following problems. Decide on an appropriate number of significant figures for your answers.
   (a) A voltmeter across a lamp read 12.5 V and the current through the lamp was measured as 0.33 A. Calculate a value for the resistance of the lamp ($R = V/I$).
   (b) A force of 46 N was required to extend a spring by 0.12 m. Calculate a value for the force constant, k, for the spring ($F = kx$).
6. Rewrite the following numbers in standard form:
   (a) 780 000, (b) 0.0066, (c) 27.5, (d) 0.000 000 000 9.
7. Here are three sets of measurements. For each set decide on what you think is the best 'average' value. Say briefly how you found the 'average'.
   (a) Student measurements of room temperature with different thermometers:
   21 °C, 21 °C, 21 °C, 22 °C, 21 °C, 23 °C, 20 °C, 21 °C, 21 °C
   (b) The mass of a set of dynamics trolleys:
   604 g, 605 g, 603 g, 604 g, 605 g
   (c) The current through a wire:
   518 mA, 22.5 mA, 478 mA, 480 mA, 520 mA, 491 mA, 502 mA
8. (a) Use your ruler to measure the lengths, L and W, in each of these two shapes.
   (b) Find the cross-sectional areas of the ends of the shapes.
   (c) Which shape has the largest volume?
   (d) What is the total volume of both shapes?

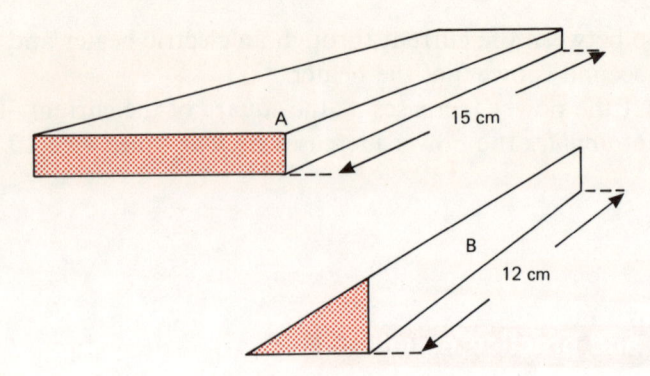

Figure 10.14

9. An equation met in this book in Unit 8 is

$$\text{pressure} = \text{force}/\text{area}$$

Use this equation to find:
(a) The pressure on the floor when a cat, weighing 12 N, stands on its four feet. Each foot has an area $= 5 \text{ cm}^2$.
(b) Force on a door of area 1.4 m^2 caused by air at a pressure of 100 000 Pa.
(c) The piston area required to cause a force of 360 N when acted on by oil at a pressure of 20 000 Pa.

10. The following sets of data came from two student investigations concerning the resistance of different conductors. Plot the sets of data on suitable axes. For each graph:
   (i) Draw the line or curve of best fit.
   (ii) Describe the relationship in words.
   (iii) Find the value of I when the p.d. is 7.5 V.

data set 1		data set 2	
p.d. (volts)	I (mA)	p.d. (volts)	I (mA)
1	6	1	14
2	14	2	28
3	20	3	32
4	24	4	41
5	28	5	48
6	34	6	51
7	44	7	54
8	48	8	58
9	52	9	58
10	60	10	60

INVESTIGATIONS

11.1 What is an investigation?

For much of the practical work you do in your course there will be instructions to tell you what to do, perhaps from a book or a worksheet prepared by your teacher. In the real world of scientific research, scientists have to plan and carry out their own experiments. Investigations give you the chance to carry out a small practical project of your own. You will have to think of the ideas, you will have to order the apparatus and you will have to make the decisions.

Your teacher will, of course, be available to give advice but he or she will also be wanting to see some work of your own. The investigation will probably form part of the *coursework assessment* for GCSE physics. This will mean that your teacher will want to see how your investigation progresses and to read a final written report of your work.

Before we talk about details of the investigation, let us read through a typical example of a student investigation. As you read through, look at the way the report is presented as this is an example of a good piece of work.

11.2 A student investigation

> GCSE PHYSICS INVESTIGATION
> MODULE ONE
> BY
> JANET EYRE   (Mr. Robson's group.)
>
> TITLE: DOES A PAPER COFFEE CUP NEED A LID?
>
> OUTLINE OF WHAT I DID: In our course we studied the heating and cooling effects of liquids and made notes about specific heat capacity and energy which can be lost from a house. I decided to investigate about why coffee cups which you sometimes get from railway cafes need lids. We don't use lids on our cups at home. I measured temperatures for

lots of the time and tried it for cups with a lid and without a lid. I also tried to find out if a windy breeze made a difference. I found out that cups with lids on did help to keep things warm.

DAY ONE   6th December

Our lesson started at 10.45 and it took me 15 minutes to find the kettle which the teacher's were using for their tea break. I boiled the water and made a cup of coffee. I didn't add milk or sugar because they would be cold and so might change the results. I wanted to see how my apparatus worked.

apparatus: from college, kettle, thermometer
            from home, coffee, cups, lids.

I wanted to see how long it took for a coffee to cool down and to plot my results.

My results are shown in the table (I used the thermometer to stir the coffee to even up the tem--perature.) I forgot to ask for a clock so Mr Robson gave me a clock.

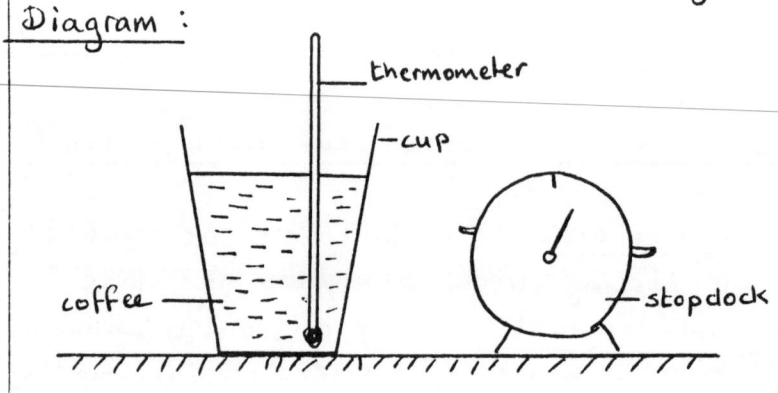

Diagram:

Ⓐ

Results:

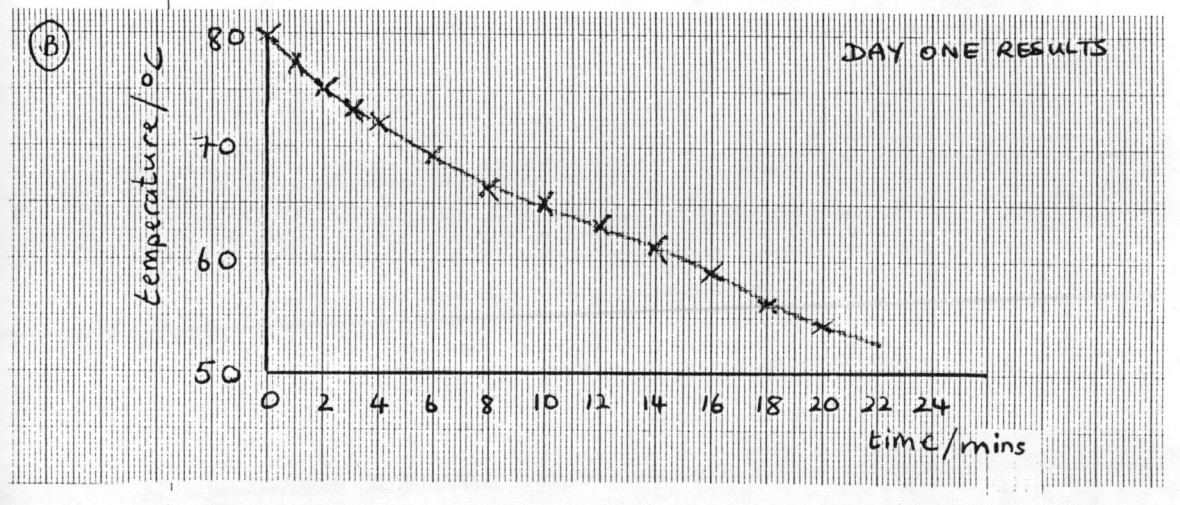

Time/m	Temp/°C		Time/m	Temp/°C
0	80		8	66½
1	77		10	65
2	75		12	63
3	73		14	61½
4	72		16	59
6	69		18	56½
			20	54

(B)

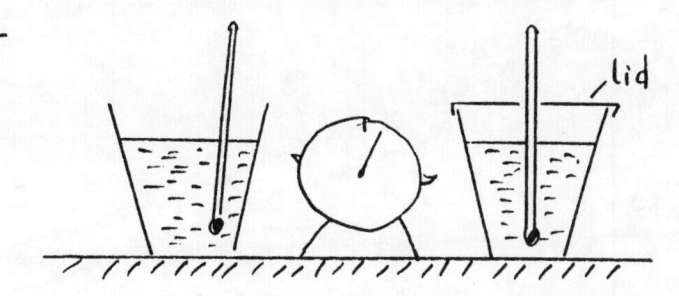

DAY ONE RESULTS

(graph of temperature/°C vs time/mins showing cooling curve from 80°C at t=0 down to ~54°C at t=20)

(C) Diagram:

(diagram of two cups with thermometers, a clock between them, one cup labelled "lid")

I tried to give both cups the same chance to cool down. To do this I put them on the same table and in the same room and with the same amount of coffee in. I made the coffee up in a 1 litre beaker and poured it into the two cups. I put the cups close so that I could tell that the levels were the same. This was important. One thermometer could not be stirred so I wiggled it about.

I wiggled both the thermometers the same amount. The results are on the next page. I have only included the graphs.

Some ideas:
I found that it took a long time for the coffee to cool down so I had to take results for only 20 minutes.
Tomorrow I will try the same experiment with two cups and put a lid on one of them.

DAY TWO   8th December

Today I knew exactly what to do. I arranged two paper (well actually polystyrene) cups just the same. The lid I had had a small hole in it. I used my pencil to make the hole bigger for my thermometer.

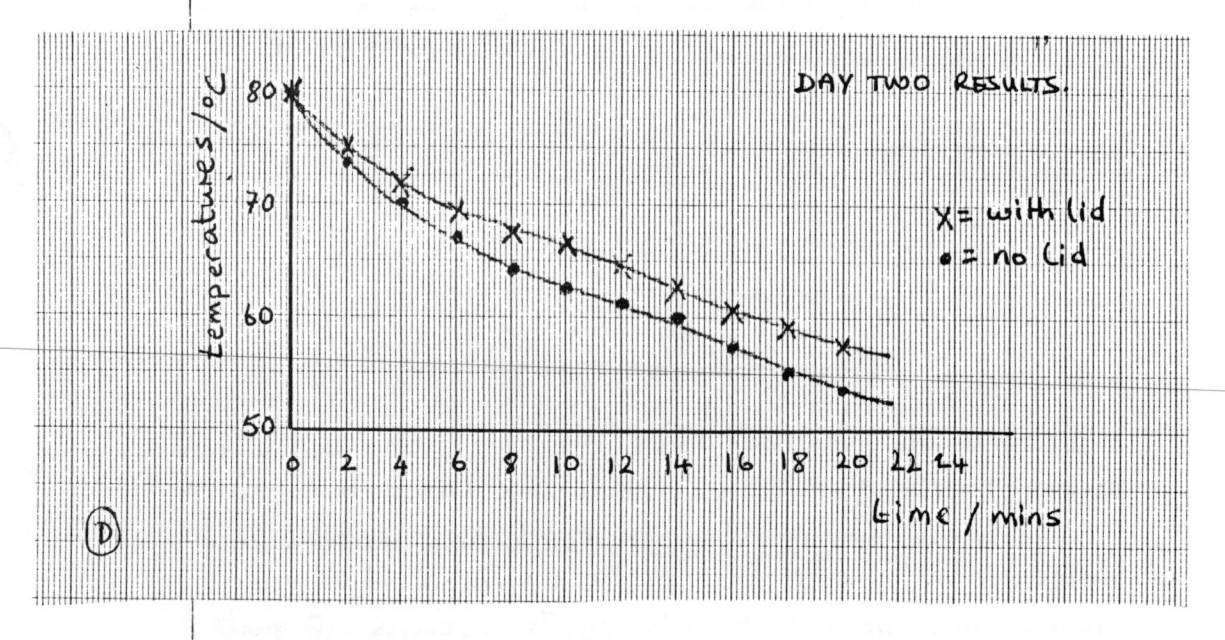

DAY TWO RESULTS.

X = with lid
• = no lid

temperatures/°C vs time/mins

Some ideas. The lid did help. It kept the heat in the coffee longer and so the coffee stayed hotter. After 20 minutes the coffee with the lid on

(E)

was still hot enough to drink. (temp = 58°C). The other coffee was too cooled. (temp = 54°C). My teacher, Mr Robson asked me why the lid made a difference and started me thinking about things. I think that the steam which comes from the hot coffee can't get through the lid and so this is how the heat is kept in. The steam must carry the heat (called latent heat) away. This is because it's really gas molecules moving very fast. (this is called kinetic energy). The lid keeps all this energy in the cup.

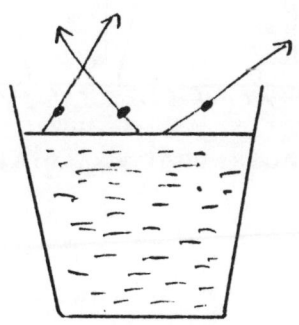

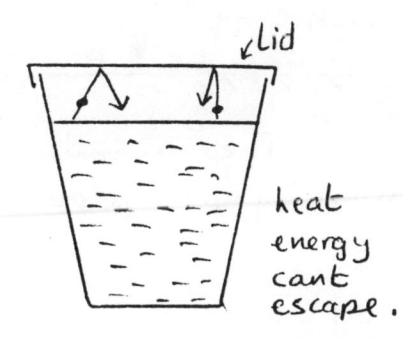

heat energy can't escape.

Some energy can get out of the cup to make the coffee cool down but this goes out through the sides and is called conduction. The next day is the last practical day. I am not sure what to do. I will think about it on Sunday.

DAY 3   13th December.

Today I had another idea to try out. I wanted to see if you could make the energy escape faster by blowing the steam away. I bought in my hairdrier (Boots vanity seven) to do the blowing. I tested my theory by blowing air over one cup and not blowing air over the other cup.

(F) I held the hair drier in a clampstand at the right level with the top of the coffee cup. I put the drier on gentle blow. Every minute I measured the temperatures.

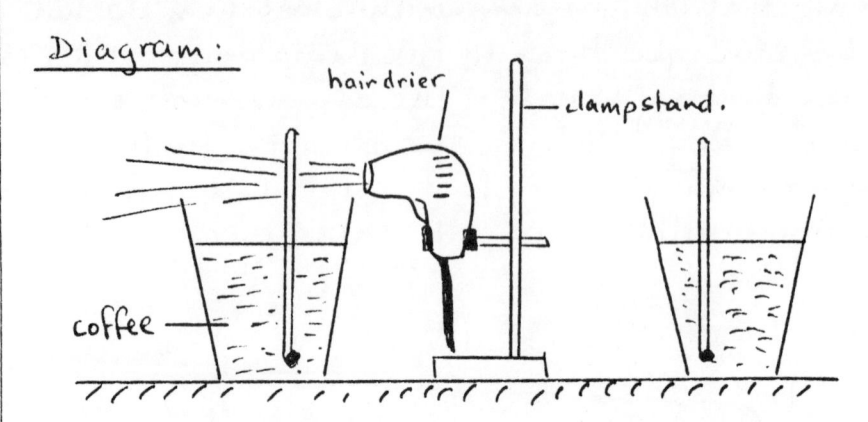

Diagram:

(G) DAY THREE RESULTS.

X = no lid
● = no lid plus blower.

temperatures/°C vs time/mins

The results of my last experiment are on the graph paper.

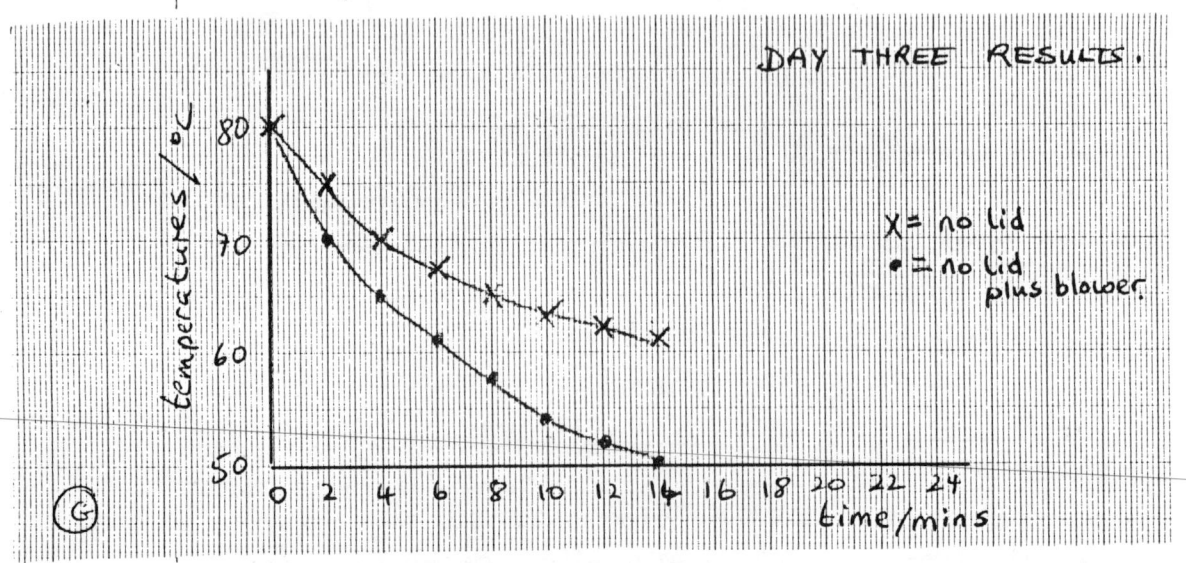

My last ideas (conclusion).

I enjoyed doing this investigation because it was easy and interesting. I think that the lid is important to stop the steam from carrying the heat away. If you blow the steam it carries the heat away faster. This is why

you blow your hot soup or hot coffee to cool it down. When you buy you're coffee from the railway cafe you will probably have to stand on the platform with it. This means that the draft will blow the steam away unless you have a lid. This is why they give you a lid. This is what I have proved.
This is a photo of my last experiment. →

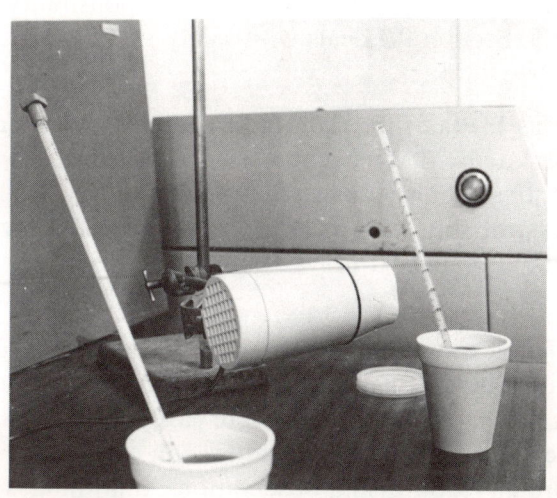

11.3 Before you start

Investigations need to be planned and planning forms part of the assessment scheme. First of all you need an idea and a title. You will feel more enthusiastic about an idea of your own rather than one allocated by your teacher. If you are struck for an idea, even after looking back over the lesson notes and talking to your friends and teacher, you might find something interesting to tackle from the list at the end of this Unit. The investigation should be related to the work you have already covered but should not be a repeat of a class practical you have already done. Do not be too ambitious. You are not expected to re-invent the television. Keep your aims simple and try to choose a topic which will interest you.

Decide in advance on exactly what you will be doing in the first laboratory session. Do not waste time thinking about it on the day. You might need to use some laboratory equipment and this will need to be ordered at least a week in advance. *Try not to be too ambitious with equipment*: complicated equipment always brings problems and some of the best investigations are done with simple equipment. You will probably have to get to know the laboratory technician, a busy professional person—be patient and polite at all times! You might also need some simple equipment from home. Discuss your plans with your teacher at all stages.

11.4 Action

On the first day of the investigation you should check that the equipment you require is available and that you have a working space somewhere in the laboratory. Are you near enough to a gas, water or electric supply should you need one? Start investigating. Some useful tips are outlined below.

(a) Safety
It is most important that you are sensible and safe when investigating on your own. Although the teacher will be at hand, the responsibility for your safety rests with you. (Unit 9, Section 9.2 deals with safety.)

(b) Time
You may have as few as three laboratory sessions in which to carry out the investigation. Make sure that what you start can be finished within the time given for each session. If you finish a piece of experimenting with fifteen minutes left in the session, it is probably wise to clear your equipment away and spend some time thinking about your next move.

(c) Notes
People have different ways to take down notes. Some people can write down their results and ideas in best straight away. Most people will use a rough note book and copy up in best later. Rough notes are easily lost unless made in a booklet. Note down everything about the investigation, the day and date, sketch the apparatus, record all readings and observations. If nothing is observed, especially when something was expected, note it down.

(d) Direction
It sometimes happens that your investigation appears to lead you away from your planned path. Do not be afraid of allowing your work to change direction. If something unexpected happens then follow a new direction. What is important is that the work you do is your own and that you carry it out safely and sensibly. It does not matter if you run out of time and manage to finish only part of the work. *How you actually do your investigation is more important than the end product.*

11.5 Your written report

You will be expected to write and submit a written account of your investigation. This need not be too long. If you find your report is two pages long, it is probably too brief. It it is twenty-two pages, then it is probably too long. Make the report neat and easy to follow. Diagrams should be clearly drawn and labelled. Tables of results and graphs should be included. Perhaps a photograph of your apparatus could be included.

A good way of presenting your report is in a diary form (see the sample report). You could write up each day's work that same evening while it is fresh in your mind. There is no need to make your report too formal. It is far better to tell the story of the investigation in your own words. Start with a title and a brief summary of what happened. Explain what you intended to try to find out. Give details of every experiment you tried. Be honest about the parts which did not go smoothly.

Finally, you should try to show how your investigation linked up with physics. In which parts did you use your knowledge of physics? If you can, show that the work you did had some value to the world outside the lab, perhaps your idea came about from a problem you discovered at home, then you will be given credit for this.

11.6 Some suggestions for investigations

- *The effect of wind resistance on a lightweight home-made vehicle.*
- *Surface road resistance and wheels (bring your bicycle, pushchair or shopping wheeler in for a test).*
- *Strength and stickability, Blu-tac versus another tac.*
- *Cardboard bridges under load.*
- *Straw and pin structures. Building simple towers.*
- *Paper clips, hair clips, any clips. The physics of clips.*
- *Concrete cubes under test.*
- *The efficiency of elastic bands.*
- *Elastic in clothing. Investigate your underwear.*
- *The flow of water through holes—how fast can you empty a plastic bottle?*
- *The effect of temperature on the bouncing of a squash ball.*
- *Table tennis balls and different surfaces. How much energy is lost on impact?*
- *Inflating a football—how much work is needed?*
- *Heating a glass rod.*
- *Making tea. Keeping the pot hot.*
- *Making tea. Do Thermos flasks work?*
- *Making tea. The rate of cooling of hot tea in a cup.*
- *Iced Martinis. The effect of ice on a cool drink.*
- *Testing the mechanical properties of a condom.*
- *Packing materials. How protective are they?*
- *How much energy is stored in a 'U2' cell?*
- *Lemon batteries. How useful can a lemon be in providing power?*
- *Rotary signs are becoming more common. Make one and investigate its properties.*
- *How accurate is the stated resistance of a commercial resistor?*
- *How powerful is a clear headlamp bulb?*
- *Domestic fuse wires. Do they 'blow' as expected?*
- *Do you have a bicycle with a dynamo? Bring your bicycle into college to test how efficient the dynamo is.*
- *How far does magnetism reach through different materials.*
- *Radioactive background count. How does it vary in your college?*

- *Riples on water. What factors influence their speed?*
- *Simple musical instruments. Testing the quality of their sounds.*
- *Waves on a spring. How fast do they travel?*
- *Design and build a hazard warning system to sound an alarm.*
- *Build a simple reward system which will please a gorilla once he/she presses the correct buttons.*

VIBRATIONS AND WAVES

12

12.1 Vibrations and frequency

Why do bees buzz? The buzzing sound of a bee is not the bee singing or humming to itself but a sound produced by the *vibrations* of its wings. The wings push on the air at a **frequency** of about 80 times per second. This repeated forcing effect starts a sound wave in the air which spreads out and is captured by our ears. The air vibrations bash our eardrums about 80 times each second and we recognise this as the sound of a bee. Each vibration has its own **amplitude**. For a tall building, the amplitude is the greatest sideways distance moved by the building, perhaps up to 3 metres. The time for one complete, there and back, vibration is called the **period**. For a bee's wing, the period is about 1/80th second. The period of a tall swaying building might be about 6 seconds.

i.e. 80 cycles of force every second

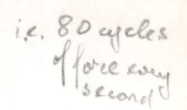

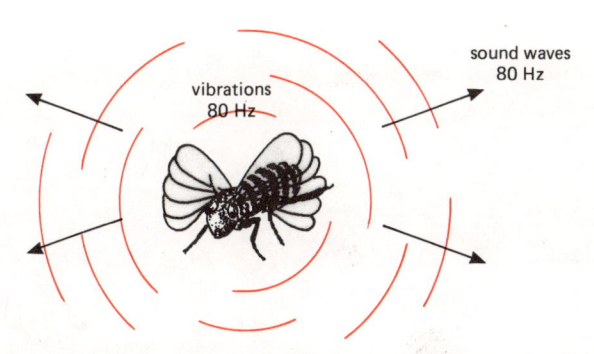

Figure 12.1 Sound waves start from vibrations

The frequency of sound vibrations can be measured in the laboratory using an oscilloscope and microphone. The microphone detects the vibrations and the oscilloscope displays the shape of the sound as a wave. High frequencies appear as many waves on the screen. The height or amplitude of the signal shows how loud the sound is.

The unit for measuring frequency is the **hertz**, **Hz**. Heinrich Hertz (1857–1894) pioneered the study of radio waves. Most people can hear sounds within the frequency range of about 40 Hz to 19 000 Hz (19 kHz). Middle C on a piano is 264 Hz. The piano string vibrates 264 times every second. Some sounds just cannot be heard.

Frequencies below 40 Hz are called '**infrasound**' and although we cannot hear

a pure note   a higher frequency   the signal from a trumpet

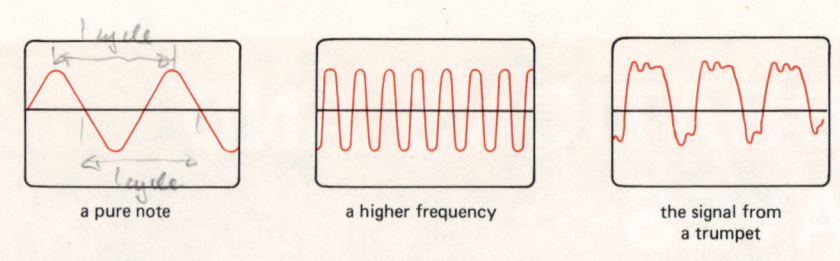

Figure 12.2   Sound waves can be displayed on an oscilloscope screen

them, these low-frequency pressure waves can have unpleasant effects on humans. At about 8 Hz infrasound is thought to induce epilepsy in some people. Frequencies above 19 kHz are called '**ultrasound**'. The echoes from ultrasound signals are used in hospitals to create images of unborn babies, and in therapy by helping to break down unwanted tissue. Ultrasonic vibrations are used by dental hygienists to destroy bacteria between teeth.

12.2 The size and speed of waves

You can easily hear the frequencies of sound waves but you cannot see them. Waves on water are easier to measure. A holiday photograph might show up the shape of a wave. It captures the shape of a wave at one particular moment. The height of wave is called the **amplitude** and the length of a wave is called the **wavelength**.

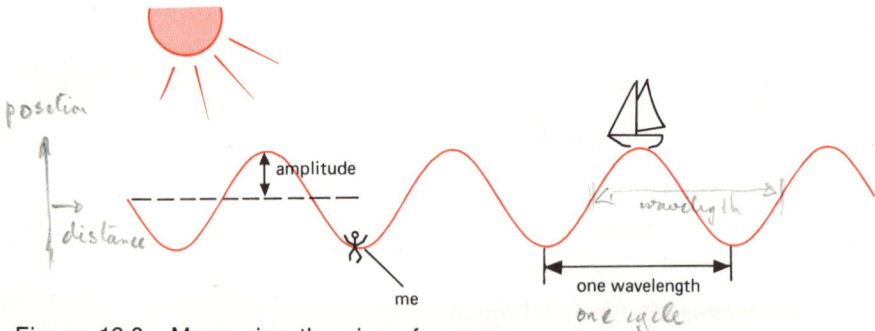

Figure 12.3   Measuring the size of a wave

As you bob up and down in the sea, you can measure the **frequency** of water waves. If, for example, you time two seconds for one wave to pass by, then the **period** of one wave is 2 seconds. The period is the time for one complete wave cycle, for example, up, down and back to the middle. This means that the waves are being produced at a rate of half a wave each second. The wave frequency is 0.5 Hz.

Waves like water waves and sound waves which move away from a vibration are called **travelling** or **progressive** waves. They have a wave speed which can be measured. The frequency and wavelength of a wave are related to how fast the wave moves. To calculate the **speed** of a wave, you simply need to **multiply the frequency and the wavelength**.

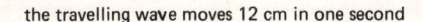

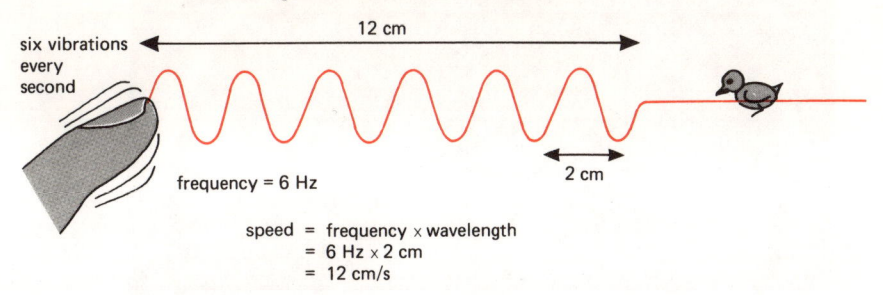

Figure 12.4 Calculating the speed of a wave

12.3 Longitudinal and transverse waves

Waves involve movement. When water waves move through water, the water itself moves up and down as the wave moves sideways. These waves are called **transverse waves**. Light waves are another example of transverse waves. Sound waves are **longitudinal waves**. This means that the movement of the air particles is along the same direction as the travelling wave. A slinky spring can be used to show these two kinds of wave.

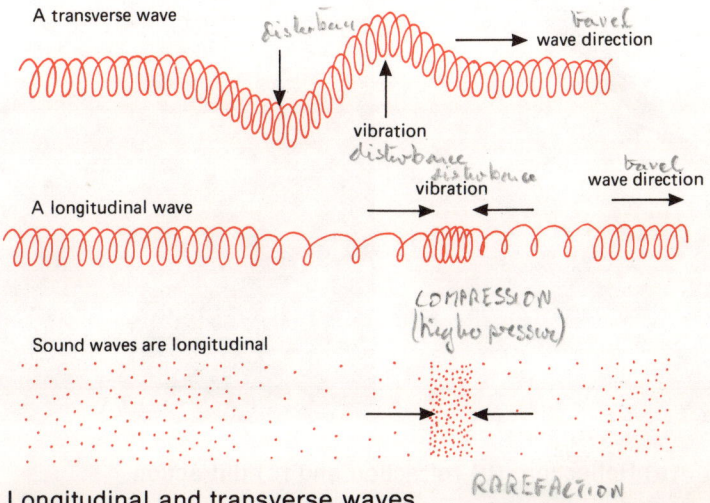

Figure 12.5 Longitudinal and transverse waves

12.4 Some properties of waves

(a) Reflection

When a wave hits a barrier it bounces back. We call this **reflection**. Whenever you look into a mirror you see reflected light waves, and when you hear an echo you hear reflected sound waves. Waves on a string reflect back off a fixed end. Some reflections are unwanted. In a concert hall the sound reflections can lead

Figure 12.6 (a) Reflection, (b) refraction and (c) diffraction

to a muddled noise, and reflections of sunlight on a wet road can temporarily 'blind' a driver. Your reflection in a mirror and the reflection of waves on a guitar string are both useful reflections.

(b) Refraction
Waves can travel at different speeds. The speed depends on the material carrying the wave. The speed of sound in air is about 330 m/s but in water sound travels at about 1500 m/s. Light travels at 300 000 000 m/s in air but only at about

200 000 000 m/s in glass. The change in speed when a wave goes from one medium to another can make the wave change direction. This is called **refraction**. Waves in sea water change direction as they approach shallow shores. This is refraction because water waves travel slower in shallow water. A glass lens uses refraction to bend the path of light waves. Swimming pools often look shallower than they are because of the refraction of light as it leaves the water.

(c) Diffraction

Waves often hit the edges of objects. When this happens the waves will tend to bend around the object edge and spread out more. This spreading is called **diffraction**. Waves will show diffraction when they pass through a gap. The gap in a harbour wall allows ships to pass but also allows water waves to come through and spread out. Sound waves will diffract when they come out of the end of a trumpet. Light waves diffract as they pass through a slit, especially if the gap is narrow and the wavelengths are long. One reason why we find it difficult to read small writing from a distance is because of the diffraction of light as it passes through our pupils. If you look at a street light through squinted eyes or through some stretched material, you will see a diffraction pattern. Diffraction through gaps can be a problem. We can minimise its effect by avoiding small gaps or by using waves with wavelengths smaller than the size of the gap.

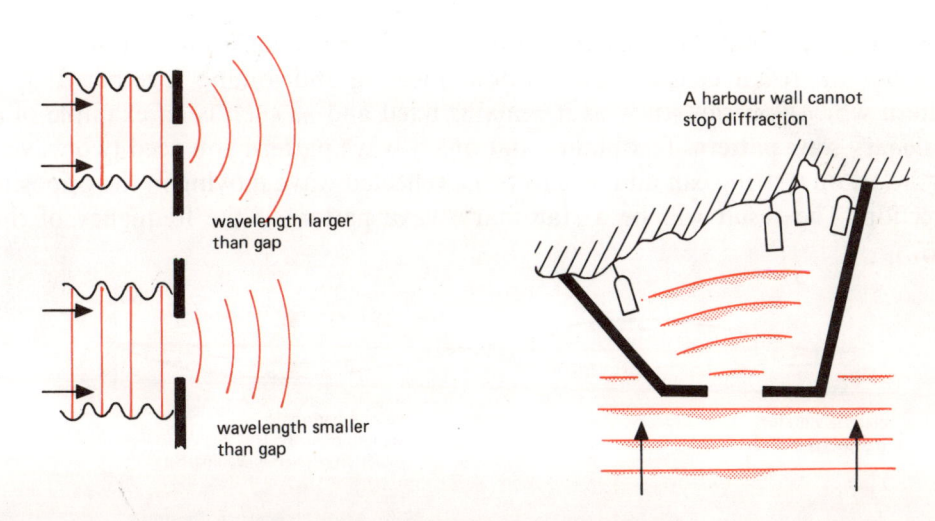

Figure 12.7 Waves diffract when they pass through a gap

(d) Interference

This happens when two waves meet. When two waves meet they combine their effects. The result can be either to reinforce each other or to cancel each other out. This addition or subtraction is called **interference**. If two waves have the same wavelength and start together from the same vibration, it is possible for them to meet and form an interference pattern. An **interference pattern** can be demonstrated using water waves, light from a laser or sound waves.

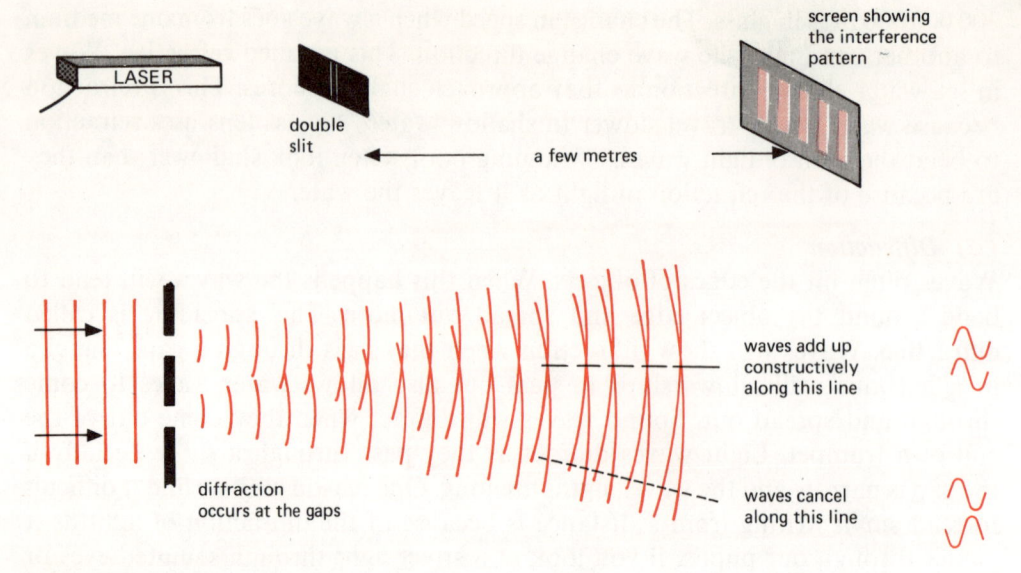

Figure 12.8 Waves can add up or cancel out to form an interference pattern

12.5 Stationary wave patterns

The interference pattern obtained from waves (see Section 12.4) is not a wave itself but the result of two wave motions meeting and joining together. It is a pattern which you can study as it remains fixed and as such is an example of a **stationary wave pattern**. To obtain a stationary wave pattern you need two waves.

A wave on a string can add its effect to a reflected wave moving in the opposite direction. The result will be a stationary wave pattern if the frequency of the

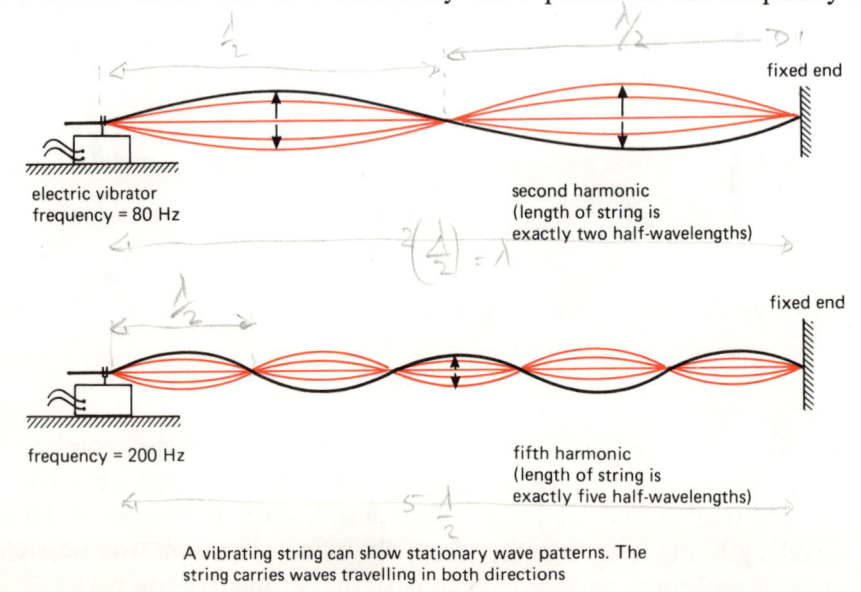

A vibrating string can show stationary wave patterns. The string carries waves travelling in both directions

Figure 12.9 Stationary wave patterns can be shown on a vibrating string

waves is just right. For a guitar string, the frequencies which produce stationary wave patterns are called '**harmonics**'. The stationary wave pattern will only appear if the length of the string is exactly a whole number of half-wavelengths. On a guitar string you can hear the harmonics by stopping the string at particular fret intervals.

12.6 Related reading: Sound in buildings

Building engineers and designers must consider how noise and sound may affect the comfort or pleasure of people living in buildings. An understanding of the reflections of sound is most important. Sound reflects many times off walls and ceilings, and on each reflection a fraction of the sound is absorbed. This makes the sound eventually die away. The time it takes for a sound to die away is called the **reverberation time**. Small buildings have short reverberation times because the sound frequently bounces off the walls. The reverberation time for a classroom might be 0.2 s but for a large cathedral it might be as long as 2 s. This will mean that when a cathedral organ plays, the sound of one note will become mixed with the next note. This gives church music its distinctive echo sound. The reverberation time in a church full of people will decrease because large numbers of people will absorb some of the sound.

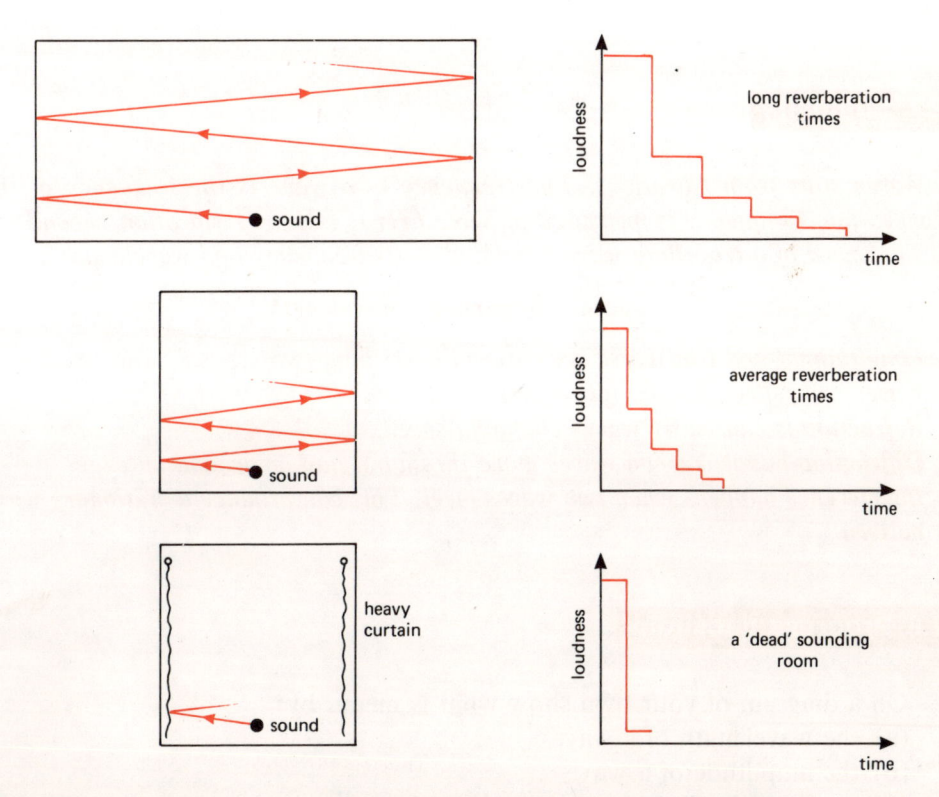

Figure 12.10 How long does a sound last? The reverberation time

In a concert hall, the reverberation time of echoes needs to be limited but not cut out altogether, otherwise the sounds will be 'dead'. To achieve a desirable reverberation time of about 1.1 s some concert halls have used heavy curtains to absorb the sound or reflectors to make the concert hall appear smaller. Reflections from curved ceilings can lead to the concert hall having loud spots where the reflections are focussed. Once again, reflectors can diffract and scatter the sound to avoid loud spots.

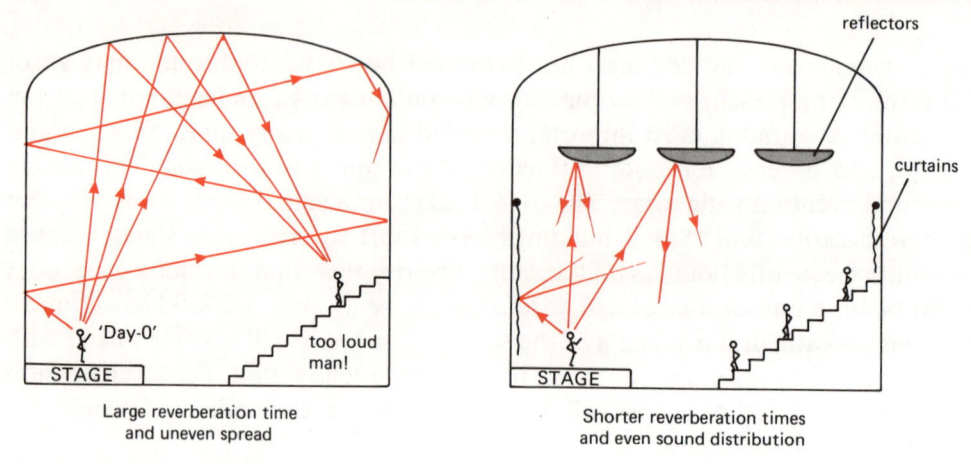

Figure 12.11 Sound engineers can improve the acoustic performance of old concert halls

12.7 Summary

- *Waves start from vibrations. The **frequency** of a wave is the frequency of the vibration. Frequency is measured in **hertz (Hz)**. 1 Hz = 1 vibration/second.*
- *The speed of a **travelling wave** is related to its frequency and wavelength by*

$$speed = frequency \times wavelength$$

- ***Longitudinal** and **transverse** are ways of describing two types of wave motion.*
- *Waves can **reflect** as they hit objects.*
- ***Refraction** is caused by waves changing speed.*
- ***Diffraction** happens when waves move through a gap or around an edge.*
- ***Interference** happens when two waves meet. This can produce a **stationary wave pattern**.*

12.8 Progress questions

1. On a diagram of your own show what is meant by:
   (a) the wavelength of a wave
   (b) the amplitude of a wave.
2. If the wings of a fly beat 60 times in each second:

(a) What would be the frequency of the sound produced by the wings?
(b) Would you expect a person to be able to hear this sound?
(c) Is there a reason why our ears are the shape they are, or are they designed for us to wear ear-rings?

3. (a) A radio station sent out waves with a frequency of 250 000 Hz. Their wavelength was 1200 metres. What value does this give for the speed of radio waves through air?
(b) Is there anything special about this speed?
(c) The speed of sound in water is 1500 m/s. If a whale made a 30 Hz vibration under water, what would be the wavelength of the resulting sound wave?

4. Use diagrams to show what would happen to the waves in each of the examples shown in Figure 12.12.

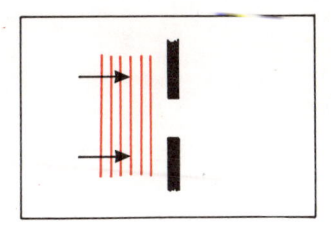

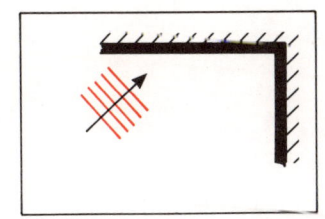

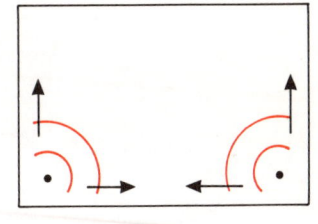

Figure 12.12

5. How would you explain to a friend who did not study physics just what a stationary wave pattern was. Try to explain your answer here.

THE ELECTROMAGNETIC SPECTRUM

13.1 Light and the visible spectrum

There have been few areas in physics which have caused as much interest as the nature of light. One early idea about vision said that 'seeing' an object involved something leaving your eye and travelling to the object. What about light itself? What exactly is light? Isaac Newton thought that light consisted of a stream of particles. This 'corpuscular' theory was first proposed by Pythagoras, the ancient Greek. Alongside this was the alternative view of Christiaan Huygens that light was a continuous wave. Another idea was that the darkness at night-time was caused by a dark gas which descended on the Earth each evening and which, if breathed in, gave you a weary tired feeling!

Modern theories about light are equally strange. It is suggested that light is a stream of 'photons' which travel at 300 000 000 m/s and can be thought of as wave-like or particle-like!

The fact that light comes in a variety of colours was first noticed by Newton using sunlight and a glass prism. You can easily repeat this observation in a

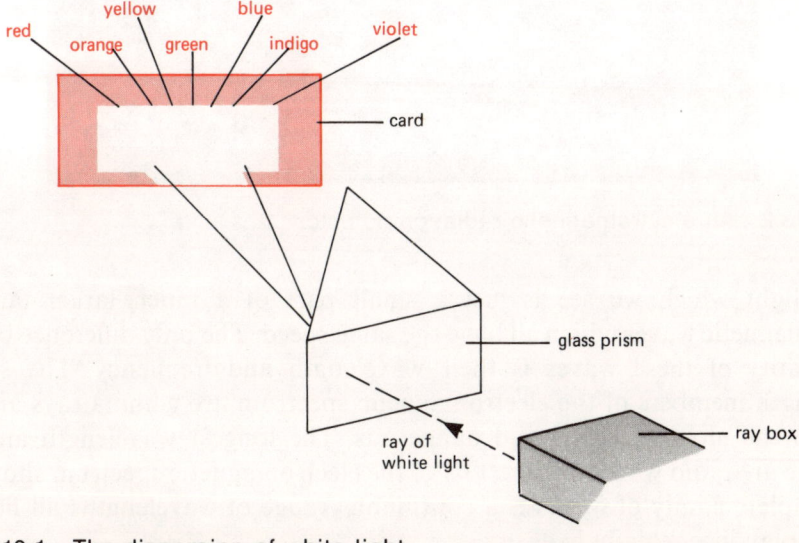

Figure 13.1   The dispersion of white light

laboratory. A beam of white light will refract as it slows down when it passes through glass. Blue light slows down more than red light and as a result is deviated more. The colours, the same as those of a rainbow, show that what we see as white light is actually a mixture of red, orange, yellow, green, blue, indigo and violet. These colours form what we call the **visible spectrum**.

The colours of the visible spectrum have the same speed in air, the speed of light. They form a family of waves of different wavelength. Violet light has the shortest wavelength, red has the longest.

13.2 The invisible spectrum

As you read this line, you are being bathed by invisible radiations from all directions. It is not surprising that the existence of these radiations was not discovered until 1800. William Herschell discovered that there was invisible 'light' beyond the red end of the visible spectrum. We call this 'infra-red' radiation and it gives us a heating sensation. In 1801 a similar invisible radiation was detected beyond the violet end. Ultra-violet radiation will fog a photographic film and causes a sun-tan on human skin. In 1888 Hertz experimented with electromagnetic radio waves and found that they had the same speed as light. During this time it became clear that there was more to light than met the eye!

Figure 13.2   An electromagnetic radiation detector

The light which we see is just a small part of a much larger family of electromagnetic waves which all have the same speed. The only difference between the identity of these waves is their wavelength and frequency. The shortest wavelength members of the electromagnetic spectrum are gamma rays and they are also the most energetic and dangerous. The longest wavelength and least energetic are radio waves. Figure 13.3 of the electromagnetic spectrum shows that the complete family of waves is a continuous range of wavelengths all having a part to play in our daily lives.

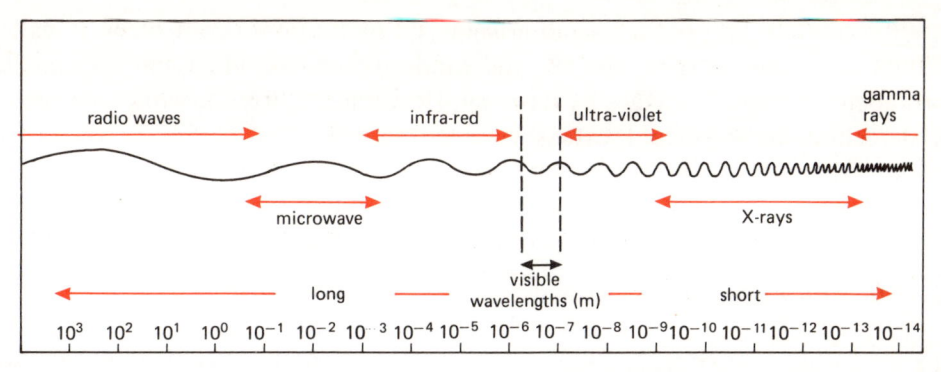

Figure 13.3 The range of the electromagnetic spectrum

13.3 Producing and using electromagnetic waves

(a) Gamma rays

These rays are the most dangerous of all electromagnetic waves. They are emitted randomly from the nuclei of radioactive isotopes (see Unit 14) of which some occur naturally and some are deliberately made by particle collisions. In a hospital, a patient with a suspected cancer may be injected with a small amount of gamma-emitting radioisotope. Gamma rays can then be collected and detected by a gamma camera placed outside the body to give a photograph of the cancerous region.

(b) X-rays

We receive small amounts of both gamma rays and X-rays from our surroundings and from outer space. Controlled X-rays are used to give X-ray shadow photographs in hospitals and for airport security checks. X-rays cameras are used to show up defects in building structures. An X-ray generator works by firing electrons at a metal target converting their kinetic energy to X-rays energy. Some low-energy X-rays are given off by television screens.

(c) Ultra-violet rays

It is ultra-violet (UV) radiation which shows up our white shirts in some discos and gives us a tan under UV lamps. The glow from UV-illuminated objects is used to security label valuables. A common scientific use of UV is to help to identify chemical compounds by their absorption of certain frequencies of UV radiation. Atoms absorb and emit UV radiation by changing their electron energies.

(d) Visible radiation—light

This is the very narrow band of frequencies which our eyes and photographic film are sensitive to. Light is produced from hot objects at temperatures above about 600°C, for example, a filament lamp, or spark discharges like lightning.

(e) Infra-red radiation

It is the infra-red (IR) component of sunshine which we detect through its heating effect. IR radiation is emitted by all objects at temperatures above absolute zero.

IR radiation can be used for sending signals. Some remote control switches for a video or television send out IR, and modern cameras which can 'see in the dark' focus and detect images by receiving IR radiation. Rescue workers now use IR detection cameras to locate survivors buried under rubble following an earthquake or explosion. Unknown chemical substances can be identified by the exact frequency of IR radiation which their molecules absorb and emit as they vibrate. This technique is known as IR spectroscopy.

(f) Microwaves and radio waves

These radiations form the long wavelength end of the electromagnetic spectrum. The very longest wavelength radiowaves have wavelengths over 1000 m. Medium band radio waves are about 100 m and short band radio waves about a metre or so. Very short wave radio waves are called microwaves and have wavelengths from a few millimetres up to a metre. All these waves are used for communication. Microwaves are used to send television signals bouncing off satellites and also for cooking. Microwaves in cookers are the most energetic members of this radio group. They heat up food by forcing water molecules to vibrate more energetically.

13.4 What exactly is an electromagnetic wave?

Do not expect to receive a totally satisfactory answer to this question at GCSE level. Sunlight travels to us through a vacuum, space. The fact that electromagnetic waves can travel through a vacuum without any medium to carry them makes it difficult for us to visualise what is actually doing the waving. If you want to start to understand what light is, then think about the effects of magnetism and static electricity. The forcing effects of a magnet or a charged balloon seem to reach through space without anything to connect them. In physics we describe these distant forces by saying that around magnets and charges there are magnetic and electric '**fields**'. You can start to think of electromagnetic radiation as being the vibrations which travel through these fields. If you are confused about this strange idea, then join the rest of us. There are some ideas in physics which most human minds find very difficult to understand.

13.5 Related reading: Radiation and the Earth's atmosphere

It was quite by accident in 1901 that Guglielmo Marconi, a young Italian experimenter, discovered that long wavelength radio waves were reflected back to Earth by the Earth's atmosphere. In his attempt to send radio waves across the Atlantic from Cornwall to North America, Marconi discovered the **ionosphere**, a layer of ionised gas surrounding the Earth. Present day communication systems make use of the ionosphere to send signals anywhere across the globe.

The layers of gas in the atmosphere act like a protective shield. Electromagnetic radiations from the Sun, other stars and the depths of the universe rain down on the Earth from space. Fortunately, most of these radiations are absorbed or scattered by the atmosphere. Some radiation does break through. UV radiation

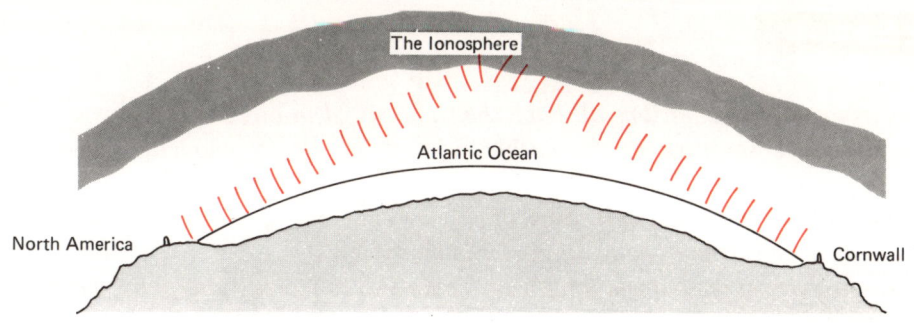

Figure 13.4 The ionosphere

from the Sun manages to give us a tan in the summer and can cause skin cancers. There is no doubt that visible light can penetrate through the atmosphere (just look at the stars!). There is concern, however, that the use of some chemicals, particularly those in aerosol sprays, is slowly reducing the protective effect of the ozone layer in parts of the atmosphere. Without the ozone layer we face a greater risk of skin cancer from UV radiation.

Finally, spare a thought for the astronomer. The only '**windows**' in the atmosphere through which the astronomer can observe are in the narrow visible and the short-wave radio band of the spectrum. Optical and radio telescopes are in constant operation across the Earth's surface. To make use of IR signals from space, modern telescopes are perched high upon mountains to capture the IR radiation before water in the lower atmosphere has a chance to scatter it. There are now X-ray telescopes which operate outside the atmosphere on satellites. 'X-ray' astronomers are on the look out for black holes.

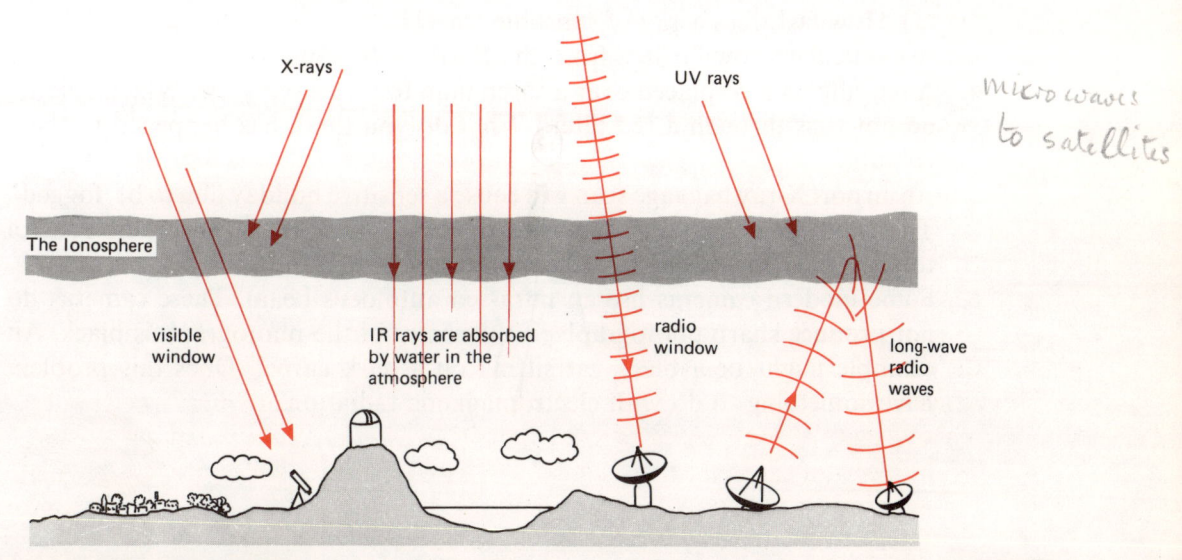

Figure 13.5 Only selected frequencies are allowed through the atmosphere

13.6 Summary

- *Electromagnetic radiations all have the same speed in air, 3×10^8 m/s.*
- *Our eyes are sensitive to the visible part of the electromagnetic spectrum of radiation.*
- *White light is composed of a series of colours each having a different wavelength.*
- *Most of the electromagnetic spectrum is invisible.*
- *The spectrum extends from long wave radio waves to very energetic short wave gamma rays.*

13.7 Progress questions

1. Which of the following radiating waves belong to the electromagnetic spectrum?
   (a) The light from a candle.
   (b) The sound of thunder.
   (c) Ripples on a still pond.
   (d) Sunshine.
   (e) Microwaves in a microwave cooker.
2. Arrange the following waves in order of wavelength. Put the longest wavelength first.

   Infra-red radiation
   Ultra-violet radiation
   Short-wave radio waves
   Blue light
3. It takes about eight minutes for rays of sunshine to travel from the Sun to the Earth.
   (a) How fast does a ray of sunshine travel?
   (b) Calculate how far it is from the Earth to the Sun.
4. A red filter can be placed over a torch bulb to give a red glow. Which colours do not pass through a red filter? What do you think has happened to these colours?
5. An airport X-ray baggage scan will cause a sensitive holiday film to be 'fogged'. The same film will not be affected by the signals from the airport radio control tower. Can you explain why this is the case?
6. Some modern cameras use an infra-red autofocus beam. These cameras do not produce sharp photographs if the centre of the photograph is black. An example might be a black cat sitting on a dark carpet. Does this problem have something to do with electromagnetic radiation?

14 RADIOACTIVITY

14.1 Discovering radioactivity

It was by accident that Henri Becquerel, in 1896, discovered radioactivity. Becquerel found that some crystals of a uranium salt which he had kept near a photographic film in a drawer caused the film to become exposed. Radiation from the uranium salt had travelled through the air and paper surrounding the film and had affected the sensitive film. Film badges are worn today by people who work with radiation. The badges are regularly changed and each time the film is developed to check on the amount of exposure.

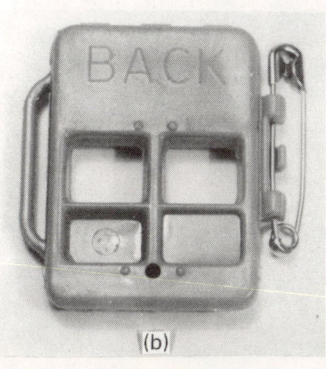

Figure 14.1 (a) Henri Becquerel. (b) A safety film badge. (c) Marie Curie

Marie Curie had been Becquerel's young assistant. She discovered two more sources of radiation: the elements polonium and radium. For many years the radioactivity of one gram of pure radium was used as the standard measure of radioactivity. One gram of radium emitted 3.7×10^{10} particles per second. This **activity** was called one curie. The modern unit of activity is the **becquerel**, **Bq**. An activity of 1 Bq is an activity of just **one particle per second**.

The particles from radioactive elements were found to have the effect of knocking electrons out of the atoms in their path. This effect, called **ionisation**, is the reason why radiations can be so harmful and yet so useful. Even in the early pioneering days of radioactivity, radium together with X-rays (see Unit 13) was used in hospitals to treat tumours.

14.2 Types of radiation

There are three main types of radiation which are known to be emitted by radioactive elements. They are called **alpha**, **beta** and **gamma** radiations. These radiations can be thought of as streams of fast moving particles.

(a) Alpha (α) particles
An alpha particle consists of two protons and two neutrons. The particle carries a double positive charge and moves at a high speed of about 10^7 m/s. Because of their relatively large electric charge and mass, the trail of ionisation which alpha particles leave behind them is very dense but short. A thin piece of paper or a few centimetres of air will be enough to stop most alpha particles. However, if you are contaminated by a small amount of alpha-emitting substance, the effect of the alpha particles on your local body tissue will be serious. Alpha particles can be deflected by a strong magnet.

(b) Beta (β) particles
A beta particle is a fast moving electron with a speed of about 10^8 m/s. It carries a single electric charge and has a mass which is about 1/7000 of that of an alpha particle. The ionisation caused by a beta particle is therefore not as intense and so beta particles can travel a few metres in air before losing their kinetic energy.

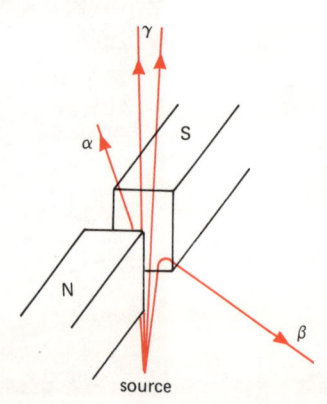

Figure 14.2 A magnet will deflect alpha and beta particles

A thin sheet of aluminium will stop most beta particles. Beta particles can be easily deflected by a magnet.

(c) Gamma (γ) particles
A gamma particle belongs to the high-energy end of the electromagnetic spectrum (see Unit 13). It therefore moves at the speed of light, has no mass, no charge and has wave-like properties. Gamma 'particles' will show diffraction and are often called gamma 'rays' or 'photons'. It is very difficult to stop and detect a gamma photon as they are not affected by a magnet and they produce little local ionisation. Several thick layers of lead and concrete are needed to stop gamma photons.

(d) Neutrons and X-rays
These are another two types of fast moving radiations. They are used in hospitals and industry to produce images. However they are **not** emitted by radioactive elements and so will not be covered in this Unit.

Particle	Identity	Charge	Speed	Mass	Penetration
alpha α	2p, 2n	2 +	10^7 m/s	4 units	few cm in air
beta $β^-$	fast electron	1 −	10^8 m/s	$\simeq$ 1/2000 unit	few metres in air
gamma γ	photon	0	3×10^8 m/s	0	several cm of lead

Figure 14.3 The properties of alpha, beta and gamma particles

14.3 Safety and radioactivity

Radioactive sources for educational use are usually of low activity, about 200 000 Bq or 5 microcurie. The radioactive sources which you will see in school and college are sealed in containers. They will be kept in lead-lined boxes and clearly labelled. **It is a legal requirement that you must be supervised by your teacher if you handle a radioactive source.** In general, sources must be handled using tongs or tweezers to avoid the possibility of **contamination**. To avoid the problem of **irradiation**, sources should never be pointed at any person.

14.4 Detecting and measuring radiations

(a) Detectors
The use of a film badge was mentioned in Section 14.1. A more immediate way of detecting the presence of radiations is to use a **Geiger–Muller (GM) tube** attached to a counter. A particle entering the tube through the thin window will cause the gas inside to ionise. A high potential difference across the inside of the

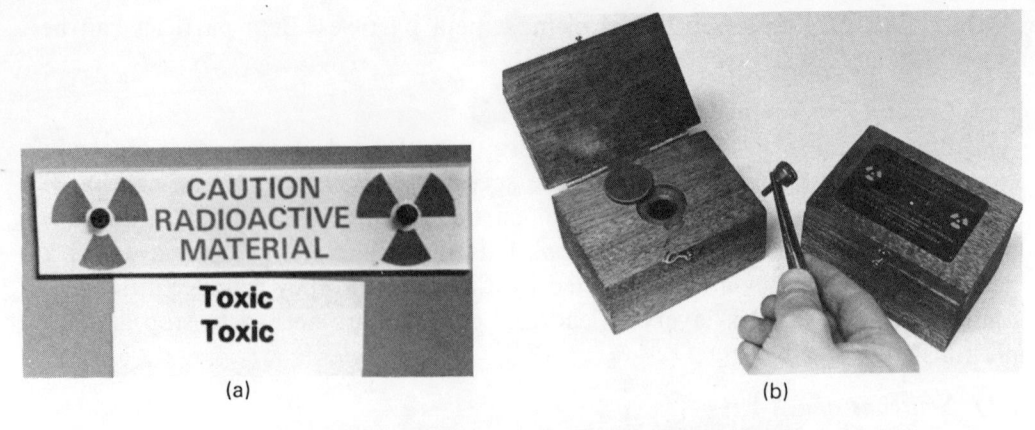

Figure 14.4 (a) A radiation warning. (b) A radiation source and its lead-lined box

tube collects these ions and amplifies the sudden burst of ion activity. The number of events in a period of time can be recorded as 'counts per minute'.

To enable the paths of alpha and beta particles to be seen a **diffusion cloud chamber** can be used. The trail of ions left behind as a particle moves through the chamber shows up as a line of tiny vapour droplets. The vapour is alcohol which is cooled by solid carbon dioxide (dry ice) placed in the base of the chamber.

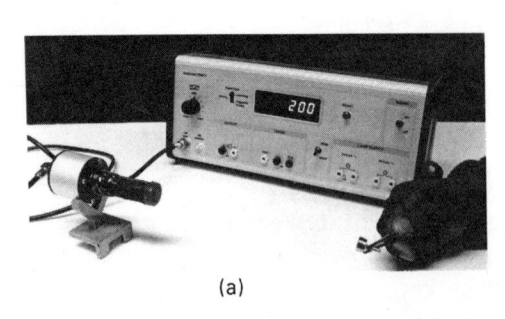

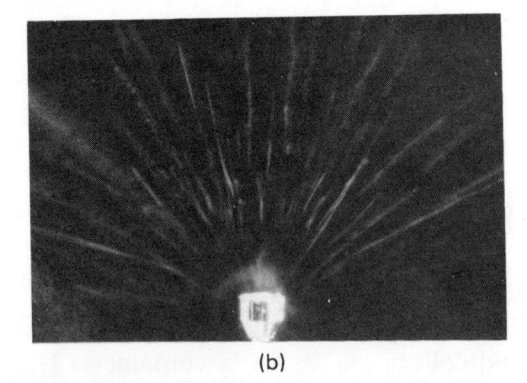

Figure 14.5 Radiation detection using: (a) a GM tube and (b) a cloud chamber

(b) Background count

If you switch on a GM tube and counter when all the known radioactive sources are locked safely away, you will still register a small count. This is called the background count and it is always present. The background count shows that we are being bombarded continuously by alpha, beta and gamma particles. These particles come from a number of sources. A small proportion of radioactive elements occur naturally in rocks and minerals. A major source of background is the building material used to make bricks, floors and ceilings. Areas like Cornwall and Aberdeen contain a particularly high concentration of radioactive elements in the local building material. People living in these areas will be subjected to larger background doses than people living in other places.

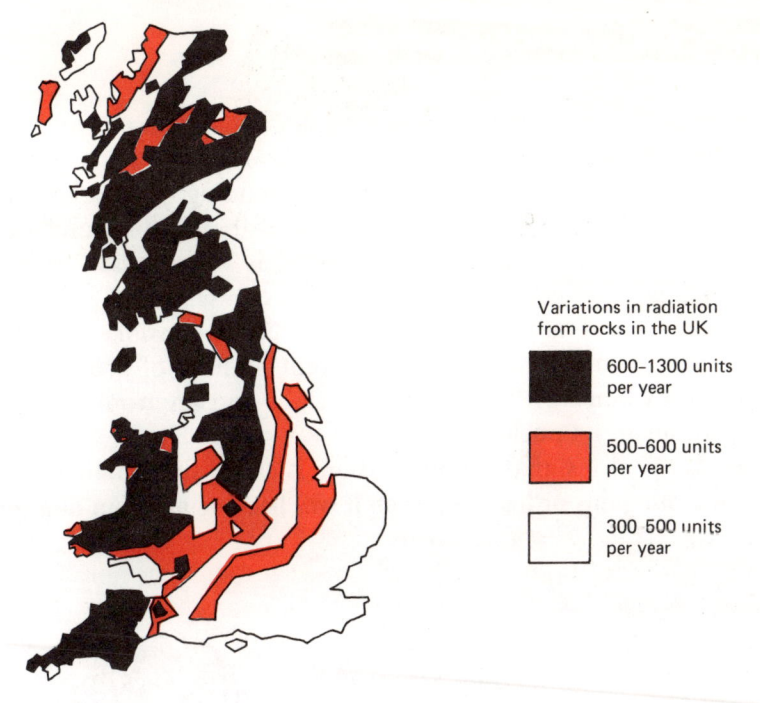

Figure 14.6 Background radiation from rocks in Britain

Another source of background is the atmosphere which is constantly bombarded by cosmic rays from space.

Radioisotopes, such as potassium 40 and carbon 14, naturally occur in our bodies and contribute to our annual dose.

As the background count is always present, it is important to take a reading of the background count before you use your apparatus to monitor another radioactive source. You can then allow for the background by **subtracting the background count from all your other counts**. For example, see Figure 14.7.

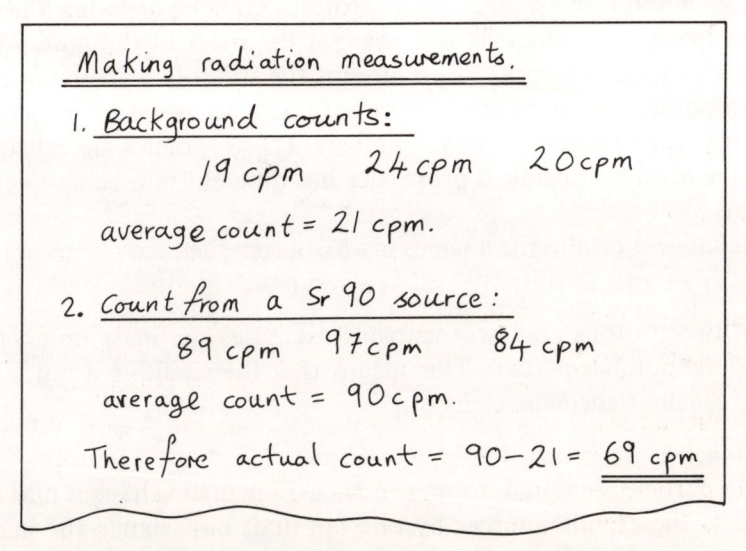

```
Making radiation measurements.

1. Background counts:
        19 cpm    24 cpm    20 cpm
   average count = 21 cpm.

2. Count from a Sr 90 source:
        89 cpm    97 cpm    84 cpm
   average count = 90 cpm.
   Therefore actual count = 90 - 21 = 69 cpm
```

Figure 14.7 Dealing with a background count

14.5 Isotopes and radioactive changes

It would be surprising if elements which radiate alpha, beta or gamma particles underwent no change. Changes do occur and they happen to the central part of the atom, the **nucleus**. It would help your understanding of these changes if you looked back to Section 13.18 to revise some ideas about atoms and models.

A simple model of the structure of an atom is of a dense central nucleus containing protons and neutrons surrounded by a sea of negatively charged electrons. To understand radioactive change you need to consider only the nucleus. Atoms of different elements will have a different number of protons. Hydrogen has one proton, carbon has six, oxygen has eight and an atom of uranium has ninety two protons in its nucleus.

The number of protons, that is **6** for carbon, is called the **atomic number** of the element. **If an atom gains or loses a proton it will become an atom of a totally new element.**

hydrogen $^{1}_{1}H$ (one proton)

carbon $^{12}_{6}C$ (six protons, six neutrons)

uranium $^{235}_{92}U$ (92 protons, 143 neutrons)

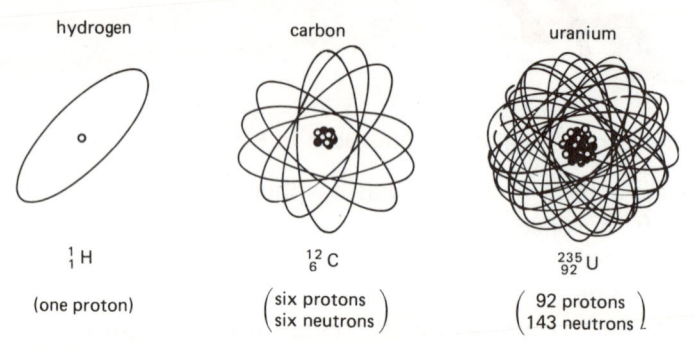

Figure 14.8 Atomic numbers and mass numbers

Making up the rest of the nucleus are neutrons. These are particles without charge but with about the same mass as protons. **Gaining or losing a neutron has no effect on the type of atom. It just changes the mass of the atom.** The **mass number**, for example, carbon **12**, of an atom is the sum of its proton and neutron numbers. In nature, atoms of an element naturally occur with a variety of mass numbers because of different neutron numbers. These varieties are called **isotopes**. Isotopes have identical chemical properties but different numbers of neutrons in their nucleus.

So what changes occur to the nucleus of an isotope when radiations are emitted?

Alpha emission
The loss of two protons and two neutrons decreases the mass number by four and the atomic number by two. This means that the resulting atom is an atom of a totally different chemical element.

Beta emission
When a beta particle is emitted from the nucleus, a neutron changes into a proton. This increases the atomic number by one but does not change the mass of the atom. Once again the atom becomes an atom of a totally different element.

Some isotopes of hydrogen	^1_1H	^2_1H	^3_1H
	1 proton	1 proton 1 neutron	1 proton 2 neutrons
Some isotopes of carbon	$^{12}_6C$	$^{14}_6C$	$^{15}_6C$
	6 protons 6 neutrons	6 protons 8 neutrons	6 protons 9 neutrons
Some isotopes of uranium	$^{235}_{92}U$	$^{238}_{92}U$	$^{239}_{92}U$
	92 protons 143 neutrons	92 protons 146 neutrons	92 protons 147 neutrons

Figure 14.9 Some examples of isotopes

$$^{238}_{92}U \longrightarrow {}^{234}_{90}Th + {}^4_2\alpha \qquad\qquad ^{14}_6C \longrightarrow {}^{14}_7N + \beta^-$$

(a)   (b)

Figure 14.10 Representing (a) alpha and (b) beta decay

Gamma emission
Losing a gamma photon causes no change. This can be thought of as the atom losing some excess energy. The mass number and atomic number remain the same.

14.6 Radioactive decay and half-life

Radioactive change is a random process. This means that you cannot tell which atom in a material is about to emit a particle and you cannot say exactly when a particle will be emitted. The mathematics of chance describe the process of radioactive change. It is most unlikely that all the atoms in a sample will emit a particle at the same time. It is more likely that particles will be emitted over a period of time.

Let us consider a fresh sample of 1000 unstable atoms. At first, many particles will be emitted each second. This is because there are many atoms available to 'decay'. After a while, the activity will have decreased. This is because there are fewer remaining atoms available to decay. After some time, the activity will be very low. This is because, with only a few atoms still remaining to decay, the chance of one decaying is small. It must be remembered that at the end of the decay period there are still 1000 atoms but they will be atoms of another element.

How long does a sample of radioactive isotope take to decay completely? This question is difficult to answer because you could theoretically wait for many years for the last few atoms to decay. It is much more sensible to measure the time taken for half the number of atoms to decay. This is called the **half-life** of the material and is a constant for a particular radioisotope. In a time of one half-life, the activity of a radioisotope will have decreased to 50 per cent of its original

Figure 14.11 The statistics of decay

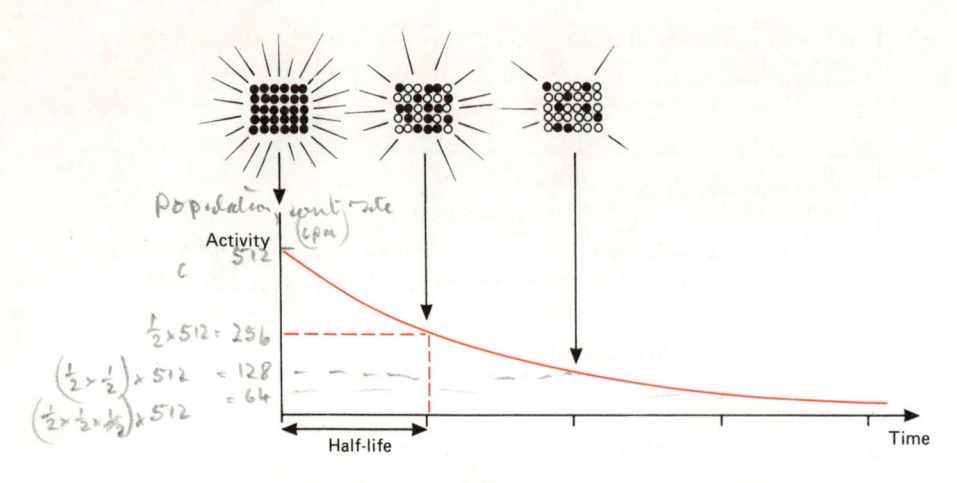

At the start of its life a sample is very active. There are lots of chances that nuclei will decay
After a time, called the half-life, only half the nuclei are left to decay. The activity is a half
After a longer time the activity is low. Very few nuclei are left to decay

activity. In two half-lives, the activity will reach 25 per cent of its original value, and so on.

The reality of radioactive decay is a little more complex than outlined in this Section. Some radioisotopes decay to a stable '**daughter**' product. Others, however, decay to a daughter isotope which itself is radioactive and has its own half-life as it decays to a '**granddaughter**'. This leads to the possibility of whole families of radioactive isotopes. There are three naturally occurring families of radioisotope. Part of one decay series is shown in Figure 14.12.

$$^{238}_{92}U \xrightarrow{\alpha} {}^{234}_{90}Th \xrightarrow{\beta} {}^{234}_{91}Pa \xrightarrow{\beta} {}^{234}_{92}U \xrightarrow{\alpha} {}^{230}_{90}Th \xrightarrow{\alpha} {}^{226}_{88}Ra \xrightarrow{\alpha} {}^{222}_{86}Rn \xrightarrow{\alpha} {}^{218}_{84}Po$$

Figure 14.12 Part of the uranium 238 decay series

14.7 The biological effects of radiation

Exposure to radiation is referred to as **dose**. The effect of a dose depends on the type of particle, the duration of exposure, the energy of the particles and the precise area of the target. A unit for measuring a dose is the **sievert, Sv**. A convenient unit to work with is the **microsievert**. We shall use the microsievert as our 'radiation unit'.

Cells in the body may have their chemistry changed by the impact of an alpha, beta or gamma particle. The body has a repair mechanism which constantly copes with the damage caused by background radiation. Occasionally the affected cells die (this is how radiation treatment helps to kill cancer cells). If a body is exposed to larger than average 'doses', then the effects will depend on whether the dose was a large sudden dose (**early effect**) or a gradual long-term build up (**late effect**).

An early effect of a sudden dose of about 100 000 radiation units is temporary sterility; a million units will result in hair loss, nausea and skin burns; ten million units would be fatal.

The effects of a gradual build up of dose are much less severe. The effect of living in, say, Cornwall where the background is about 2000 units per year (average background is 1000 units/yr), is to increase the annual risk of getting cancer by 1 in 80 000. Compare this with the annual risk of death from a road accident of 1 in 7000 and the annual risk of death from heart disease of 1 in 300. The relative risk of death from background radiation compared with the risk caused by medical and other doses is shown in the pie diagram of Figure 14.13.

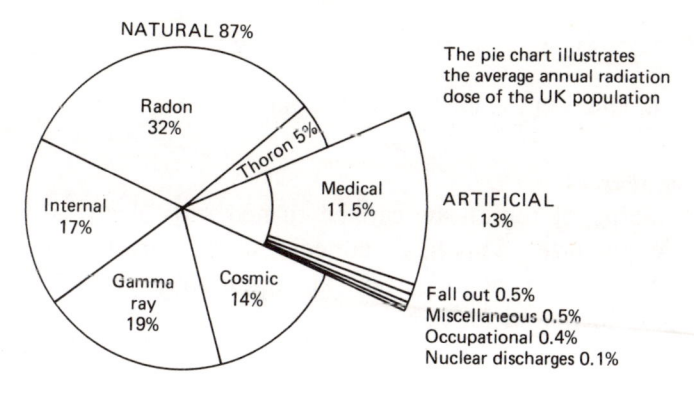

Figure 14.13 Contributions to the annual radiation dose for an average member of the population

14.8 Applications of radioactivity

The uses of radioactivity are numerous. A selection of the more common uses is given below.

Radio-carbon dating
Living things take in and give out carbon atoms all the time. Because of this dynamic equilibrium a certain fixed proportion of radioactive carbon 14 is to be found in all living things. When living things die they no longer take in carbon and so the proportion of carbon 14 in their bodies decays. By measuring the activity remaining in a once-living object, it is possible to say just when it stopped living. The radiocarbon dating techniques can be used for objects which are about 1000 to 10 000 years old.

Radioactive underground tracers
Geologists use radioactive tracers to follow the paths of underground rivers. A small amount of radioactive liquid is introduced to the flowing water and by placing detectors in the water downstream, the path of the tracer can be followed.

Monitoring the thickness of paper
Paper is made in a continuous rolling process. To check that the thickness of the paper is just right, a beta emitter and GM tube are placed on either side of the

rolling paper. The paper will absorb the beta particles. A decreased GM tube reading would mean that the paper were too thick. The rolling process would then adjust its speed to correct for the error.

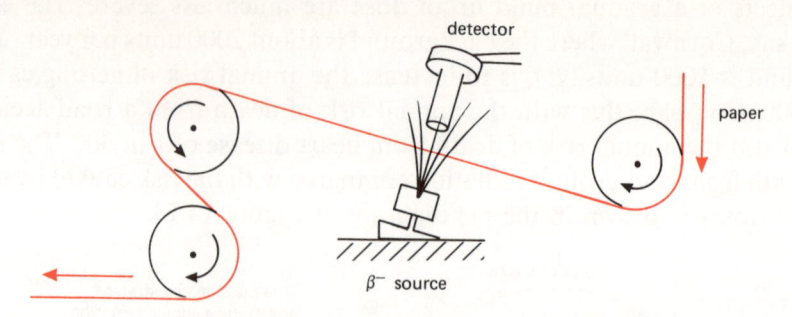

Figure 14.14 Monitoring the thickness of paper

Mobile power sources
The kinetic energy of radiations can be turned into electrical energy using a thermoelectric converter. This has enabled a small, portable radioactive source to act as a battery for heart pacemakers, for space vehicle computers, for underwater amplifiers and for lights on remote arctic airstrips in Alaska.

Sterilisation
Gamma photons can have just the right energy to destroy bacteria. It is for this reason that many doctors and hospitals use a gamma photon source to sterilise their equipment. Plastic equipment can now be cheaply sterilised whereas before the equipment had to be made of glass to withstand the high sterilisation temperature.

14.9 Related reading: Medical imaging using gamma radiations

Until recently there was only one way to find out about the interior of a person's body—dissection! Fortunately, this century, X-rays have allowed shadow photographs to be taken without damaging patients. Today, images of the inside of human bodies can be made using a gamma camera.

A radioisotope is injected into the bloodstream and it is tagged on to a chemical which will take it to the particular organ or body region in question. During its time in the body the radioactive source continues to emit gamma rays. These gamma rays are picked up outside the body by a gamma camera, and a photograph of the region can be seen. This photograph can be a moving picture to show how the organ changes with time.

The particular radioisotope used needs to be a good gamma emitter whose particles are not so energetic that they pass right through the back of the camera. Iodine 131 was very common until recently. Its drawback was that it was also a strong beta emitter. Technetium 99 is now commonly used. Te 99 emits only gamma photons and has a half-life of about 6 hr which means that it will not linger in the body for much longer than is necessary.

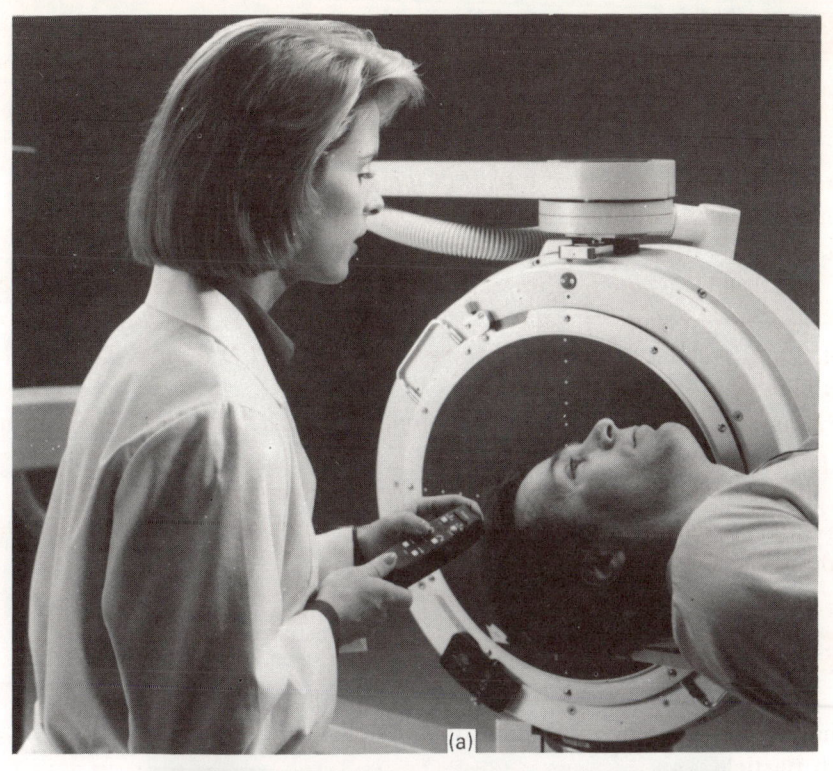

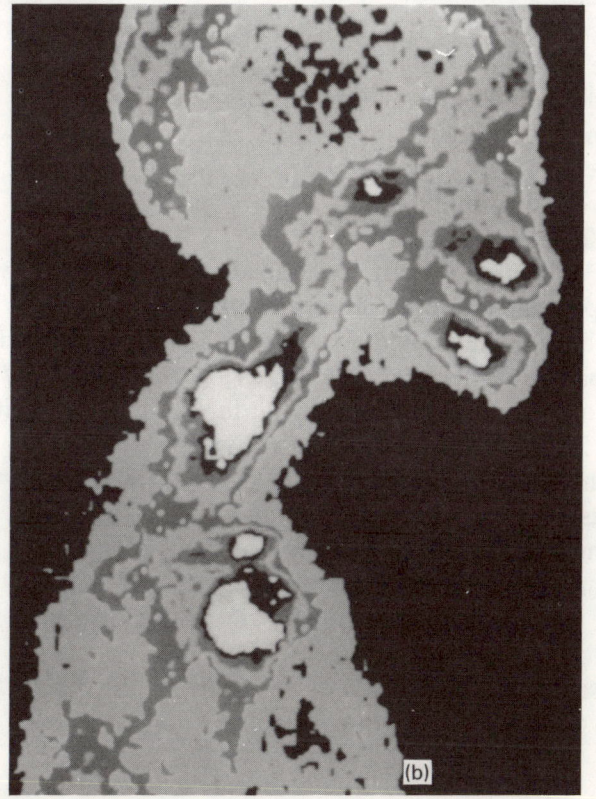

Figure 14.15 (a) Using a gamma camera. (b) An image from a gamma camera

151

14.10 Summary

- *Particular materials, called radioisotopes, randomly emit ionising radiations.*
- *The activity of a sample of radioisotope is measured in becquerels, Bq.*
- *Alpha particles create a dense trail of ionisation but over a short range.*
- *Radiation detectors use the ionising properties of alpha, beta and gamma rays to detect them.*
- *The background count is always present and should be considered whenever a measurement of counts is made.*
- *Numbers of particles in a nucleus are described by the atomic number and the mass number.*
- *The emission of a beta or alpha particle will change the nucleus both chemically and physically.*
- *The time for the activity of a radioisotope to halve is called the half-life.*
- *The effect of radiation on humans depends on the type of radiation and the time period of the exposure.*

14.11 Progress questions

1. What are the differences between an alpha particle and a beta particle? Describe each particle.
2. What do you think are the most important safety rules when dealing with radioactive sources?
3. Why are radioactive sources kept in lead-lined boxes?
4. Explain what you understand by the terms
   (a) Isotope
   (b) Background count
   (c) Half-life.
5. You were told that a box contained a small quantity of low-activity radioisotope with a half-life of four hours.
   (a) Describe how you would measure the activity of the radioisotope. Briefly say what instruments you would use.
   (b) How long would you have to wait for the initial activity to become less than 25 per cent of the original activity?
6. Atoms of the radioisotope magnesium 28 are represented by the symbol $^{28}_{12}Mg$. $^{28}_{12}Mg$ emits beta particles and has a half-life of 21 hours.
   (a) How many protons are there in a nucleus of $^{28}_{12}Mg$?
   (b) How many neutrons are there?
   (c) If you started off with a million atoms of $^{28}_{12}Mg$ how many would you expect to have after about sixty hours?
7. It can be said that the benefits of radioactivity outweigh the disadvantages. What do you think? Give your reasons.

15 ELECTRONS AND ELECTRICITY

15.1 Sparks

The spark which you sometimes feel after walking on a nylon carpet or taking off a synthetic fibre sweater is often called **static electricity**. In fact, as you will find out, there is nothing at all very static about sparks. Static effects are caused by the build up of **electrons**, electric 'charged' particles. Frictional forces may cause an electron to be freed from its atom. The resulting attraction between positively charged atoms, called **ions**, and **free electrons** will cause them to be forced together again. A spark occurs at the place where the electrons rush towards the positive charges.

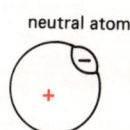

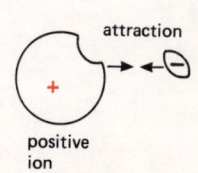

Figure 15.1 Opposite charges attract

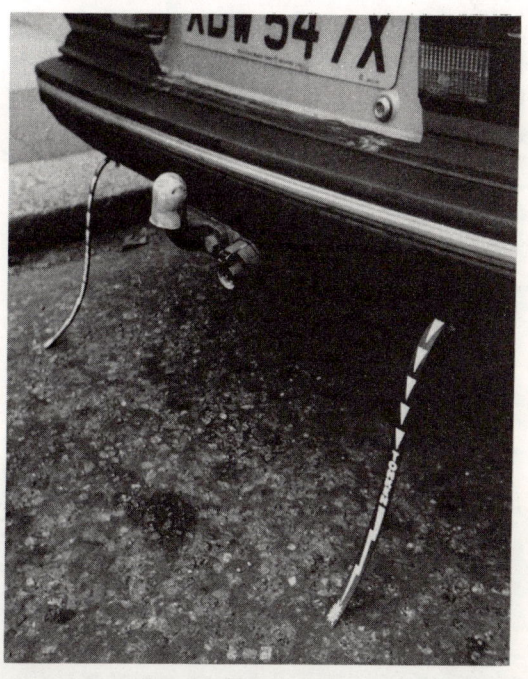

Figure 15.2 An 'earthing lead' will prevent the build up of static charges on a motor car. Charges are conducted to the ground

Sparks can be very useful as in the case of a spark-operated gas lighter or a glowing discharge lamp. Quite often, however, sparks will ignite an explosive gas

or a spark plug

accidentally. The anaesthetic used in hospital operating theatres and the products from oil refineries give off explosive vapours. To prevent sparks in these environments, any free electrons which might gather on equipment are allowed to trickle down to the ground by a conducting chain or wire. You may have noticed such a conductor hanging down from the back of a motor car.

15.2 Electrons in wires

As we have never seen an electron, we need to use simple models to help us to imagine a picture of what happens when a metal wire conducts electricity. Atoms in metals are arranged in a regular crystal structure. Some of the more energetic electrons will be free to move through the crystal. These free electrons are sometimes called a 'sea' of electrons. When they are attracted by an electric force they will drift through the metal, colliding with the atoms as they pass by.

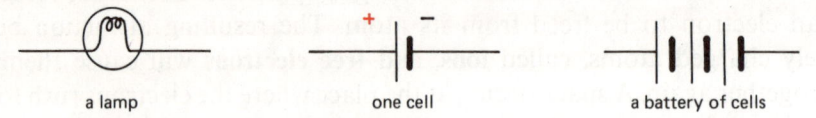

Figure 15.3 Symbols for circuit diagrams

The collisions result in the atoms in the wire gaining internal energy. This is how an electric current heats up a wire. There must be a complete circular path for the electrons if they are to be expected to keep moving. We call the path an **electric circuit**.

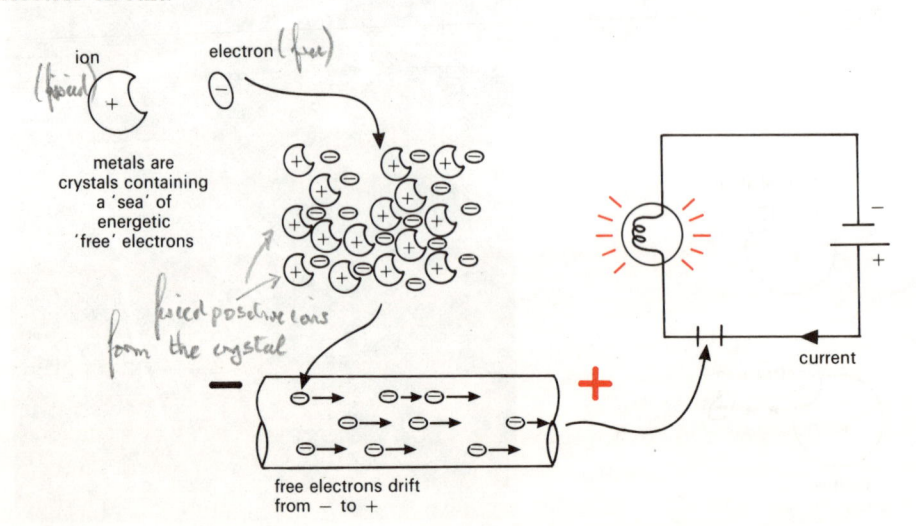

Figure 15.4 'Free' electrons move electric charge around a complete circuit

Each electron carries a certain amount of electric charge. (It is not clear to physicists just what this thing called 'charge' actually is. It is an idea without an easy explanation. It is a concept.) Electric charge is measured in units of coulombs. As electrons are very small, the charge they carry is a tiny fraction of a coulomb.

You need about a million million million electrons before you have one coulomb of charge. (Charles Coulomb, 1736–1806, was a French military engineer.) The direction of an electric current was traditionally agreed to be from + to −. Electrons in fact move in the opposite direction, from − to +.

15.3 Electric current and potential difference

What measurements might be made concerning moving charges? How fast the charge is flowing is one. Another is how much energy is being transformed. Let us consider these measurements one at a time.

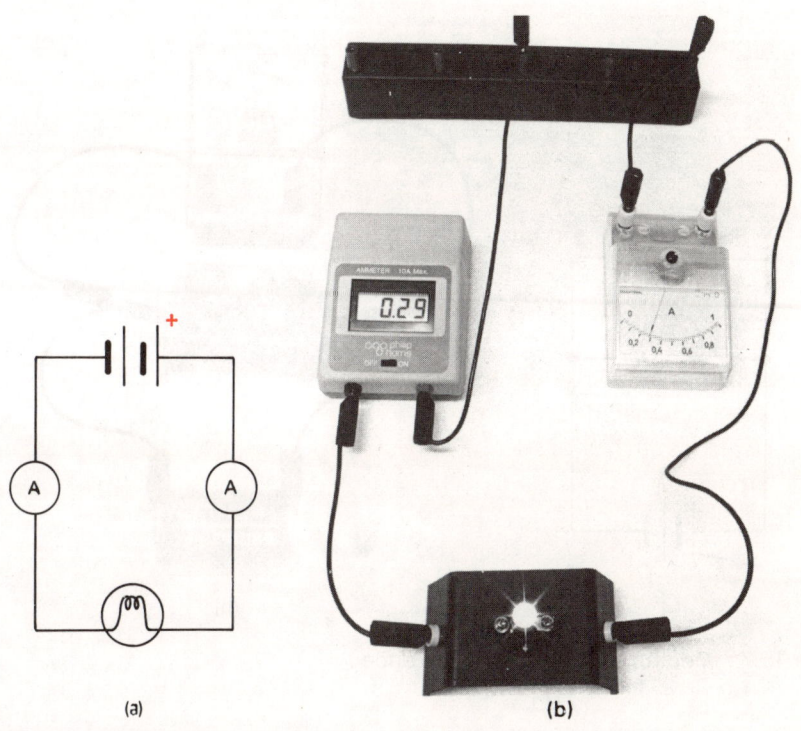

Figure 15.5 Measuring an electric current

Ⓐ is in series with lamp – i.e. on the same current path.

To measure the amount of charge passing any point along a wire, we use an ammeter. The ammeter can be a moving needle type or have a digital display, but it must be connected so that the charges flow through it. We call this **connecting in series**. An **ammeter** measures the electric **current**, the rate of flow of charge. A rate of flow of one coulomb per second is called **one amp** (AMPERE). A milliamp is one-thousandth of an amp. A flow of charges in one direction is called **direct current** or d.c. It is possible for charges to move repeatedly backwards and forwards in a wire. We call this **alternating current** or a.c.

A **voltmeter** will tell us just how much energy the charges are transforming as they battle their way through a wire. This energy difference is called **potential difference**, p.d. or sometimes **voltage**. To measure a potential difference a voltmeter

(or potential energy difference)

ammeter   voltmeter   switch

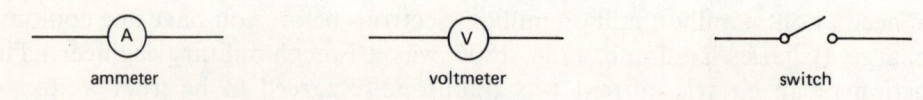

Figure 15.6 More symbols for circuit diagrams

must be connected across that part of the circuit which is of interest. We call this **connecting in parallel**. If each coulomb of charge transforms one joule of energy, then the p.d. is **one volt**. A battery or mains operated power unit provides the supply of energy. (Remember that the charges are part of the wire in the circuit. They are not supplied by the battery.)

(a)   (b)

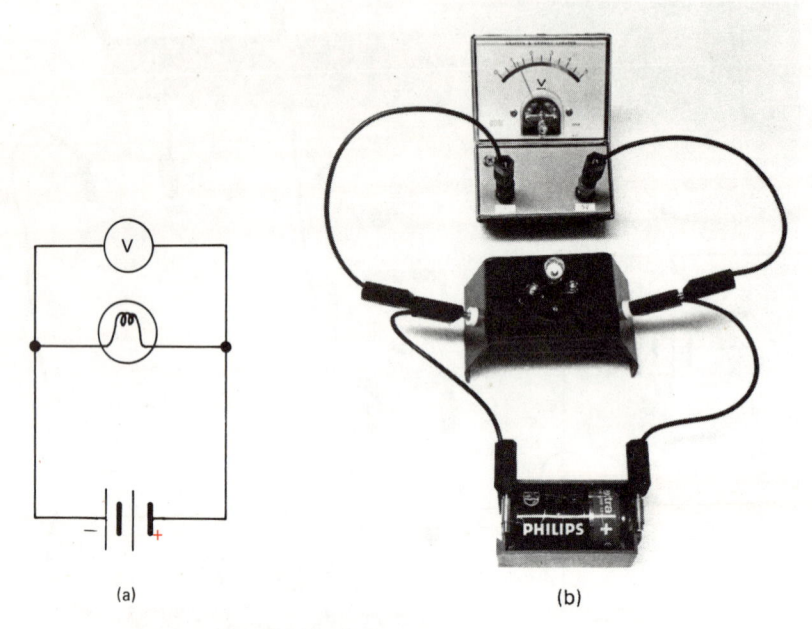

Figure 15.7 Measuring potential difference

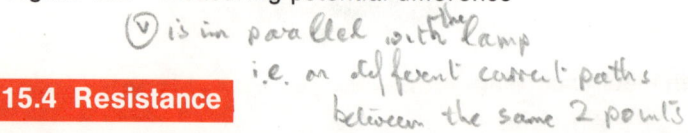

*V is in parallel with the lamp
i.e. on different current paths
between the same 2 points*

15.4 Resistance

Not all wires are equally good at conducting electricity. In some materials, glass and wood for example, there are few free electrons to carry charge. Such materials are called electrical **insulators** and have a **high resistance**. A small group of materials have electrons which are easily given enough energy to conduct by a little heating or illumination. We call these materials **semiconductors**. Silicon and germanium are semiconductors.

Some metals are better conductors than others. For any one material, the shape of the conductor has a major effect on its resistance. If you remember that an electric current is the flow of free electrons, it is easy to see why a long, thin wire will be a much poorer conductor than a short, fat wire. Short, fat wires provide the electrons with a much wider path. If you had to design a by-pass road to

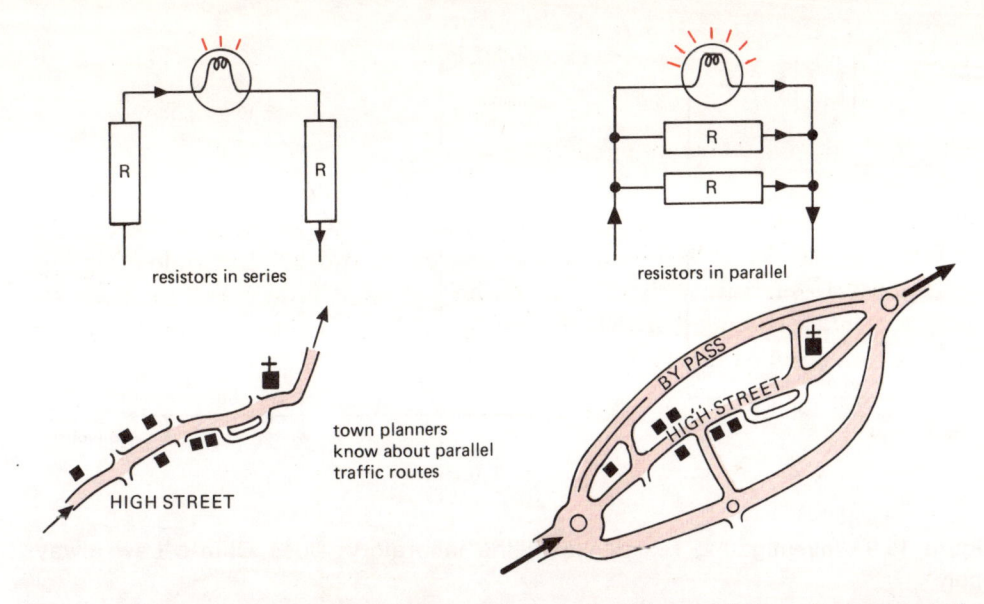

Figure 15.8 The flow of charges, like traffic, is helped by providing alternative paths

carry most of the traffic around the outside of a town, would you build a long thin road or a short, wide road?

Wires and lamps connected **in parallel** with each other will allow more current to flow than wires and lamps connected one after the other **in series**. Resistors in series add to the total resistance. Resistors in parallel decrease the total resistance.

15.5 Measuring resistance

The resistance of a wire or a lamp can be found experimentally. You need to complete an electric circuit using a supply of energy, a battery perhaps, and measure the p.d. across your resistor as well as the current in the circuit. In physics we define resistance as **the potential difference divided by the current**.

$$\text{resistance} = \frac{\text{p.d.}}{\text{current}}$$

$$R \text{ (ohms)} = \frac{V \text{ (volts)}}{I \text{ (amps)}} \quad \text{or} \quad V = I \times R$$

The unit of resistance is the ohm, written Ω. Georg Ohm, 1787–1854, was a German school teacher. Ohm found that the resistance of a conductor was constant provided the temperature remained constant. This result is known as **Ohm's Law**. Another way of expressing Ohm's Law is to say that the **current is directly proportional to the potential difference**. Most wires obey Ohm's law up to a point. The filament of a lamp is designed to glow white hot and so a lamp will not have a constant resistance and so will not obey Ohm's Law. The behaviour of resistors at different temperatures can be investigated by changing the current using a variable resistor or by using a variety of p.d. values.

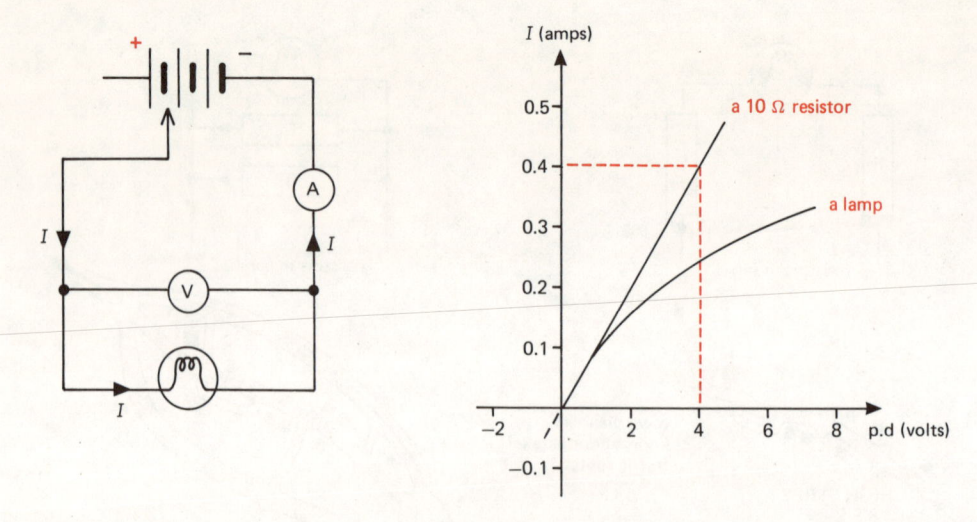

Figure 15.9 Investigating resistance in the laboratory. Does Ohm's Law always apply?

15.6 Dividing circuits

(a) Dividing current

When conductors are connected in parallel they provide more than one path for the flow of charges. In parallel circuits, paths with less resistance will carry most current. When paths join up again, the currents add up.

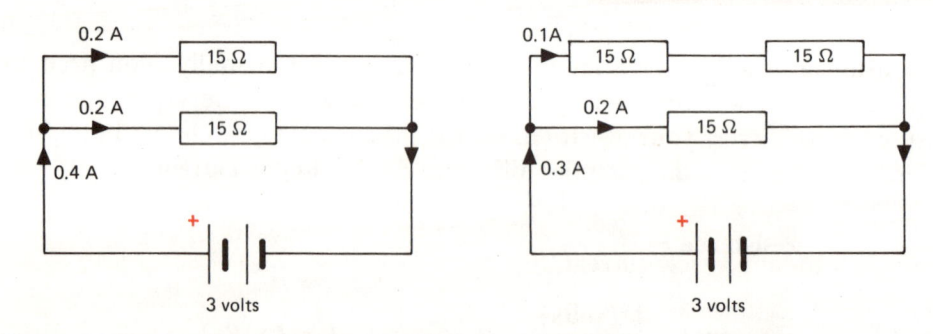

Figure 15.10 Parallel circuits will divide up the current

You will notice that the current divides in the ratio of the resistances, with less current in the path with most resistance. It is possible to calculate the current in any part of the circuit using the resistance equation given in Section 15.5.

(b) Dividing potential difference

Conductors can be connected so that there is only one path for the charges to follow. This is called a **series** circuit. In a series circuit the current is the same at all places around the circuit. The charges transform energy in every resistor

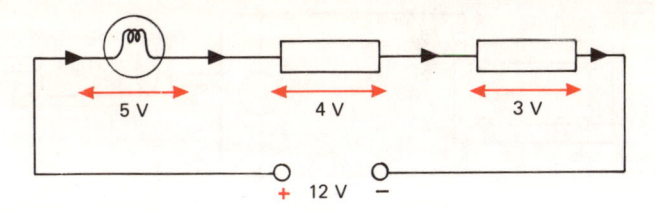

Figure 15.11 Potential difference is divided by a series circuit

through which they pass and so potential difference across the circuit is divided up between the components. The total p.d. supplied by the battery will be the sum of the p.d.s around the circuit.

Now consider a circuit with two resistors in series with a 12 volt battery. They form a **potential divider** circuit. If the resistors are equal, say 100 ohms each, they will each have a p.d. of 6 volts across them.

If one resistor is altered to 200 ohms, the p.d. will be unequally divided in the ratio 1 to 2, that is, 2 volts and 4 volts.

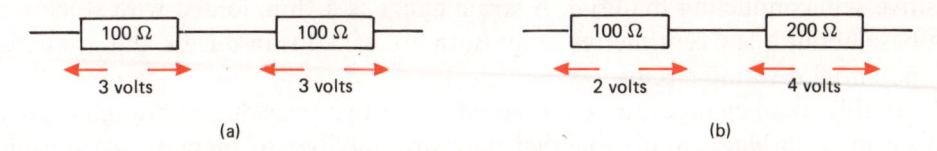

Figure 15.12 Potential difference divides in the ratio of resistances

You could use the resistance equation to help to calculate these p.d. values but the ratio of resistances is a useful and quick method. You will find the idea of potential dividing returning in the reading at the end of this Unit and in Units 20 and 21.

15.7 Energy and power in electric circuits

Most electric circuits are used to transform energy. A battery-operated torch, a hair drier, a food mixer and a portable radio can all be considered as devices for changing electrical energy into other forms. A 400 W food mixer changes energy at a rate of 400 joules every second. The electrical energy becomes mechanical work. How can the power of an electric circuit be measured or calculated? There are two ways of looking at the power of an electric circuit: the power input and the useful power output.

A laboratory joulemeter will tell you the total amount of energy your circuit has transformed. Divide this energy by the time taken and you will have a measure of the input power. A wattmeter will automatically read the power input. Alternatively, the power can be calculated from the current and the p.d.

power of an electric circuit = p.d. × current = $V \times I = I^2 \times R$

(1 watt = 1 volt × 1 amp)

power input
= V × I

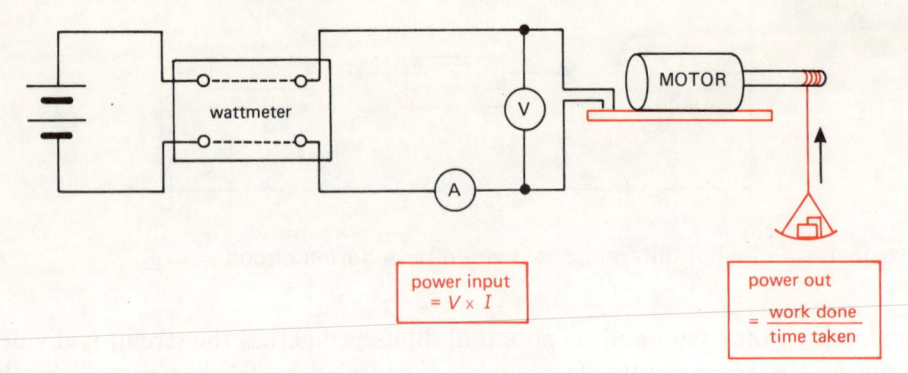

power out
= work done / time taken

Figure 15.13 Measuring the power of an electric circuit

15.8 Related reading: Making use of resistance changes in industry

You have seen that the resistance of a wire will change with its shape and also when its temperature changes. A **thermistor** is a resistor made of a temperature sensitive semiconducting material. A **strain gauge** is a thin, folded wire stuck on to a base about a few centimetres long. Both are called **transducers** and are used in a potential dividing circuit.

To enable small changes to be measured, these two transducers are often used in a sensitive '**bridge**' circuit together with an amplifier to increase the output signal.

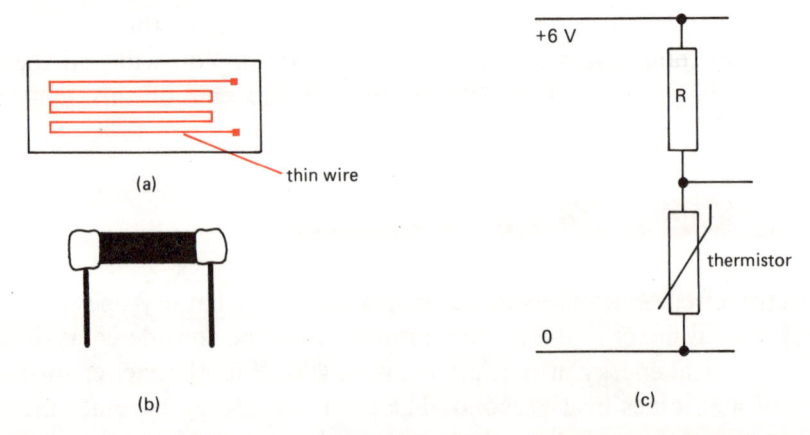

Figure 15.14 (a) A strain gauge. (b) A thermistor. (c) The 6 volts will be divided between the two resistors

The bridge circuit is first adjusted to balance the two sides so that they divide the potential difference in the same ratio. When the transducer, for example, the strain gauge, extends fractionally, its resistance changes and so the balance of p.d.s is disturbed. The amplified output signal can be displayed on an oscilloscope or stored and displayed using a computer.

Strain gauges have been used in this way to check the stretching of aircraft wings and road bridges. Thermistors can be used as thermometers which can be

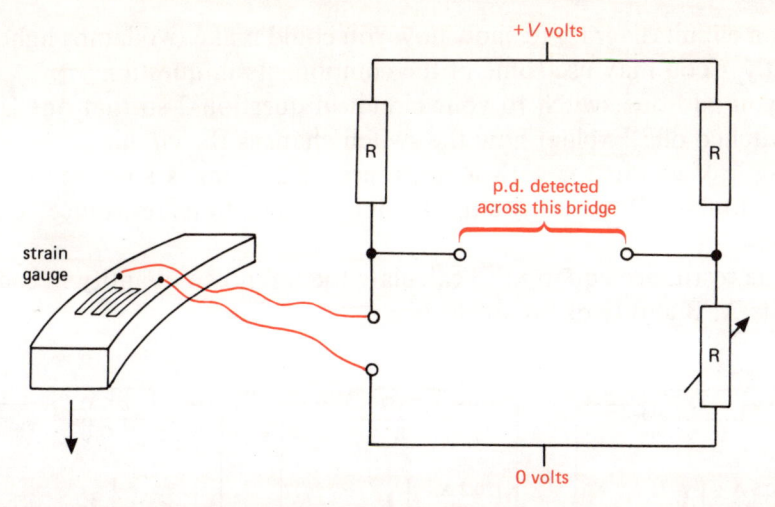

Figure 15.15 A strain gauge as part of a 'bridge' circuit

put in inaccessible places such as the inside of an oil pipeline or the inside of a very cold refrigerator.

15.9 Summary

- *In metals, electric charge is carried by free electrons.*
- *Some materials are better conductors than others. Resistance can change with shape or temperature.*
- *The **resistance** of a conductor is measured in ohms and can be found from:*

$$R = V/I$$

- *The rate of transport of charges is the **current** and is measured in **amps** using an ammeter.*
- *The energy transformed when charges move between two places in a circuit is called the **potential difference** between those places. P.d. is measured in **volts** using a voltmeter.*
- *Components can be connected in series or parallel. A parallel circuit divides up the current. A series circuit divides up the p.d.*
- *The rate at which an electric circuit transforms energy can be calculated using*

$$\text{Power} = V \times I \qquad \text{or} \qquad \text{Power} = I^2 \times R$$

15.10 Progress questions

1. Which electrical component is shown by each of the circuit symbols in Figure 15.16?

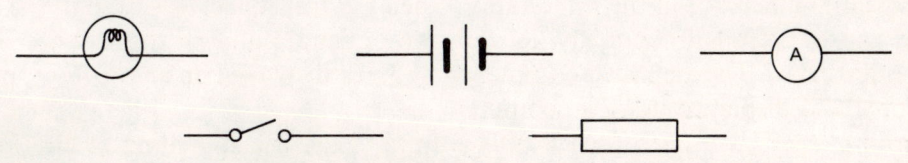

Figure 15.16

2. Draw a circuit diagram to show how you could make two lamps light equally brightly. (You may use some of the components in question 1.)
3. Can you add one switch to your circuit in question 2 so that one lamp can be switched off? Explain how the switch changes the circuit.
4. A length of conductor with a resistance of 2 ohms is stretched so that its length doubles. What do you think might happen to its resistance? Give your reasons.
5. Use the resistance equation to calculate the unknown quantity in each of the circuits A, B and C of Figure 15.17.

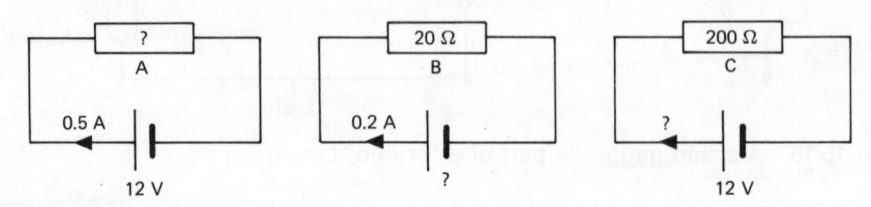

Figure 15.17

6. Draw a circuit diagram for yourself. Make sure that it is a series circuit and that it contains some 10 ohm resistors and a 6 volt battery. Explain how the 6 volts are divided up in your circuit.
7. Draw for yourself a circuit diagram for a parallel circuit. Use a 6 volt battery and some 10 ohm resistors. Explain how the current is divided by your circuit.
8. (a) Which of the circuits drawn for question 5 is most powerful? Show how you arrive at your answer.
   (b) If circuit B in question 5 had a second 20 ohm resistor connected in series with it what would happen to:
   (i) the current flow?
   (ii) the power of the circuit?

ELECTROMAGNETISM

16.1 Magnetic fields

Exactly why two magnets attract or repel each other is a question which still puzzles modern physicists. However, magnetic forces do exist and we can describe their size and direction by using the idea of a **magnetic field**.

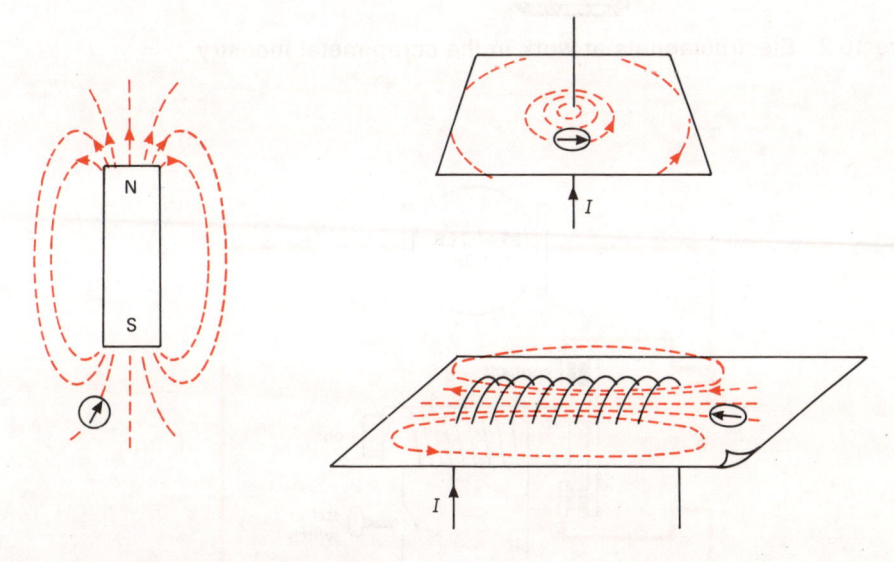

Figure 16.1   Magnetic field shapes

A sprinkling of iron filings or the needle of a small plotting compass will reveal that there are permanent magnetic fields around magnets and temporary magnetic fields around electric currents. The importance of a magnetic field caused by an electric current is that it can be switched on and off. It is controllable.

16.2 Using electromagnets

A coil of wire, called a solenoid, will create a magnetic field around itself whenever an electric current passes through the wire. We say that the solenoid becomes an **electromagnet**. The shape of the field is shown in Figure 16.1. Tightly winding the coil strengthens the magnetic field and placing a piece of iron inside the solenoid greatly increases the field strength. Electromagnets have a variety of applications in our daily lives. Some common uses are outlined below.

Magnetic cranes
In the steel and scrap metal industries, large masses of metal are moved around using cranes fitted with electromagnets. The load is released by switching off the current to the electromagnet.

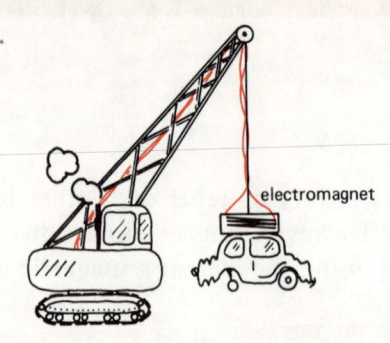

Figure 16.2 Electromagnets at work in the scrap metal industry

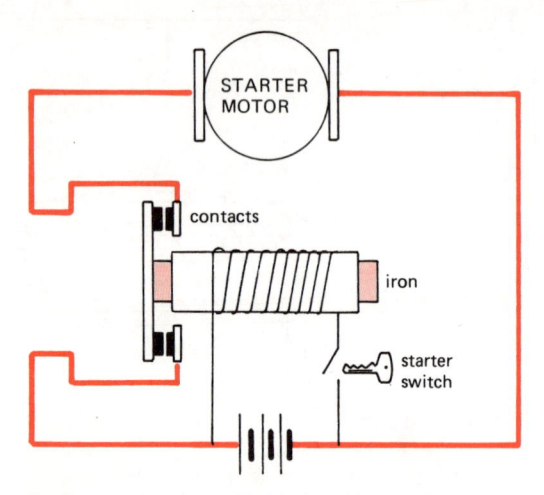

Figure 16.3 A car starter motor is switched on by a relay

Relay switch
A small current flowing in the relay solenoid will cause an iron bar to be attracted to the electromagnet and so close the two terminals. This is a good way of using a small current to switch on a large current safely. In a car, a relay operated by the ignition key switches on the starter motor circuit which may carry about 60 amps for a few seconds.

Reed switch
Thin strips of unmagnetised metal can be temporarily magnetised by a solenoid. The magnetised strips attract and touch each other to make their own circuit. Reed switches are used in some burglar alarms. A tiny magnet concealed in a door operates the reed switch as the door is opened.

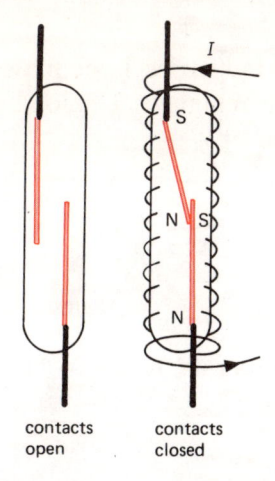

Figure 16.4 A reed switch in operation

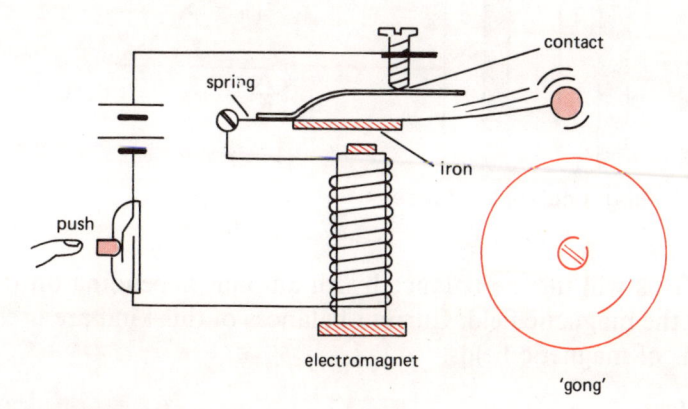

Figure 16.5 An electric bell

Electric bell
When the switch is pushed, current passes around the circuit. The coil becomes an electromagnet and attracts the iron bar... 'gong'. This movement breaks contact and the current stops. The coil releases the iron bar which springs back to remake the contact. The current flows and so the process starts again.

16.3 Getting things moving with magnets

The magnetic field around a wire carrying current will interact with another magnetic field, resulting in a force between them. As the wire is usually free to respond, the force will cause the wire to move. The direction of motion can be predicted by a simple rule called the left-hand rule.
  This idea has many applications and some are outlined below.

The current balance
A delicately balanced wire in a magnetic field will be forced when a current passes

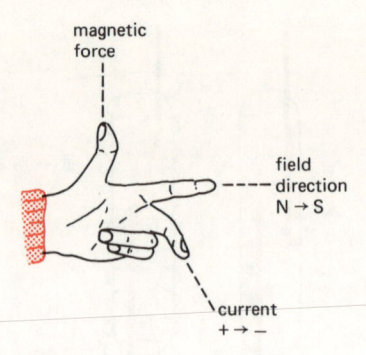

Figure 16.6 Fleming's left hand rule. A rule of thumb—and two fingers

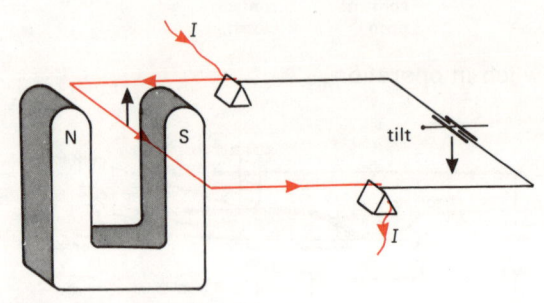

Figure 16.7 Tilting a current balance

through it. This will tilt the balance by an amount depending on the size of the current and the magnetic field. Current balances of this kind are used to measure the strengths of magnetic fields.

Electric motors
A coil of wire in a magnetic field will tend to rotate when a current passes through it. One side of the coil is forced upwards as the other is forced down. (Use the left-hand rule to check this for yourself.) By arranging the current in the coil to keep flowing in the same direction, this motion can be continued so that the coil spins. Electric motors are designed so that a moving commutator touches two fixed contacts, called brushes, to keep the coil rotating in the same direction.

16.4 Converting motion to electricity

A bicycle dynamo produces a potential difference which can light up a headlamp bulb. Where do these volts come from? What actually happens inside the dynamo case to produce electricity apparently from nowhere? The electric current in the dynamo circuit lights up a lamp. This represents an output of energy. The energy input is from the cyclist whose legs provide the force to keep the dynamo turning. All dynamos and generators are devices for converting kinetic energy to electrical energy. The principle is known as **electromagnetic induction**.

Inside a bicycle dynamo there is a small magnet which spins around near to a coil of wire. The coil is part of the lamp circuit, see Figure 16.9. When a magnetic

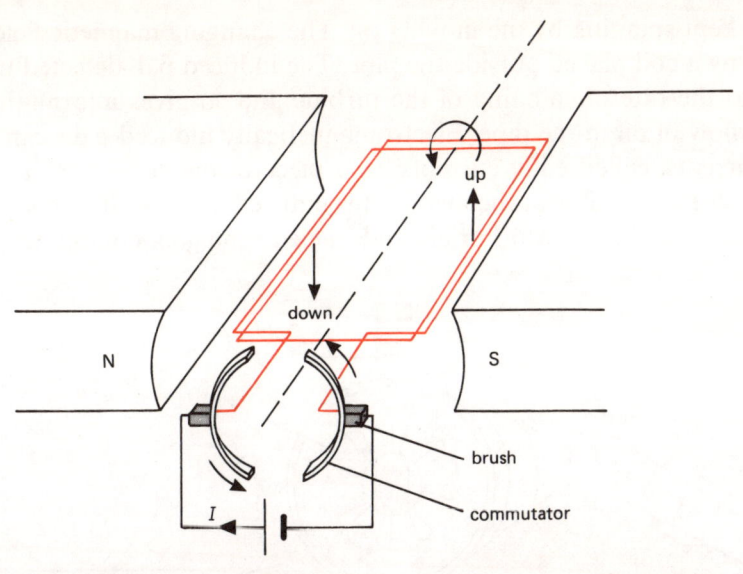

Figure 16.8 A simple electric motor

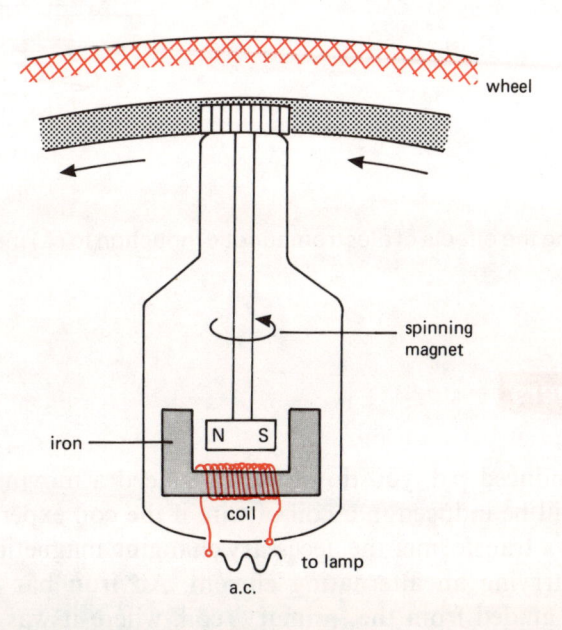

Figure 16.9 A bicycle dynamo—the inside story

field and a conducting wire move relative to each other, a p.d. is developed across the wire. In the bicycle dynamo this p.d. lights up a lamp. The generator or alternator in a power station uses the same principle. It rotates 50 times each second to produce a 50 hertz alternating current which is connected to our homes. You can find out more about the production of 'mains' electricity in Unit 17.

The flow of oil in a pipe can be measured using electromagnetic induction. This technique is used in the Sullom Voe Oil Terminal in Scotland to measure the oil flow from the Brent and Ninian fields. A turbine carrying a set of permanent magnets is kept spinning by the moving oil. The changing magnetic field pattern is detected by a coil placed outside the pipe. The induced p.d. detected in the coil is related to the rate of spinning of the turbine and so gives information about the rate of flow of oil in the pipe. Electromagnetically induced p.d.s can be made to drive currents, called eddy currents, in a piece of metal, such as aluminium. These eddy currents will heat the metal. This induced heating effect has been used in the design of industrial sand driers and in electromagnetic induction cookers.

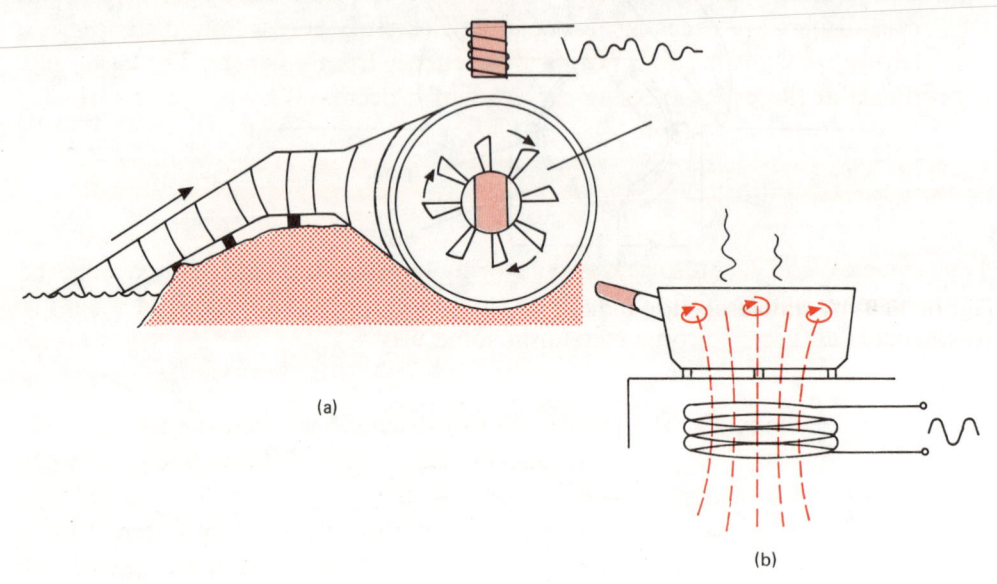

Figure 16.10   Using the effects of electromagnetic induction to (a) measure oil flow and (b) cook food

16.5 Transformers

To produce an induced p.d. you do not always need a moving wire or moving magnet. A p.d. will be induced in a coil of wire if the coil experiences a **changing** magnetic field. In a transformer the necessary changing magnetic field is produced by a solenoid carrying an alternating current. An iron bar ensures that this magnetic field is guided from the '**primary**' coil, where it was produced, to the '**secondary**' coil, where the result is an induced alternating p.d.

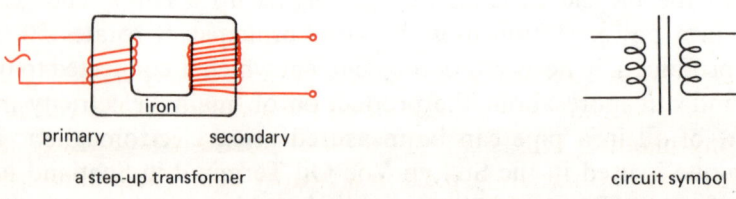

Figure 16.11

a step-up transformer

circuit symbol

The size of the alternating p.d. in the secondary coil depends on the **turns ratio** of the transformer. With more turns on the secondary coil then the primary coil, the induced p.d. will be greater. This is called a **step-up** transformer. If the turns ratio is such that there are fewer turns on the secondary coil, then the induced p.d. will be smaller. This is a **step-down** transformer.

A mains adaptor can be bought if, for example, a 120 volt electric drill is to be operated from a 240 volt mains supply. The required turns ratio of this step-down transformer would need to be 120 to 240 or 1 to 2. Unit 17 explains why transformers are necessary for sending electricity across long distances.

A step-up transformer does not produce energy from nowhere. The larger p.d. is produced at the expense of the current which decreases by the same ratio.

16.6 Related reading: Coils and magnets in home entertainment

Tape cassettes and records are ways of storing information which can be retrieved by the listener with a hi-fi system. The storage, retrieval and playback stages in this process all use electromagnetism in some way.

Cassettes
These contain 'magnetic' tape. This is a thin plastic base coated with an oxide of iron or chromium. The oxide contains tiny magnetic grains which can rearrange themselves in patterns to store information. When a tape is played it is allowed to run past a tiny gap in the iron core of a pick-up solenoid (see Figure 16.12). The magnetic field patterns from the tape cause a changing induced signal to be produced in the solenoid. These signals are sent to an amplifier.

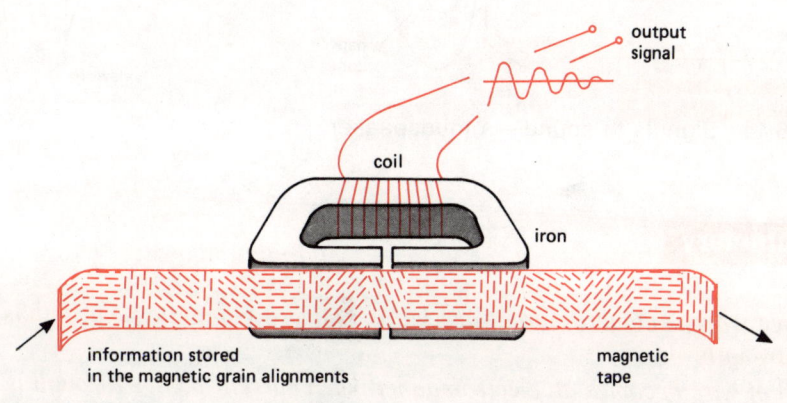

Figure 16.12 'Reading' magnetic tape

Records
The information on a record is stored in a pattern of tiny narrow grooves. The diamond needle vibrates as it tracks along the grooves. At the end of the stylus arm is a tiny magnet. Vibrations of the needle cause vibrations of the magnet which induce small alternating p.d.s in a nearby coil. These alternating signals carry the information to an amplifier.

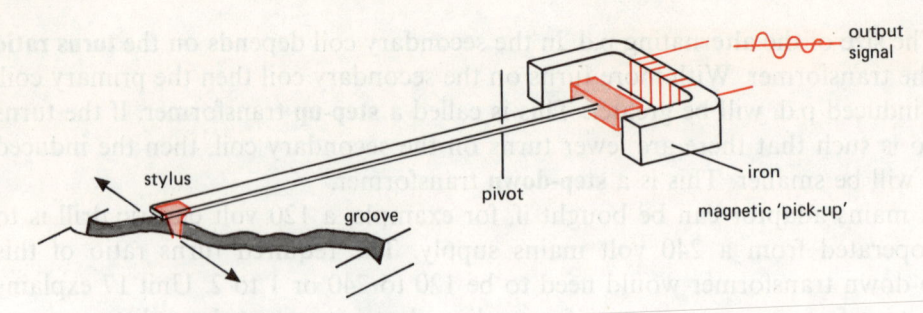

Figure 16.13 Signals from a record

Loudspeakers

The amplifier sends energetic electric signals to a very lightweight solenoid attached to the paper cone of the loudspeaker. The solenoid sits neatly in a narrow gap in the magnetic field of a permanent magnet. As currents pass through the coil, the magnetic force on it causes the coil and the paper cone to move in and out of the gap. The surrounding air in turn vibrates and so information is carried by sound to the listener.

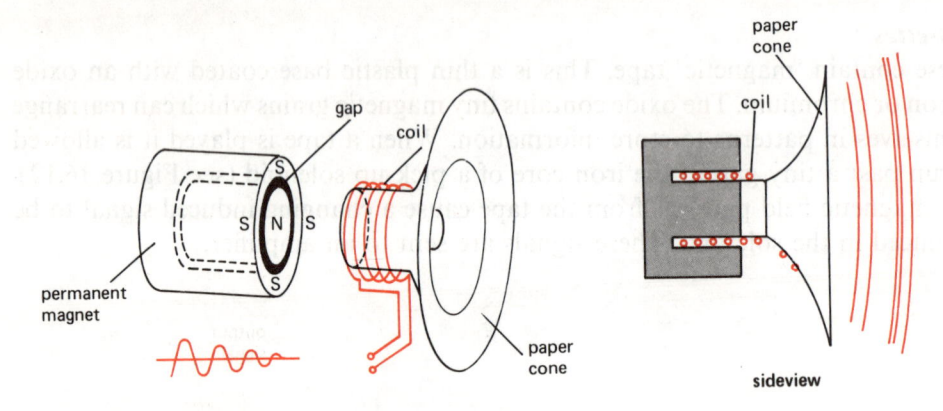

Figure 16.14 Signals to sound—a loudspeaker

16.7 Summary

- A place where magnetic forces are felt is called a magnetic field. It has a shape and strength.
- A coil of wire becomes an electromagnet when current passes through it. An iron core strengthens the field.
- Currents in wires will be forced by other magnetic fields. This leads to the motor effect.
- A potential difference can be induced in a wire if it moves relative to a magnetic field. This is called electromagnetic induction.
- In a transformer a changing magnetic field induces an alternating p.d. in a secondary coil.
- Transformers can be step-up or step-down depending on the turns ratio.

16.8 Progress questions

1. (a) Draw a diagram to show the shape of a magnetic field around a long coil of wire.
   (b) On your diagram indicate where you think the field strength is greatest.
2. Iron becomes a strong magnet but is easily demagnetised. Steel is harder to magnetise but keeps its magnetism.
   (a) Why is iron used rather than steel for the core of an electromagnet?
   (b) Why are transformers so heavy?
3. Draw a diagram of a magnetic relay. Explain how a very small current might switch **off** a much larger current.
4. Study the diagram of a coil in a magnetic field shown in Figure 16.15.

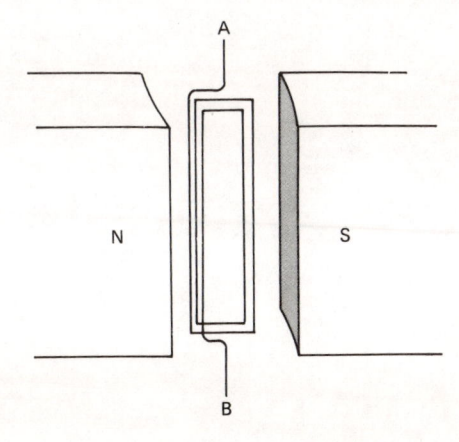

Figure 16.15

   (a) What will happen if a current is conducted from A to B?
   (b) How could this apparatus be converted to a moving coil ammeter?
5. A bicycle becomes harder to pedal when the dynamo is attached. Can you think of two reasons why an extra force is needed?
6. A transformer is needed to operate a 12 volt toy electric train set from the 240 volt mains supply.
   (a) What type of transformer will be needed?
   (b) What will be the required turns ratio?
   (c) What other features would a transformer designer need to think about?

17 SUPPLYING ELECTRICAL ENERGY

17.1 Cells and batteries

It was in 1800 that the Italian Professor, Alessandro Volta, built the very first battery. Volta piled up a number of 'cells' to make his battery. Each cell was a zinc and copper disc, separated by moist fabric. A potential difference was produced across the ends of the battery. Volta's was a **primary** cell battery. This meant that once the chemical reaction which provided the p.d. had finished, the cell was no longer useful. The chemical reactions in some cells can be reversed by an electric current supplied from an outside source. Such rechargeable cells are called **secondary** cells.

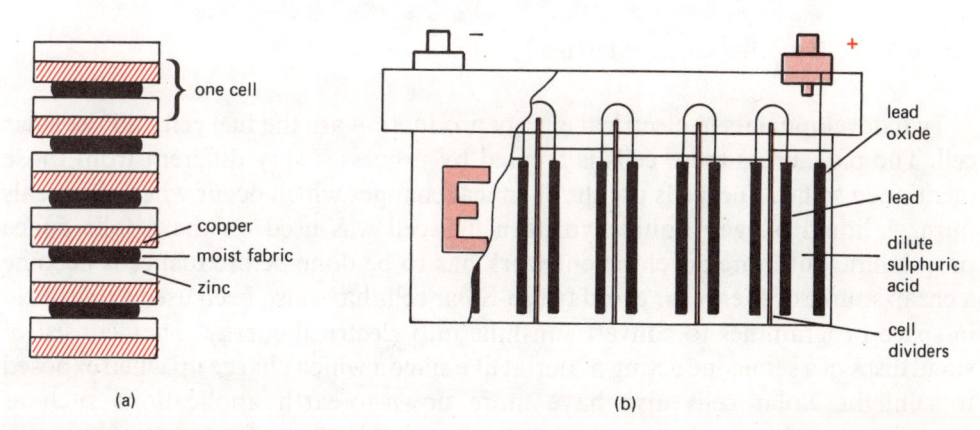

Figure 17.1 (a) Volta's early 'wet pile' battery. (b) A modern 'wet' car battery

In a lead–acid car battery, called an accumulator, lead (−) and lead oxide (+) plates are immersed in sulphuric acid. Six individual lead–acid cells connected in series form the complete 12 volt battery. Car batteries have to conduct large currents and need to be recharged constantly by the car dynamo. In a battery, electrical energy is produced from the energy of chemical reactions. Batteries 'run down' as their chemicals become exhausted. The battery in a parked car with its headlights left on will soon become discharged or 'drained'.

The batteries which are used in portable torches and radios are made from a number of separate dry primary cells. A carbon–zinc dry cell, sometimes sold in shops as a 'battery', contains a chemical paste sandwiched between a carbon (+)

173

and zinc (−) electrode. Most dry cells like these are primary cells. They can be used for one life cycle only. It is possible to buy rechargeable dry cells. These are more expensive but, with a charger, will last many times longer.

A standard 1.5 volt dry cell might typically store enough chemical energy, about 3600 J, to light a 0.5 watt torch bulb continuously for two hours. A 12 volt car battery labelled '100 amp.hours' will store about 4 000 000 J of chemical energy. This means, for example, that it can supply a current of 1 amp for a hundred hours or 2 amps for fifty hours, etc. Car batteries and some dry cells are recharageable. This means that their chemical reactions can be reversed by turning electrical energy from an external supply back into stored chemical energy.

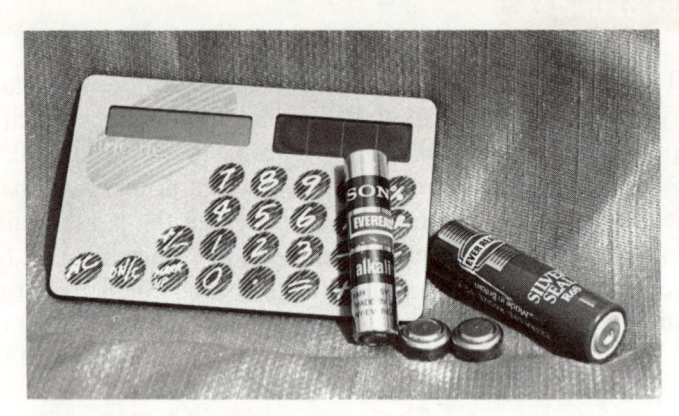

Figure 17.2 Batteries for everday use

Two developments in electrical energy production are the **fuel cell** and the **solar cell**. The p.d. across these cells is created by processes very different from those mentioned so far. Fuel cells use the chemical changes which occur when chemicals burn. A liquid oxygen/liquid hydrogen fuel cell was used on the Apollo space programme but more development work has to be done before fuel cells become a cheap source of energy for everday use. Solar cells have also been used extensively in space programmes to convert sunshine into electrical energy. They consist of small discs of a semiconducting material like silicon which charge up when exposed to sunlight. Solar cells also have more down-to-earth applications such as powering portable electronic calculators, charging batteries for hot water heating and for operating solar powered bicycles!

17.2 Alternating current and direct current electricity

The cells and batteries mentioned in Section 17.1 all deliver d.c., **direct current**. This means that their potential difference drives a current in one direction around a circuit. Direct currents produce both a heating effect and magnetic field. The mains electrical supply to our homes is a.c., **alternating current**. Electric currents can alternate at any frequency. A mains-operated low-voltage a.c. power supply used in a laboratory will carry an a.c. signal with a frequency of 50 hertz, the same frequency as the mains supply. A variable frequency signal generator, also used in laboratories, can produce a.c. voltage signals from 1 hertz up to perhaps 100 000 hertz (0.1 MHz).

An oscilloscope is a voltmeter which can display an a.c. or a d.c. signal.

Both a.c. and d.c. signals have heating and magnetic effects but it is the **changing** magnetic field around a wire carrying an alternating current which makes a.c. such a useful way of sending electrical energy around the country.

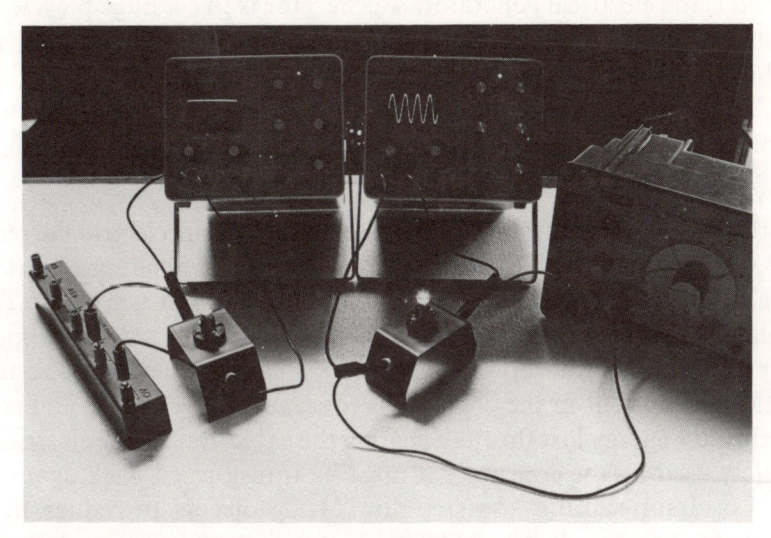

Figure 17.3 Power supplies: d.c. (left) and a.c. (right)

17.3 Supplying electricity to the country

(a) Generation
Batteries supply only a tiny fraction of the electrical energy demanded by an industrial nation. To meet Britain's power demands, which exceed thousands of

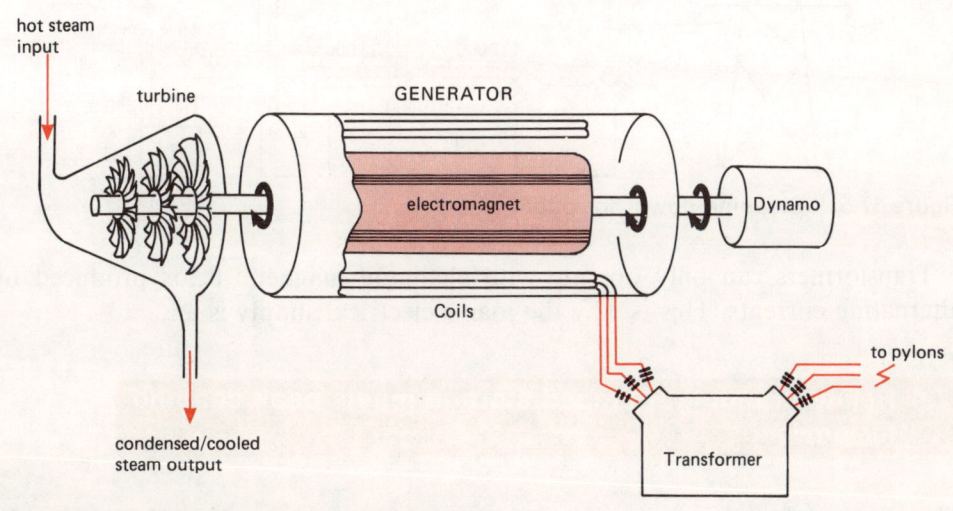

Figure 17.4 Generating electrical energy

175

millions of watts, there is a nationwide network of power stations all connected together. This is the **National Grid**. Each power station has its own type of energy source. These sources of energy, their advantages and disadvantages will be the subject of Unit 19.

All power stations in operation in Great Britain today use the same basic method, called **electromagnetic induction**, to produce electricity. At the heart of this method is the electrical generator. A generator is like a huge bicycle dynamo.

A turbine forces the electromagnet to rotate at exactly 50 times each second. (The turbine is forced by either steam or water, depending on the type of energy source.) The rotating magnetic field induces an alternating p.d. of about 25 000 volts, 50 Hz, in a coil of wire surrounding the electromagnet.

(b) Transmission

Cables attached to the output of the generator carry an electric current to the National Grid network and then on to the consumers. Sending electric current over long distances results in energy losses as the current warms up the many kilometres of cable. To decrease these energy losses, the p.d. is stepped up to about 400 000 volts at the power station by a transformer. As a result of the transformer, the current in the cables falls to a much lower value and so there is considerably less energy lost through heating the cable. Before the electrical energy can be safely used by the consumer it must be transformed back again to lower voltages. Local sub-stations use step-down transformers to reduce the p.d. to 33 000 volts for heavy industry, 11 000 volts for light industry and 240 volts for use in homes.

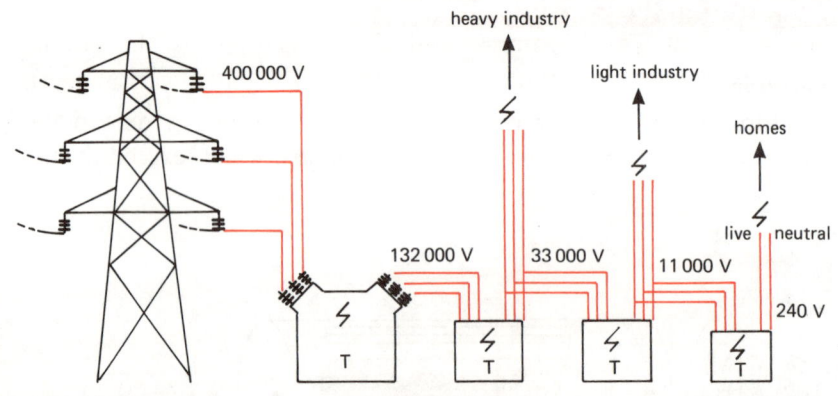

Figure 17.5 'Stepping down' for public use

Transformers can only operate with changing magnetic fields produced by alternating currents. This is why the mains electrical supply is a.c.

17.4 Related reading: Pumped storage meets peak demand for power

The demand for electrical energy is never constant. On 22nd January 1984 there was a sudden demand for energy just after 9 pm when a film, *The Thorn Birds*, ended. The National Grid was able to meet this demand within ten seconds thanks to the energy supplied by two **pumped storage** power stations at Ffestiniog and Dinorwig in Wales.

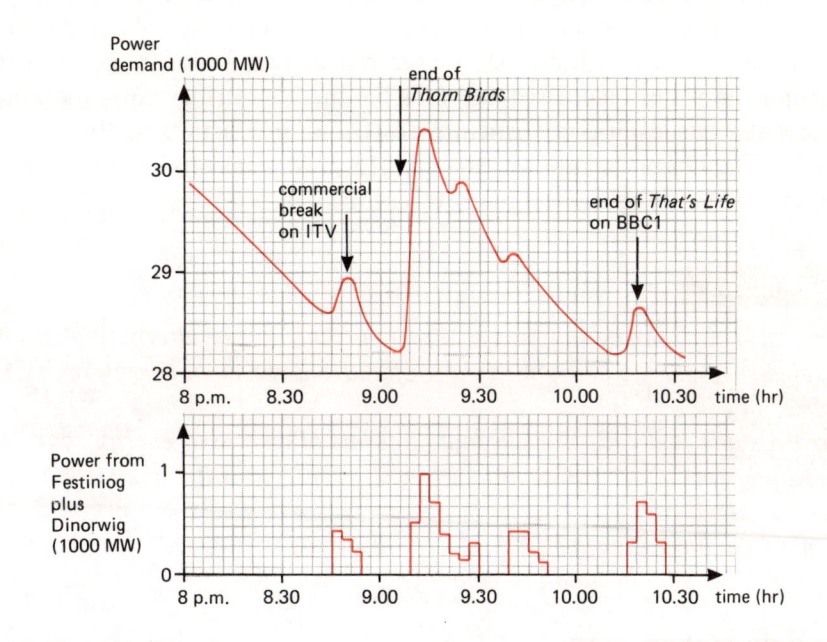

Figure 17.6 Demand and supply on 22 Jan. 1984

The power stations at Ffestiniog and Dinorwig convert the gravitational potential energy of water stored in mountain reservoirs into electrical energy. The water gains kinetic energy as it gushes down pipes built into the Welsh mountains.

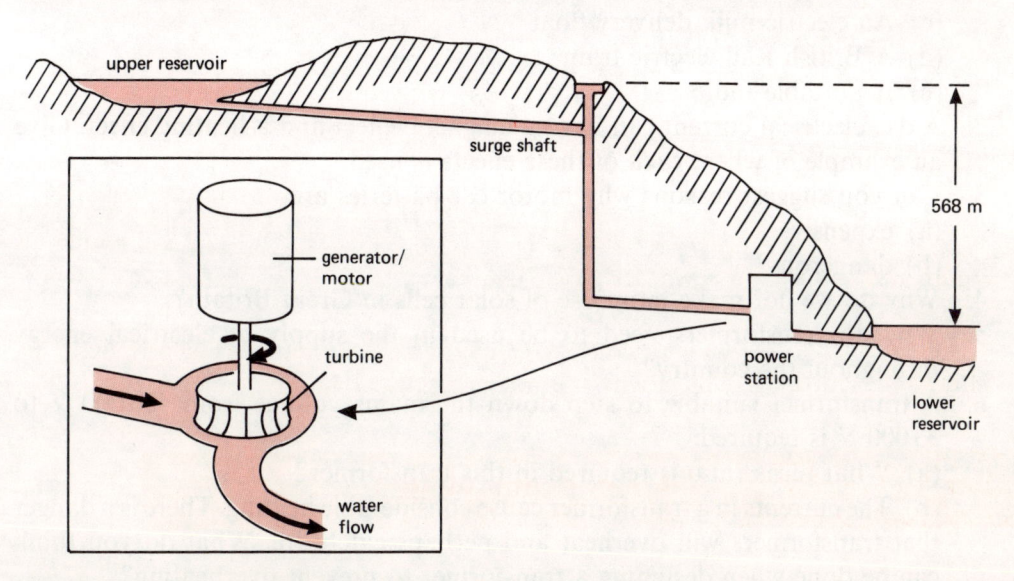

Figure 17.7 Power generation at Dinorwig, North Wales

177

This is then converted into electrical energy by generators. The graph shows that on the 22nd January 1984 the demand in Britain rose by 2600 MW. The two Welsh stations satisfied 1000 MW of this demand between them.

When the demand for power is low, usually at night, the generators at Ffestiniog and Dinorwig are operated in reverse. They are used as electrically operated pumps to pump water back up to the reservoirs ready for the early morning breakfast demand. The Ffestiniog reservoir provides 2 000 000 cubic metres of storage and the water level rises and falls 5.4 metres during daily operation. On demand, water rushes 300 m vertically down two inlet shafts to the four 90 kW generators. The Dinorwig station uses six 313 MW generators situated inside the hillside about 500 m below the main reservoir.

17.5 Summary

- *Electrical energy can be supplied as direct current, d.c., or alternating current, a.c.*
- *D.C. electrical energy is supplied most often from chemical energy in dry cells or batteries of cells.*
- *Solar cells and fuel cells are alternative forms of electrical energy sources.*
- *Generators, forced to rotate by turbines, supply us with a 50 Hz a.c. mains electrical supply.*
- *In order to reduce heating effects, electrical energy is 'stepped up' to high voltages before transmission around the country.*

17.6 Progress questions

1. The following situations all use electrical energy. Which uses a.c. and which uses d.c.?
   (a) An electric toaster
   (b) A compact camera
   (c) An electric milk delivery float
   (d) A British Rail electric train
   (e) A portable radio.
2. A d.c. electrical current can have a magnetic effect and a heating effect. Give an example of where each of these effects is used.
3. Can you suggest reasons why motor car batteries are
   (a) expensive
   (b) dangerous?
4. Why do we not make more use of solar cells in Great Britain?
5. Why do transformers need to be used in the supply of electrical energy throughout the country?
6. A transformer suitable to step down the mains voltage from 400 000 V to 33 000 V is required.
   (a) What turns ratio is required in this transformer?
   (b) The currents in a transformer cause considerable heating. There is a danger that transformers will overheat and perhaps catch fire. What do you think can be done when designing a transformer to prevent overheating?

18 AT HOME WITH ELECTRICITY

18.1 The mains electrical supply

Mains electricity is supplied to almost every home in the country. From your local transformer substation, a cable containing the live and neutral wires runs underground, often under your local roads. Each home is connected in parallel across this mains supply.

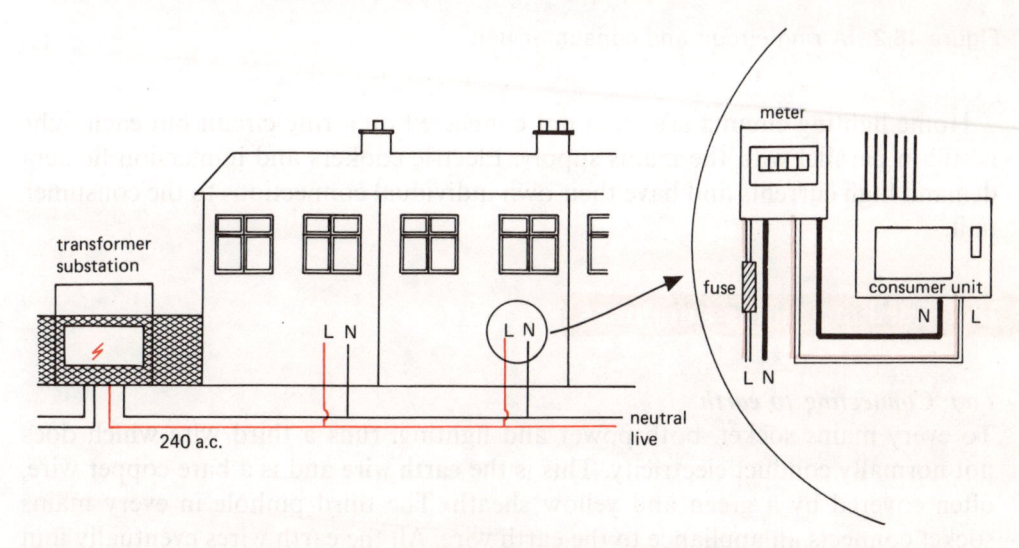

Figure 18.1 Electricity arriving at the consumer

The **live** (red) and **neutral** (black) mains wires lead through an Electricity Board fuse, through a meter and to a **consumer unit** which is the property of the home owner. Some homes have two meters, one for off-peak electricity. The consumer unit contains a mains switch, an earthing block and household mains fuses or circuit breakers, and is often found by the main door or in a cupboard.

18.2 The ring main

Connections to the 240 V mains supply voltage are made through a number of power sockets which are joined together on a **ring circuit**. Each 240 V socket is connected in parallel across the live and neutral mains supply to become part of the ring circuit. Each ring starts and ends in the consumer unit where a separate fuse, usually 30 amp, is placed in the live path for each ring.

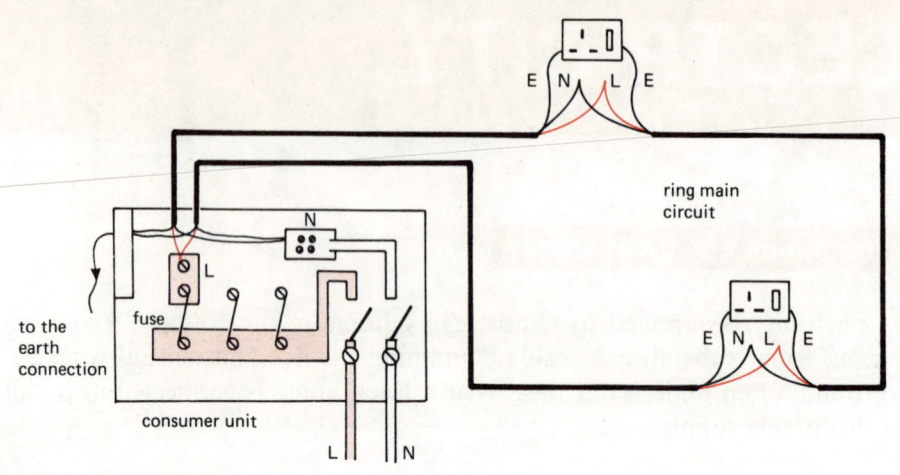

Figure 18.2 A ring circuit and consumer unit

Home lighting circuits are often not connected on a ring circuit but each light is still in parallel with the mains supply. Electric cookers and immersion heaters demand high currents and have their own individual connections to the consumer unit.

18.3 Earthing, plugs and fuses

(a) Connecting to earth

To every mains socket, both power and lighting, runs a third wire which does not normally conduct electricity. This is the **earth wire** and is a bare copper wire, often covered by a green and yellow sheath. The third pinhole in every mains socket connects an appliance to the earth wire. All the earth wires eventually join together in the consumer unit and are connected to a large copper plate buried in the ground. This direct route to the ground is an essential safety requirement.

(b) Plugs and fuses

A plug, usually three pin, connects an electrical appliance to the 240 V main supply. The three pins connect to the live, neutral and earth wires in the socket. Between the appliance and plug run three colour-coded wires. The brown wire (**live**) connects the appliance to a cartridge fuse in the plug. The blue wire (**neutral**) connects the other end of the appliance wire to the plug. The third wire, green and yellow (**earth**) connects the metal body parts of the appliance to the earth connection.

In normal operation there is a complete circuit carrying current from the live pin, through the appliance and back through the neutral pin. In the event of a **short circuit** when a 240 V live wire loosens and touches the body of the appliance,

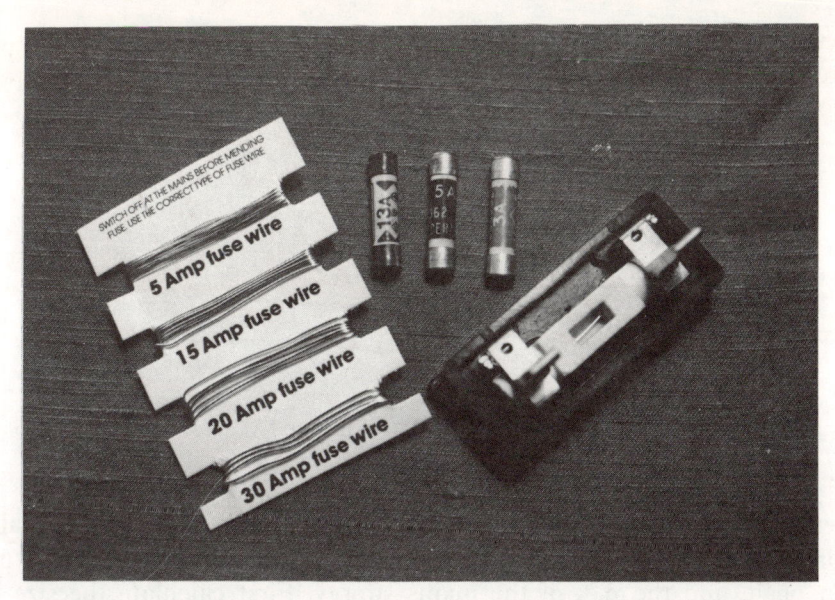

Figure 18.3 Domestic fuses

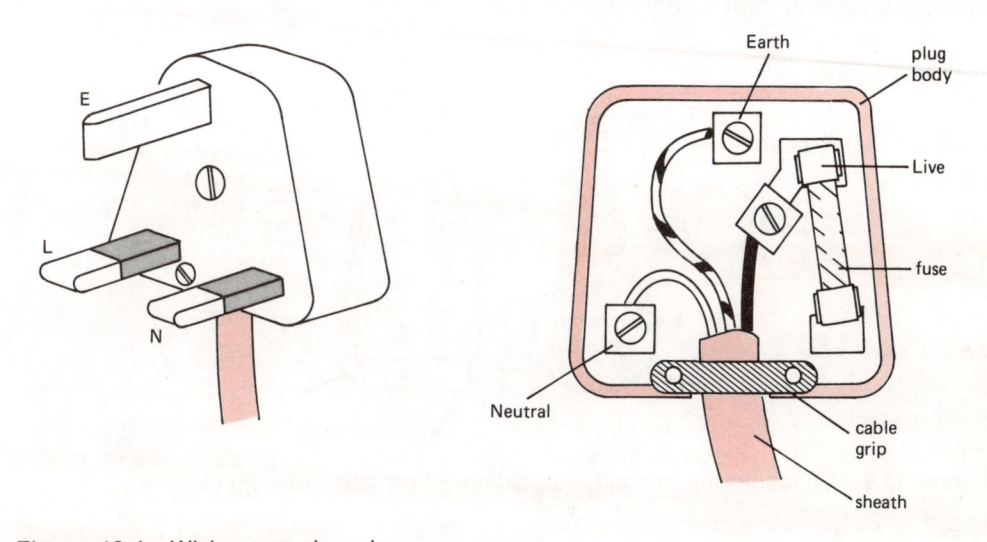

Figure 18.4 Wiring a mains plug

a surge of current will immediately rush down the earth connection to the ground. This will blow the fuse in the plug and automatically **isolate** the appliance from the 240 V supply. The appliance will then be safe to unplug and repair.

Without the earth connection, the unsuspecting user will provide the current with an easy route down to the ground and so suffer shocking consequences. Appliances with plastic, insulating bodies often have no green and yellow earth wire.

(c) Choosing a fuse
The size, or rating, of the fuse needed depends on the power of the appliance. The fuse must be such as to allow a normal working current to pass but to

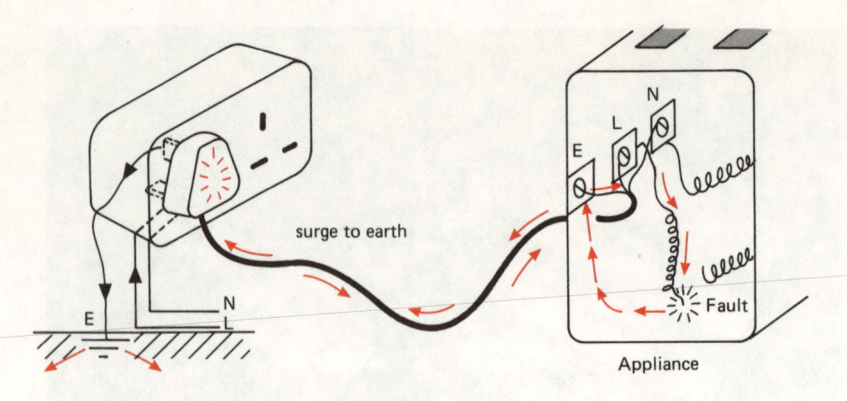

Figure 18.5 A short circuit to earth will 'blow' a fuse

overheat and melt ('blow') when a larger surge of current passes. To calculate the correct fuse rating you need to know the power of the appliance, usually written on it, and the p.d. of the mains supply. First calculate the size of the working current and then choose a fuse rated at a greater current. Fuses available in most electrical shops are 3 A, 5 A and 13 A.

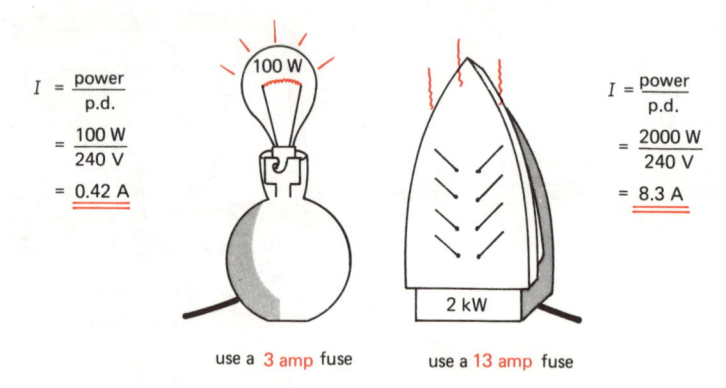

$$I = \frac{\text{power}}{\text{p.d.}}$$
$$= \frac{100 \text{ W}}{240 \text{ V}}$$
$$= 0.42 \text{ A}$$

use a **3 amp** fuse

$$I = \frac{\text{power}}{\text{p.d.}}$$
$$= \frac{2000 \text{ W}}{240 \text{ V}}$$
$$= 8.3 \text{ A}$$

use a **13 amp** fuse

Figure 18.6 Choosing the correct fuse rating—first calculate the current

(d) Circuit breakers

Blown fuses need replacing. A more modern isolating device is the **circuit breaker**. A circuit breaker in the consumer unit will break a contact electromagnetically. When the current exceeds a set limit, a magnetic switch will 'trip' and cut off the supply. Once the fault has been remedied, the trip button is simply pressed to reset itself. The ELCB (earth leakage circuit breaker) is a more sensitive and even faster electromagnetic switch. It will isolate an appliance if the current in the earth wire exceeds a small value, typically 30 mA. Plugs and sockets containing circuit breaker switches are readily available in electrical stores.

Fuses and circuit breakers should not be a substitute for common sense. **Electricity can kill**. Be careful at all times. Always switch off at the socket, never with wet hands, before unplugging an appliance.

18.4 Paying for energy

Supplying the country with energy is a costly business. Paying wages to coal miners, paying for the transport of fuel, paying for the maintenance of generating machinery, paying for waste disposal are just some of the costs. This cost is passed on to the consumer through the electricity bill. The bill shows the consumer how many 'units' of electrical energy have been supplied and gives the cost of a single unit.

The 'unit' used to measure electrical energy is the **kilowatt.hour, kWh**. If a 1 kW appliance is switched on for an hour, then the energy transformed will be one kWh. 1 kWh is equal to 3 600 000 J.

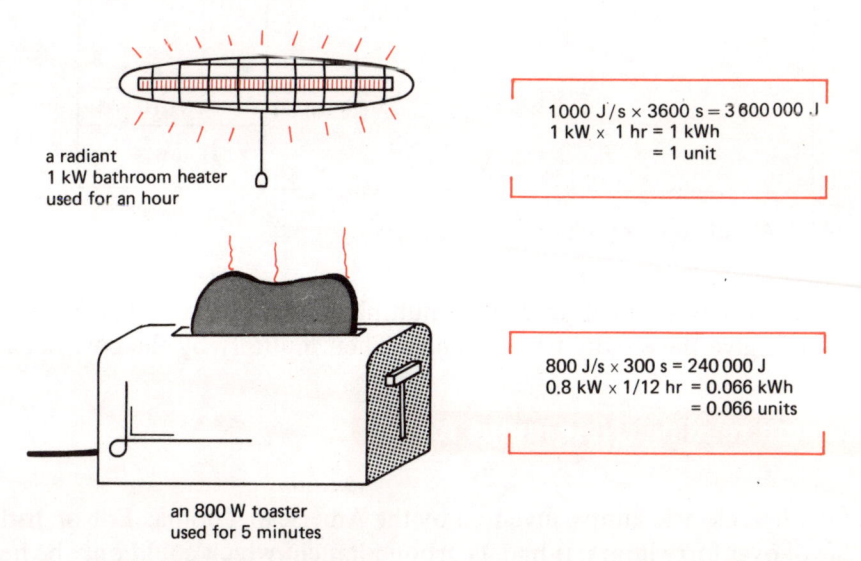

a radiant
1 kW bathroom heater
used for an hour

1000 J/s × 3600 s = 3 600 000 J
1 kW × 1 hr = 1 kWh
= 1 unit

an 800 W toaster
used for 5 minutes

800 J/s × 300 s = 240 000 J
0.8 kW × 1/12 hr = 0.066 kWh
= 0.066 units

Figure 18.7   Using electrical energy

At the time of writing this book (1989) the approximate cost per unit was 6p (3 600 000 J cost 6p). Compare this with the energy contained in a 1.5 V dry cell (see Unit 17). A 1.5 V dry cell, costing perhaps 80p, provides about 3600 J.

18.5 The electricity bill

Some consumers pay for electricity as they use it. Coin-operated meters are common in launderettes, on camping-sites and in some homes. For those people who receive a bill each quarter of a year, the charges build up to a total amount. The total amount to be paid is the sum of the cost of the energy and a standing charge. The cost of the energy is found by subtracting the previous reading from the present reading to find the number of units used and then multiplying this by the cost per unit. An example of such a bill is given in Figure 18.8.

It is possible to predict your bill in advance by looking at the cost of running each appliance in turn. To estimate the cost of running an appliance you need

LONDON ELECTRICITY	ACCOUNTS OFFICE BARTLET CLOSE, LONDON.	6 JAN. 1988
MS S. NEWTON 17, THAME ROAD, SE5		

METER READING		UNITS USED	UNIT PRICE (pence)	VAT code	AMOUNT £
PRESENT	PREVIOUS				
66 036	65 503	533	5.75	0	30.64
STANDING CHARGE				0	10.00
				AMOUNT TO PAY	£ 40.64

Figure 18.8   A typical electricity bill

first to find its power in kW and then multiply this by the number of hours of use. This will give the energy used in units. Then multiply by the cost per unit.

18.6 Related reading: New lamps for old

One of the first electric lamps, invented by the American Thomas Edison in 1879, had a life of over forty hours. It had a carbon filament which could only be heated to a yellow glow temperature. The lamps used today have tungsten filaments giving a hotter, whiter light but the general design has remained unchanged since Edison's time. Modern lamps consist of a tungsten filament, about 80 cm long and drawn to a thickness of only 1/100 mm, tightly coiled and mounted in an evacuated glass bulb sealed to a metal base. The working resistance of the filament is about 500 ohms and it reaches a temperature of about 2600°C. A major problem with incandescent (hot filament) lamps is that much of the energy supplied is wasted as the hot bulb radiates and conducts about 90 per cent of the electrical energy away as infra-red radiation. Only about 10 per cent of the energy is transformed into visible light. The lamp is 10 per cent efficient.

A new design of lamp has recently become available based on the principle of a fluorescent tube. It has an increased efficiency of about 40 per cent and lasts up to six times longer than an incandescent lamp. The main feature of the lamp is a glass tube containing low-pressure mercury gas. The tube is coated with a layer of fluorescent material. The two electrodes at the end of the tube are electrically heated, releasing electrons. The electrons are accelerated towards the positive electrode and collide with the mercury atoms in the tube. The kinetic energy of collision is radiated in the form of ultra-violet, UV, radiation. The UV

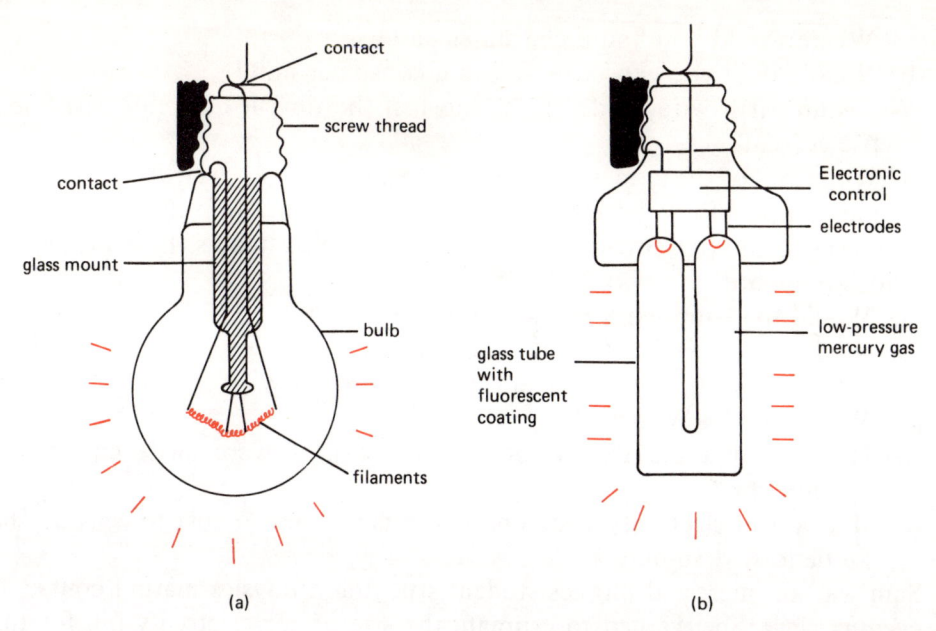

Figure 18.9 Electric lamps using (a) in incandescent filament and (b) a fluorescent tube

radiation strikes the fluorescent material which glows with visible white light. A small electronic circuit controls the electrode voltage necessary for the operation of the lamp. Because the lamp does not use high temperatures to create light, little energy is given off as infra-red radiation.

18.7 Summary

- *Mains electricity, 240 V, 50 Hz, is delivered along live (red) and neutral (black) colour-coded cables.*
- *Domestic power connections are made to a ring circuit, in parallel, across the 240 V supply.*
- *The earth conductor leads the current down to the ground in the event of a short circuit.*
- *The correct fuse rating depends on the power of the appliance and must be greater than the working current.*
- *The colour code for wiring a domestic plug is: brown (live), blue (neutral) and green/yellow (earth).*
- *Electrical energy is measured in units or kWh. 1 kWh = 3 600 000 J.*
- *The cost of operating a mains appliance can be calculated by the formula:*

   cost = power of appliance in kW × time used in hours × cost of one unit

18.8 Progress questions

1. Why do you think that electricians are given a colour blindness test before they are employed?

2. (a) Where would you find a consumer unit?
   (b) What would you expect to find in a consumer unit?
3. Why is an earth wire needed if for most of the time it does not carry any electric current?
4. What is meant by the term 'short circuit'? Explain your answer with a diagram.
5. You need a plug for your new bedside table lamp. The lamp contains a 60 W bulb. The local High Street store sells plugs labelled 'mains, 13 A protected, British Standard'.
   (a) Would the lamp work using one of these plugs?
   (b) What could be done to make the lamp safer?
6. This question is about an electric kettle labelled 2 kW.
   (a) What does 2 kW mean?
   (b) How many units would the kettle use if it were switched on for five minutes?
   (c) If a unit of electricity costs 6p, how much would it cost to operate the kettle for five minutes?
7. Sam was an interested physics student studying a physics mature course at evening class. She wanted to estimate the size of her electricity bill for the week. The table below shows information which Sam noted down about the appliances she uses. Can you complete the table and estimate her weekly bill? (One unit costs 6p and 1000 W = 1 kW.

Appliance	Power	Hours used each week	Units used
Iron	2000 W	$\frac{1}{2}$	
Fan heater	1500 W	12	
Light	100 W	22	
Kettle	2000 W	1	
Hi-fi	100 W	8	
Computer	150 W	3	

THE ENERGY BUSINESS

19.1 Demand and supply

It might appear that only crazy people would choose to work in the business of energy supply. The inefficiency of energy conversions means that about 60 per cent of all energy supplied is wasted in heating the atmosphere. Add to this problem the fact that on a planet with limited resources most supplies of energy are running out. Perhaps the greatest problem is the fact that the world demand for energy appears to be increasing by about ten times every twenty years. These problems represent a real challenge to the energy supply industry. They have speeded up research into ways of converting energy more efficiently and research into alternative sources of energy.

In Britain, the main demands for energy come from transport, industry and homes. These demands for energy have been met in the past mainly through coal, oil and gas.

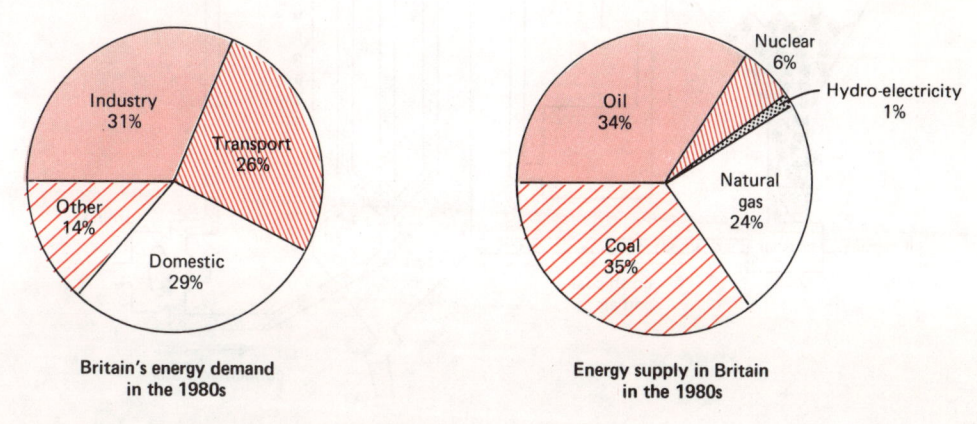

Figure 19.1 Energy demand and supply in Great Britain

Some coal is burnt directly in homes but most is used to provide electricity in coal-fired power stations. Oil is mainly used as a fuel for transport although some oil-fired power stations are in operation. Gas in the form of natural gas is used directly by homes and industry for heating purposes. Today, 1989, about 17 per cent of Britain's electricity is produced by nuclear power stations.

19.2 Fuels for electricity

The central feature of every power station is a generator which produces electrical energy from the motion of a turbine. Unit 17 gives details about generating electricity. The differences between power stations lie in the fuel which they use to provide the electrical energy and the associated problems which each type of fuel creates.

(a) Coal

Coal is a traditional fuel found in seams among the layers of rock in the crust of the Earth. Mining coal has been a hazardous process. Mining accidents and the development of silicosis from breathing coal dust are risks associated with producing coal. Improvements in mining technology have reduced the risk of being killed in a working life from about twenty deaths per hundred miners in 1930 to about one death per hundred in 1980. (Compare this risk figure to about 1 in 500 workers in the nuclear power industry and 1 in 10 workers in the deep sea fishing industry.)

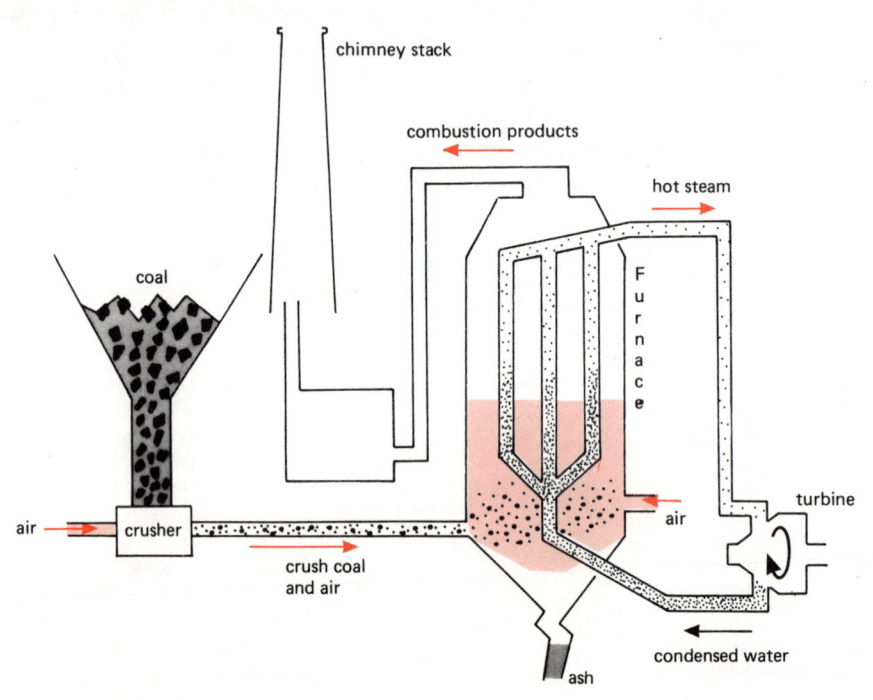

Figure 19.2 The main features of a coal-fired power station

In a coal-fired power station, a mixture of crushed coal and air is introduced into a burning furnace. Coal gives off a mixture of combustible gases including methane and carbon monoxide, called volatile matter, which burn as they rise in the furnace. The solid residue, mainly carbon, also burns to produce carbon dioxide. The energy is transported by a closed circuit of water which passes in tubes up through the furnace and past the turbine to a condenser. The water is pre-heated before returning to the furnace.

The ash from the furnace is used in road and building construction. The waste gases contain a mixture of mostly unburnt nitrogen from the air, carbon dioxide, steam, sulphur dioxide, nitrogen oxides and fine ash particles. Some of the methods of removing the more damaging oxides and ash are shown in Figure 19.3.

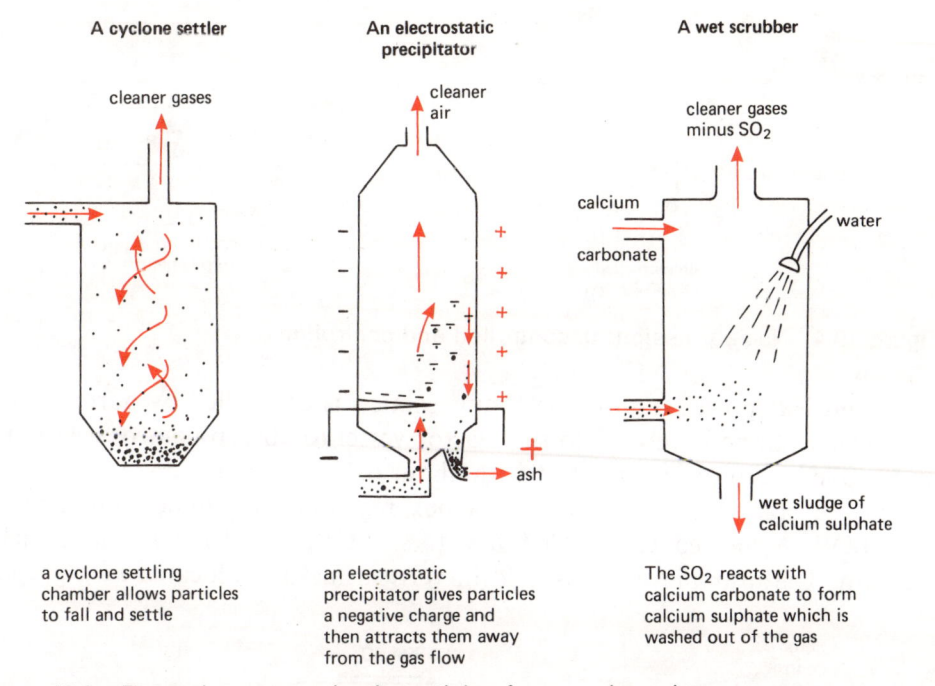

Figure 19.3 Removing gas and ash particles from coal smoke

A cyclone settler: a cyclone settling chamber allows particles to fall and settle

An electrostatic precipitator: an electrostatic precipitator gives particles a negative charge and then attracts them away from the gas flow

A wet scrubber: The SO_2 reacts with calcium carbonate to form calcium sulphate which is washed out of the gas

An issue concerning the coal industry is the production of **acid rain**. Waste gases from coal-fired power stations and car exhausts are oxidised by sunlight and react with water in the atmosphere to produce sulphuric acid. Acidic rain has a corrosive effect on building materials and damages plant and marine life. Acid rain is a strong argument to encourage ways of reducing toxic gases from combustion wastes.

(b) Uranium

Considering that the first controlled nuclear chain reaction occurred in 1942 in a squash court in Chicago, the nuclear power industry is very much a newcomer to the energy business. The raw fuel for a nuclear **fission** reaction, the 'fissile material', is an isotope of uranium called uranium 235 (U 235).

When a neutron strikes an atom of U 235 the uranium nucleus will break into two fission products, atoms with considerable kinetic energy, and release more neutrons to carry the process on in a fission **chain reaction**. The use of an uncontrolled chain reaction of this sort led to the development of atomic weapons. The kinetic energy of the fission products arises from the conversion of some of the uranium's mass into energy, a possibility reflected by Einstein's famous equation $E = mc^2$.

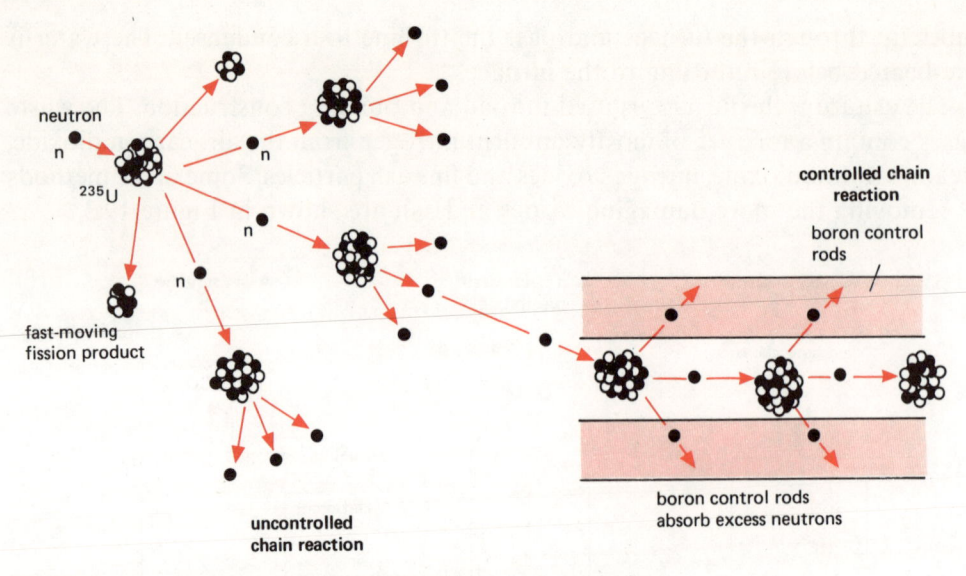

Figure 19.4 Nuclear fission: uncontrolled and controlled

In a nuclear power station, the chain reaction is controlled by boron control rods which can be lowered into the reactor vessel to absorb neutrons. Uranium oxide called yellowcake, enriched with about 0.7 per cent U 235, is used as the fuel in the older, about 500 MW, **Magnox** reactors. The higher power, about 1320 MW, Advanced Gas-cooled Reactors, **AGR**, use 2.3 per cent enriched uranium. The uranium oxide is held in vertical fuel rods located in a graphite

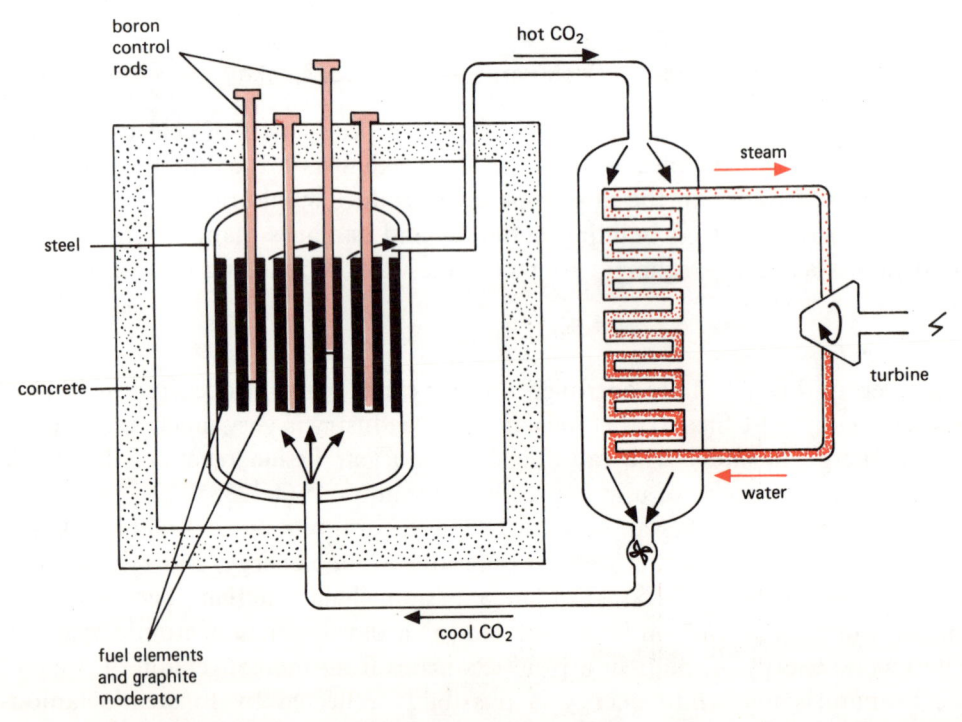

Figure 19.5 The main features of a magnox reactor

moderator to slow down the neutrons. The coolant, carbon dioxide gas for both magnox and AGR, circulates up through the reactor vessel. The hot CO_2 then exchanges its internal energy with cooling water flowing in a separate circuit. Steam from the heated water drives the turbines.

Nuclear power stations produce waste that requires special treatment depending on the type of waste. **Low-level** waste, contaminated clothing and glassware for example, is placed in steel and concrete drums and buried in underground clay pits. Liquid and gaseous low-level waste is diluted by allowing it to mix with the sea and atmosphere. The average exposure to the public from such low-level waste is much smaller than the exposure from other sources of background radiation (see Unit 14).

High-level waste, spent uranium and reactor fuel rods for example, are stored on site in cooling ponds until they are safe enough to transport to a reprocessing plant. At the Sellafield reprocessing plant, unreacted U 235 together with plutonium, a fission product, is extracted from the fuel rods. This recycled fuel will be used again.

The remaining high and **intermediate** level wastes present a disposal problem. As they remain radioactive for many hundreds of years, safe, reliable storage methods must be found. One idea has been to contain high-level waste in small glass pellets and bury them deep in the ground, about 500 m down in stable rock formations.

19.3 Looking ahead

A world with an increasing population and growing reliance on technical products will demand more and more energy. Food supplies, living space and economic necessity will contribute to limiting population growth in the long term, but what patterns can be expected for the next century?

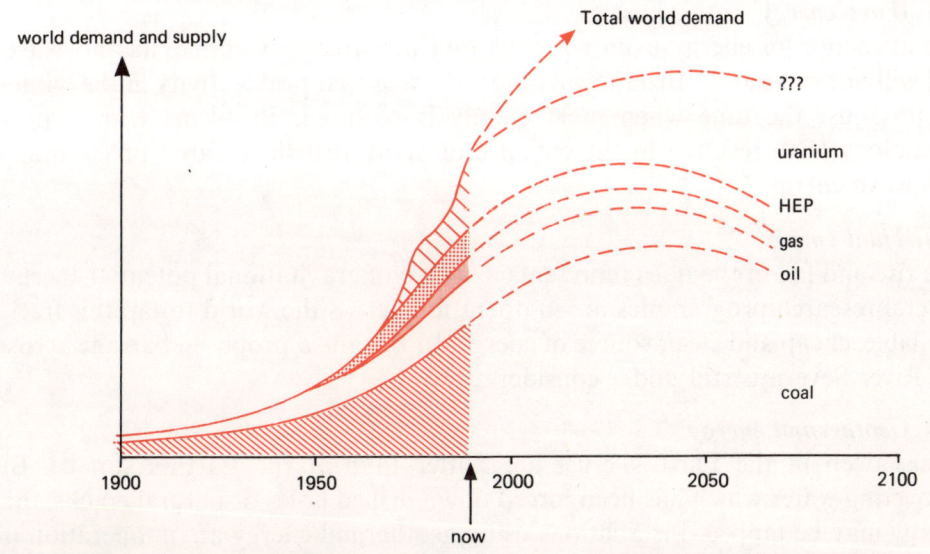

Figure 19.6   The world demand for energy: past, present and perhaps future

Predictions about exactly how long coal, oil and gas will last vary. Oil will increasingly be used for transport and producing plastics. Coal may be more wisely used to produce oil substitutes, particularly as the oil economy is subject to international tensions. There is a growing uncertainty about the safety and desirability of nuclear power. What are the alternatives?

19.4 Alternative sources of energy

(a) Hydroelectric power, HEP
Unit 17 gives an example of the use of stored water as an energy source in North Wales. Water, collected in reservoirs on high ground, represents a store of gravitational potential energy. When released and allowed to flow through turbines at a lower level, the potential energy is converted to electrical energy. Although a relatively clean and lasting method of producing energy, HEP is possible only when the geography of the land allows for rain, reservoirs and hills. Even in Britain, HEP accounts for only 1 per cent of our energy supply.

(b) Wind energy
Windmills have been a traditional small-scale source of energy in flat countries like the Netherlands. The attraction of using the kinetic energy of the wind is that it is free, has no waste problems and is not likely to run out. The problem at present is that to produce enough energy for wind-operated machines to be competitive, they will have to be designed for much larger power outputs than at present. Britain's first 'wind park' of 25 wind machines, each 30 m high, will occupy an offshore site 5 km off the Norfolk coast. The site, occupying about 4 km^2, will have a peak generating power of 8 MW. A wind park capable of generating the same power as a nuclear power station would use 300 machines over an area of 500 km^2.

(c) Wave energy
The attraction of energy from waves is that it is freely available, has no waste and will not run out. In Britain waves reach a seasonal peak activity in the winter months, just the time when most energy is required. Problems with marine technology have resulted in the collapse of many British research programmes into wave energy.

(d) Tidal energy
The rise and fall of the tides represents a source of gravitational potential energy. Several research programmes are in operation across the world to tap this freely available, cheap and clean source of energy. In Britain, a proposed barrage across the River Severn is still under consideration.

(e) Geothermal energy
Rocks deep in the Earth's crust are hotter than at the Earth's surface. By recovering water which has been forced down drilled holes or natural cracks, this energy may be tapped. Installations using geothermal energy are in operation in the United States and New Zealand where the hot rocks are relatively close to

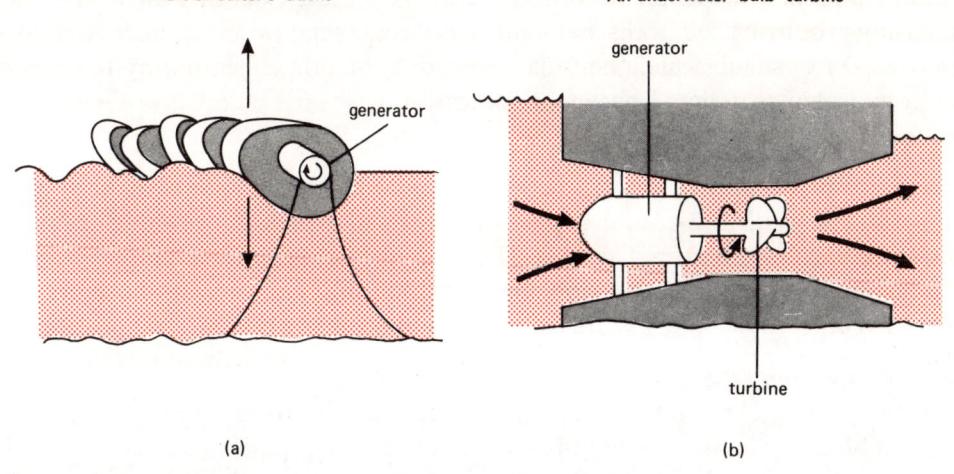

Figure 19.7 Extracting energy from (a) waves and (b) tides

the surface. In Britain, where volcanic activity is rare, much greater depths must be considered. Geothermal experiments are being carried out in Cornwall where the temperature gradient is about 40°C per km.

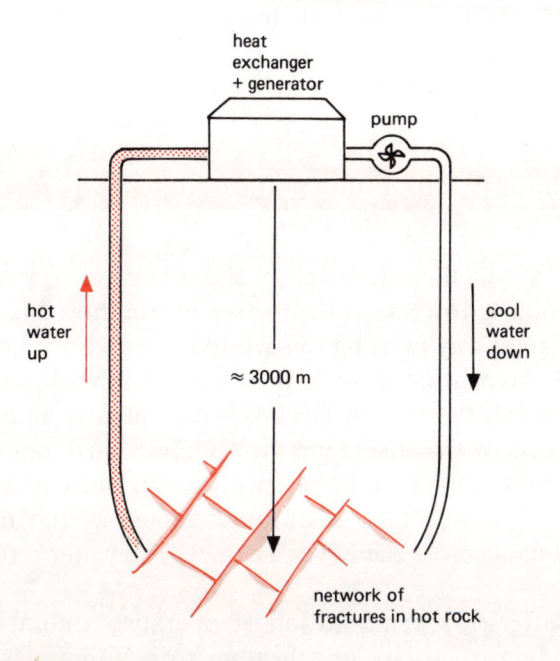

Figure 19.8 Tapping geothermal energy

(f) Solar energy
Sunshine is a freely available and virtually everlasting source of energy. The intensity of sunshine on the Earth's atmosphere is on average about 1500 W/m². Present technology can manage such a low efficiency of conversion of solar energy that a 1000 MW solar power station would require a collecting area the size of

central London. This problem, together with the variable weather in Britain and the cost of producing solar cells, has made large-scale solar power an uneconomical venture. On a small scale, the solar powering of home heating systems and electronic calculators has been more successful.

(g) Fusion

Energy from the Sun comes from the fusion of hydrogen atoms at very high temperatures. With a plentiful supply of hydrogen atoms in seawater, a fusion station on Earth is an attractive idea. JET, a joint European research programme into fusion, continues but the problems of containing the hot gases have not yet been solved. It will be many years before fusion becomes a commercial possibility.

(h) Energy from refuse

In Britain, about 24 million tonnes of domestic waste is produced each year. Most of this is buried in controlled landfill sites. A variety of initiatives uses energy from this domestic refuse. Methane, 'biogas', from the London Brick landfill sites is collected and burnt as a local energy source to fire the brick kilns, and in Warwickshire gas from decomposing waste generates 540 kW, some of which is sold to the National Grid. In Manchester, a university department is producing oil from local refuse and in Edmonton, London, refuse is burnt to produce electricity, some of which is sold to the National Grid. The Byker recycling plant in Tyne and Wear produces about 10 tonnes per hour of waste derived fuel (WDF) pellets from local refuse.

19.5 Related reading: Combined Heating and Power, CHP

All power stations are inefficient. Much of the wasted energy appears as steam or warm water. Cooling towers, so distinctive on the horizon, are a symbol of this inefficiency. A good way of using this wasted energy is to direct it to the local community to provide heating in what is called a combined heating and power scheme, CHP. Although the earliest CHP scheme operated in a sugar factory in Scotland in 1898, one of the first domestic CHP schemes ran in London from 1948 using the exhaust steam from Battersea power station. Water, heated by waste steam to 93°C, was circulated through radiators and towel rails in the Churchill Gardens flats across the River Thames. The water returned at 54°C to be reheated.

Although the Battersea scheme no longer operates, a number of local CHP schemes are providing electricity and heating to communities throughout the world. As CHP requires a local heating output, it is suited to power stations which use local town refuse for their fuel. In Neustadt, West Germany, eight tonnes of refuse are burned each hour to provide local users with 24 MW of CHP, and in Sweden 11 tonnes of refuse is burned each hour to provide the city of Stockholm with 27 MW of CHP. In Sheffield, Yorkshire, a 25 MW, soon increasing to 120 MW, CHP scheme provides district heating for 2450 homes, a nursery school, youth club, clothing factory, police station, health clinic and 26

Figure 19.9 The CHP scheme in Battersea, 1948–70

shops. All this energy comes from burning 12 tonnes of Sheffield city refuse each hour at its Bernard Road incinerator.

When planning for the best long-term use of energy, it might make economic sense to consider localised CHP schemes. Smaller local power stations could sell electricity to the National Grid and provide local heating. Such stations, being situated near to their consumers, would need improved design to minimise toxic waste products, especially from their chimney stacks. With the development of electronic devices to control demand and supply efficiently, CHP is likely to become a growth area.

19.6 Summary

- *Most of Britain's energy comes from coal, gas, oil and uranium.*
- *Using these fuels involves a degree of risk to workers and creates pollution problems for the environment.*
- *All four fuels listed above are in limited supply on Earth.*
- *The world demand for energy is increasing annually.*
- *There is a variety of alternative ways of providing electrical energy but none at present is as commercially viable as coal or uranium.*

19.7 Progress questions

1. (a) How many ways of producing electricity from fuels can you think of?
   (b) Give one advantage and one disadvantage of each.

2. (a) Which sources of energy are **unlikely** to run out?
   (b) Choose one of these and explain how electricity can be obtained from it.
3. How is your home heated? Can you say which type of energy provides your home heating?
4. Draw diagrams to explain what is meant by:
   (a) a chain reaction
   (b) control rods
   (c) fission products.
5. How do you think Britain will be producing its electricity in the year 2100?
6. One of the problems in recycling dustbin rubbish is that the rubbish needs to be sorted into glass, metal, plastics, paper, etc. Choose two of these and design a way of sorting them out from the rest of the rubbish.

INTRODUCING ELECTRONICS

20.1 The growth of electronics

Electronics has been the growth industry of the twentieth century. Advances in the science of materials, in production techniques and computer aided design have contributed to progressively smaller, faster and more sophisticated systems. The first computer used glass tubes called thermionic valves to control electric currents and could add two numbers in about 1/1000 second. The solid-state transistor, first built in 1950, used semiconductor materials which improved the speed of computers and greatly reduced their size. The development of integrated circuit 'chips' has brought electronic control into every area of everyday life from children's toys to satellite television. The latest low-temperature transistor can perform a million million operations in one second.

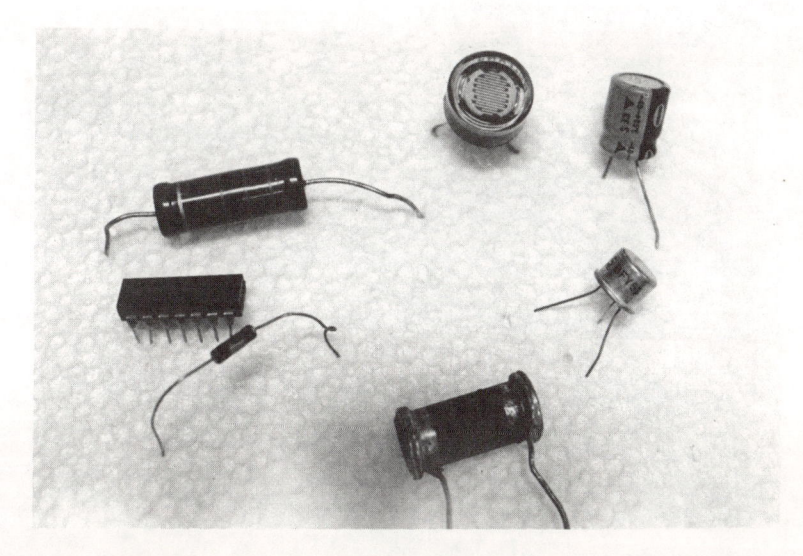

Figure 20.1 Electronic components. Clockwise from the bottom: thermistor, diode, integrated circuit chip, resistor, photocell, capacitor, transistor

Electronics as a subject can be studied from the point of view of the individual components of a system and the material properties which enable them to operate. Another approach is to consider the design of entire electronic systems, paying attention not to the components but to the overall job which they do. This Unit will start by looking at some components of modern everyday electronics. Unit 21 will introduce you to some electronic systems.

20.2 Using a cathode ray oscilloscope

The cathode ray oscilloscope, CRO, is a much used tool for looking at the variations of potential difference in electronic circuits. A bright dot is formed on a screen as a stream of electrons, fired from a hot cathode, collide with the screen material. The path of the electron beam can be bent in the vertical (Y) direction by connecting the external p.d. to be measured across the inputs to the oscilloscope.

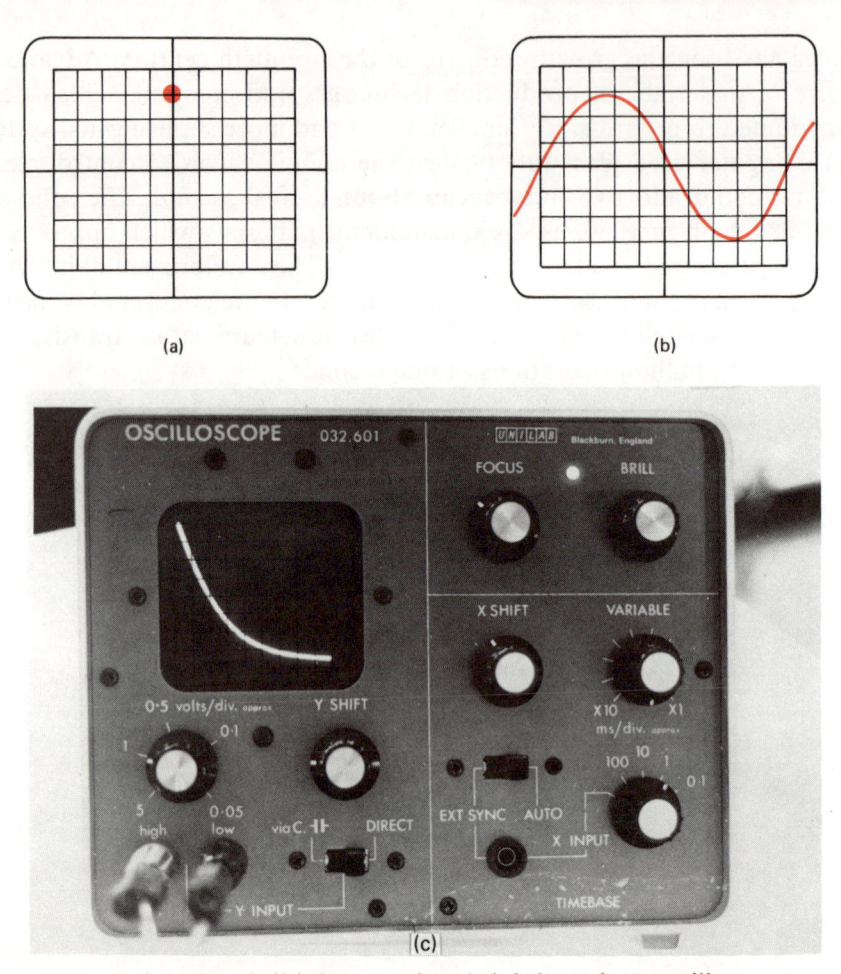

Figure 20.2 A d.c. signal. (b) An a.c. signal. (c) A student oscilloscope

The beam can be sent repeatedly across the screen in the horizontal (X) direction by a clock circuit, called the timebase, in the oscilloscope. The grid on the screen enables the user to take measurements of p.d. in the Y direction and times in the X direction.

20.3 Semiconductor devices

(a) Intrinsic devices
Between the good conducting properties of metals and the poor conduction of insulators lies a type of material known as a semiconductor. Silicon and germanium are examples of **intrinsic** semiconductors. They have few free electrons available for conducting electric charge but the number of free electrons can be increased dramatically by an external energy supply. As a result, some semiconductors are very sensitive to temperature and some to light, and become good conductors when warm or illuminated.

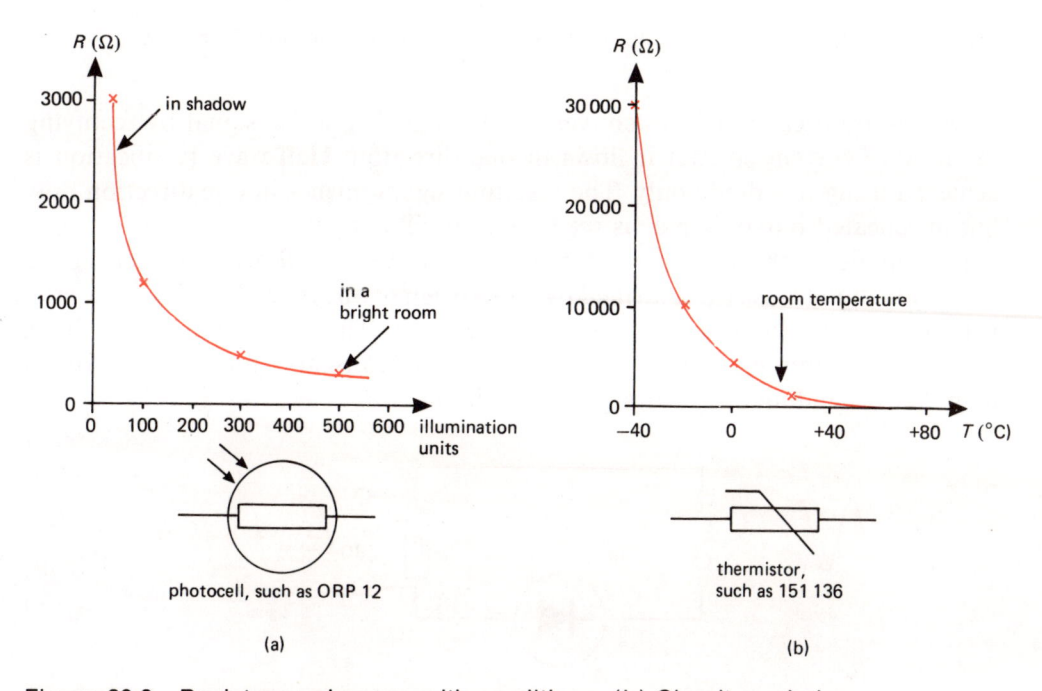

Figure 20.3 Resistance changes with conditions. (b) Circuit symbols

A **photocell** is a light-dependent resistor, LDR, with a resistance which decreases when it is illuminated. A **thermistor** is a temperature-sensitive resistor with a resistance which changes as it warms up. Both these devices are used in potential dividing circuits (see Unit 15), to switch on such things as alarms (see Unit 21).

(b) Extrinsic devices
Doping, the deliberate addition of impurities, will make a semiconductor even more sensitive to conditions. Extrinsic semiconductors, as they are known, can be *p*-type or *n*-type depending on whether the majority of their charge carriers are positive or negative charges. Electronic components can be made by joining small slices of two or more extrinsic semiconductor types. A **junction diode** is made from a *p*-type and an *n*-type of material fused together. A diode has the property that it conducts well in one direction only, called the forward direction.

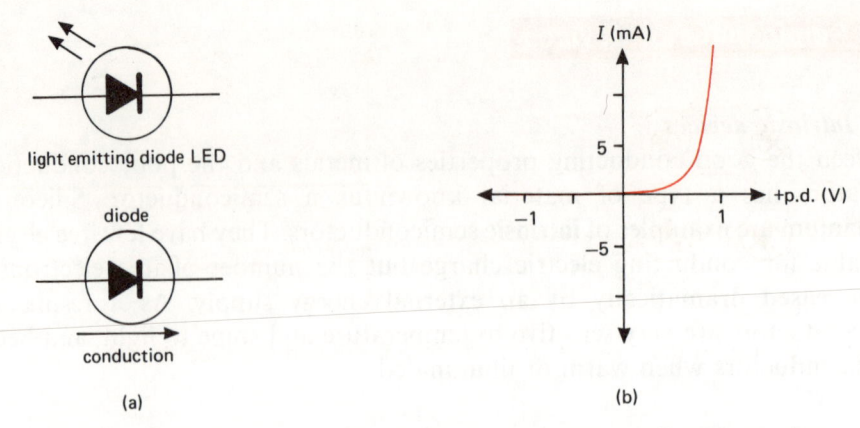

Figure 20.4 (a) Circuit symbols. (b) Diodes conduct in one direction only

Diodes are used to help to convert an a.c. signal to a d.c. signal by rectifying the flow of current so that it flows in one direction. **Half-wave** rectification is achieved using one diode only. The resulting signal pushes in one direction only but in repeated bursts of p.d. as seen on an oscilloscope.

Four diodes in the arrangement shown will produce a **full-wave** rectified signal.

The junction transistor is formed by a sandwich of one type of extrinsic material between two others in a *pnp* or *npn* arrangement. The three connections, base, collector and emitter, can be used to make the transistor into a switch or an amplifier depending on the design of the circuit.

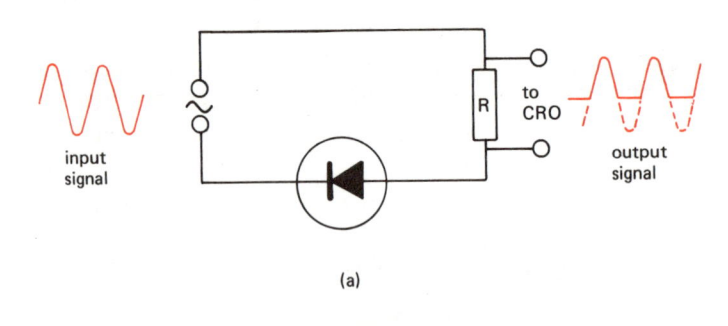

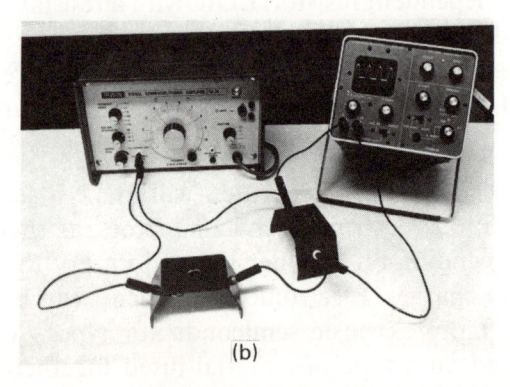

Figure 20.5 Producing a half-wave rectified signal using a diode

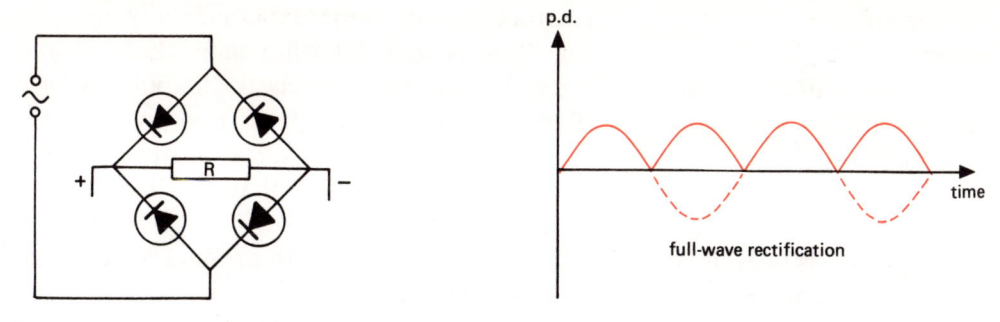

Figure 20.6 Using four diodes to produce a full-wave rectified signal

Figure 20.7 The construction and circuit symbol for an *npn* transistor

20.4 The capacitor

A capacitor does not conduct electricity. It is a component made by sandwiching an insulator between two conducting 'plates'. When connected to a battery, electrons are forced from one capacitor plate to the other as the capacitor 'charges'. This process can take time especially if the circuit resistance is large. The ability to store electric charges, the capacitance, depends on the dimensions of the capacitor. One **farad** of capacitance is an ability to store one coulomb of charge at a p.d. of one volt. Capacitance is often measured in microfarads (10^{-6} F) or picofarads (10^{-12} F). Removing the battery and allowing the electrons to redistribute themselves once again also takes time. This is called 'discharging'.

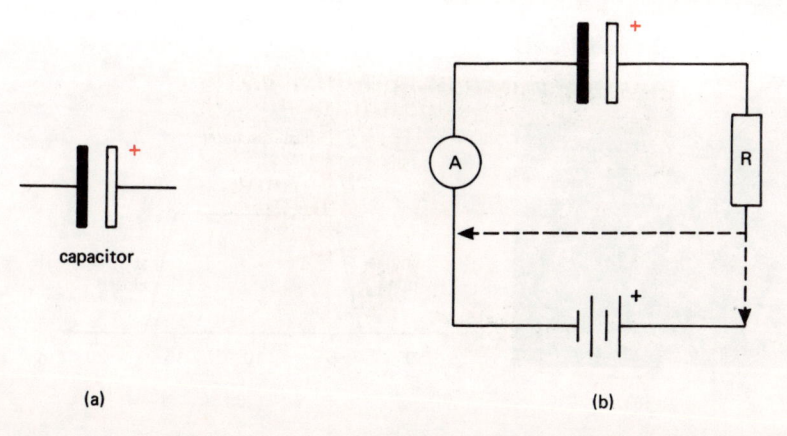

Figure 20.8 (a) A circuit symbol. (b) Charging and discharging a capacitor

Charging and discharging capacitors can be done experimentally using a battery, resistances and a capacitor. A microammeter will enable charging and discharging currents to be monitored. Do take care to check the polarity of a capacitor before you connect it. (Remember to connect positive to positive etc.) An oscilloscope will show the build up and decay of p.d. across a capacitor as it charges and discharges. Figure 20.2, in fact, shows the way that the charge stored by a capacitor decreases rapidly at first and then more slowly.

A capacitor is often used with a diode rectifying circuit to produce a d.c. signal smoother than the rectified signal alone. During the time in the cycle when the diode does not conduct, the stored charges on the capacitor take their time to discharge and so help to keep the output p.d. high. The smoothness of the final p.d. depends on the size of the capacitor and the load resistor.

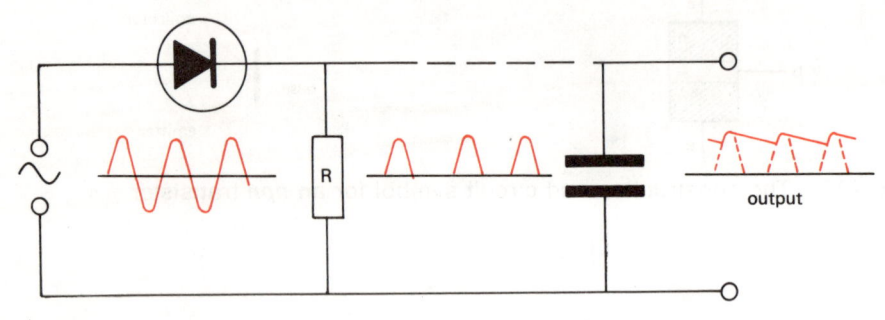

Figure 20.9 A capacitor will help to smooth a rectified signal

20.5 Related reading: Flash photography

Electronic flash units are a common feature of modern photography, either as an integral part of the camera design or as an add-on feature. A flash gun must produce a fixed light output for a short time at a required instant. This is achieved by allowing a capacitor to discharge through a tube of inert gas, usually Xenon.

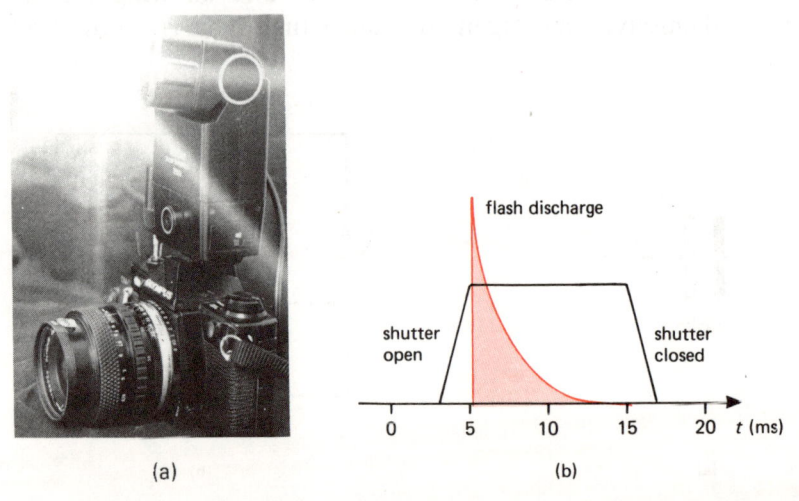

Figure 20.10   (a) Flash photo. (b) An electronic flash fires when the shutter is opened

A 500 microfarad capacitor charged up to 500 V will discharge through a xenon flash tube in a few milliseconds. This short burst of light must be synchronised to occur at the same time that the camera shutter is open to expose the film. The 500 V is needed in order that enough energy is delivered to illuminate the scene, but it needs to be supplied by a portable 6 V battery.

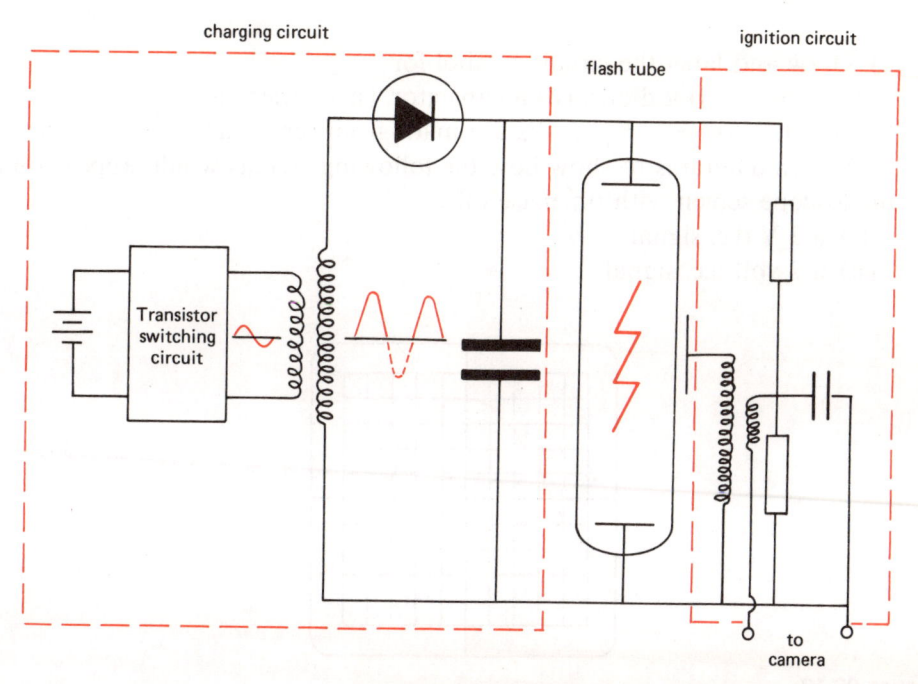

Figure 20.11 Electronic components help to charge the flash and trigger its discharge

To charge the capacitor to 500 V, a transistor switching circuit sends a series of alternating pulses from the 6V battery p.d. through a step up transformer (6:500). The 500 V output pulses are rectified by a diode and charges build up on the 500 microfarad capacitor.

To synchronise the capacitor discharge with the shutter release, a second step-up transformer, triggered on shutter release by an ignition capacitor, excites the xenon gas which then conducts the main discharge.

Each flash operation delivers about 60 J of energy in about 5 milliseconds. A 6 V dry battery would therefore be expected to last for more than 100 flashes.

20.6 Summary

- *The cathode ray oscilloscope is a voltmeter which gives a reading based on the deflection of a beam of electrons.*
- *A photo cell and a thermistor are intrinsic semiconductor devices.*
- *Doped semiconductors can be p-type or n-type.*

- *A junction diode will conduct well in one direction only and so can be used to rectify an a.c. signal.*
- *A capacitor can store charges. The ability to store charge is measured in farads.*

20.7 Progress questions

1. (a) Draw and label the circuit symbol for
        (i) a diode, (ii) a capacitor, (iii) a thermistor.
   (b) Which of these components are made from semiconducting material?
2. (a) Sketch diagrams to show how the following signals would appear on an oscilloscope screen with timebase off:
     (i) a 3 V d.c. signal
     (ii) a 2 volt a.c. signal.

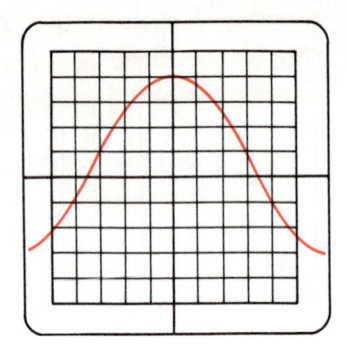

Figure 20.12

   (b) The signal shown in Figure 20.12 was displayed on an oscilloscope with its time-base set on 1 millisecond per division and its Y-gain on 5 v/division. What can you say about the signal?
3. A glass rod will become a better conductor as it gets very hot. The greater current will cause the glass to heat up even more. Explain what might happen to a piece of glass, connected to a minus voltage supply, as it is heated.
4. Electronic devices are becoming smaller and faster.
   (a) How small do you think electronic components will become? Why might there be a limit to size?
   (b) The speed of operation of electronic devices depends on the speed at which electric signals can pass along a wire. Do you think that there will be a limit to how fast electronic signals can travel? (Have you heard of fibre optic cables?)

21 ELECTRONIC SYSTEMS

21.1 The language of logic

In a court of law, a prisoner is judged to be either guilty or innocent. There is no room for uncertainty. Medically, a human body is either dead or alive (although this is hotly debated on occasions). There are very few examples in real life where a simple division can be made between two extremes. Speaking French, for example, is not just something which you can or cannot do. Some people can speak fluent French, others a little French, and others none at all. Playing a musical instrument is another skill with a variety of levels.

In electronics, it is easy to have just two 'states' for, say, a lightbulb. It can be switched either on or off. This is an example of **digital** electronic **logic**. In the language of electronic logic there are only two **states**: on and off, or high and low, or 1 and 0. State **1** represents a switch closed or an indicator lamp on. State **0** represents an open switch or a lamp off. Consider the simple circuit shown in Figure 21.1, containing switches and a lamp:

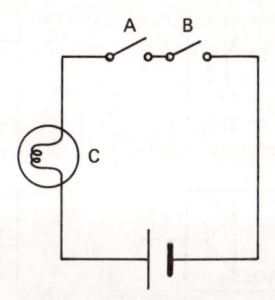

Switch A	Switch B	Lamp C
open, 0	open, 0	off, 0
open, 0	closed, 1	off, 0
closed, 1	open 0	off, 0
closed, 1	closed, 1	on, 1

Truth table

Figure 21.2 Applying logic to a series circuit

What are the conditions for the lamp to be bright (**1**)? The lamp will be bright only if both switch **A** **and** switch **B** are closed. We call this an **AND** condition. The **truth table** summarises the logic of the circuit.

Now consider the circuit of Figure 21.2 and its truth table. Can you follow the logic which results in the table? The lamp will light if either switch **A** **or** switch **B** is closed. We call this an **OR** condition.

205

Figure 21.2 Applying logic to a parallel circuit

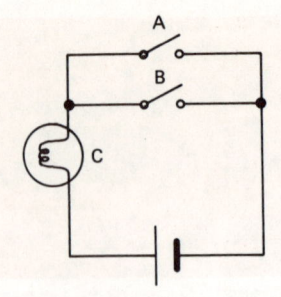

Switch A	Switch B	Lamp C
open, 0	open, 0	off, 0
open, 0	closed, 1	on, 1
closed, 1	open, 0	on, 1
closed, 1	closed, 1	on, 1

Truth table

21.2 Logic gates

It is possible to design an electronic circuit with two input terminals and one output such that the AND and OR logic conditions are followed. We call these circuits logic **gates**. Understanding the truth table for a gate is more important than knowing about the internal circuit design. A third and very simple gate is the NOT gate, or inverter. This will give an output state opposite to the input. All logic gates and transistors need to be connected to a power supply before they will function. In many circuit diagrams, including the ones in this Unit, the power supply will be omitted to help to keep circuit diagrams simple.

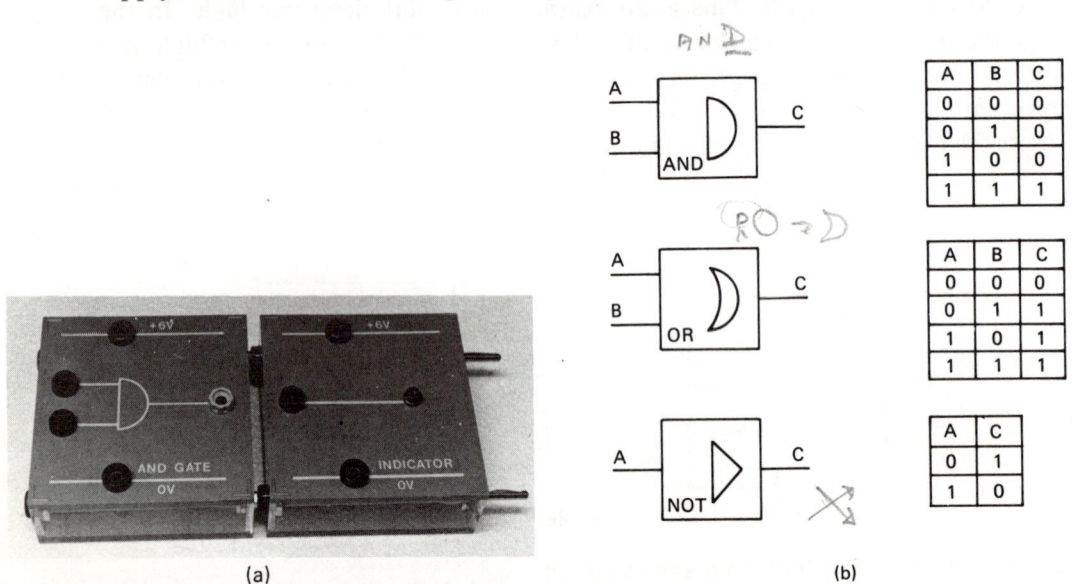

A	B	C
0	0	0
0	1	0
1	0	0
1	1	1

A	B	C
0	0	0
0	1	1
1	0	1
1	1	1

A	C
0	1
1	0

Figure 21.3 (a) An AND gate and indicator. (b) Logic gates and truth tables

21.3 Using logic gates

(a) To control two flashing lights
An aircraft carries a red and a green lamp on either wing tip. They must flash alternately but not together. *Solution*: use an **inverter**.

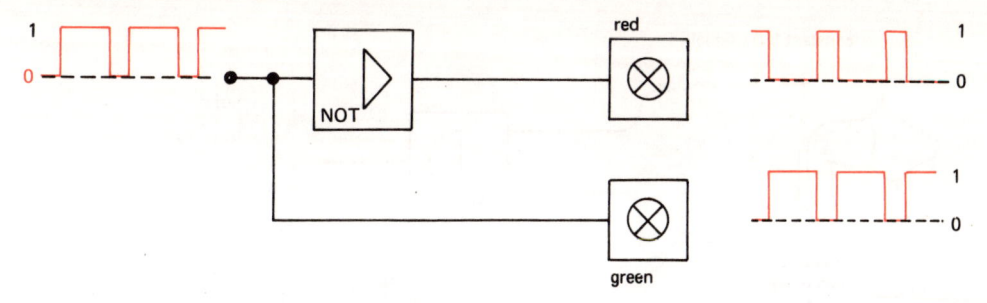

Figure 21.4 Solving the flashing light problem

(b) To ensure car passenger safety
A car designer wants to ensure that the car ignition switch does not start the engine unless the driver wears a seat belt. *Solution*: Use an **AND** gate.

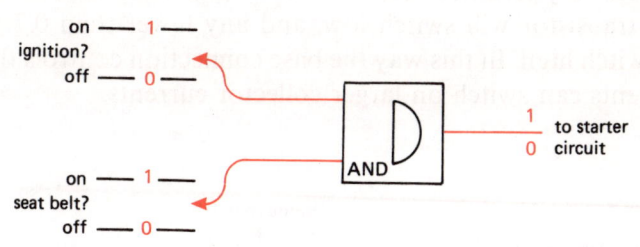

Figure 21.5 Solving the car safety problem

(c) To control the flow of traffic across a train crossing
An automatic barrier at a road and rail junction needs to ensure that the barrier is down when a train is approaching from either direction. *Solution*: use an **OR** gate and an **inverter**.

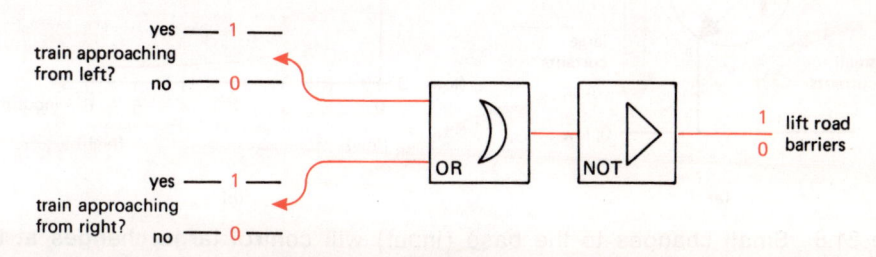

Figure 21.6 Solving the train crossing problem

(d) To ensure the safety of a baby
A baby minder wants a buzzer to sound whenever a baby crawls towards an open window. *Solution*: use an **AND** gate. see fig 21.7

21.4 The transistor as a switch

(a) Input/output
A transistor can be thought of as an inverter. Connected across a p.d. as shown

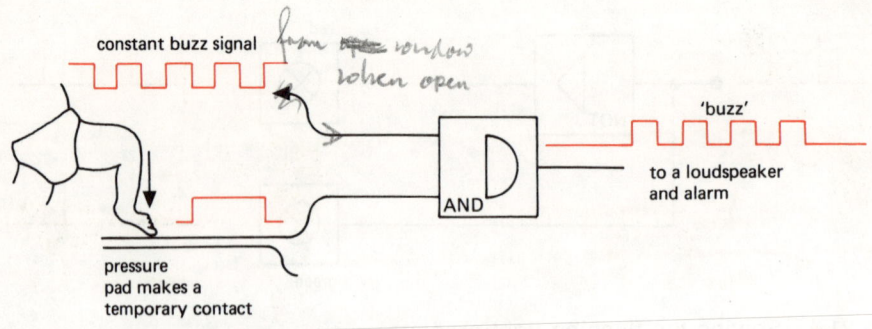

Figure 21.7 Solving the wandering baby problem

in Figure 21.8, a high signal on the input (base connection) will produce a low output signal at the collector.

The transistor is very sensitive when the base signal is at about +0.7 volt. Any higher and the transistor will switch low, and any lower than 0.7 volt and the transistor will switch high. In this way the base connection controls the transistor. Small base currents can switch on larger collector currents.

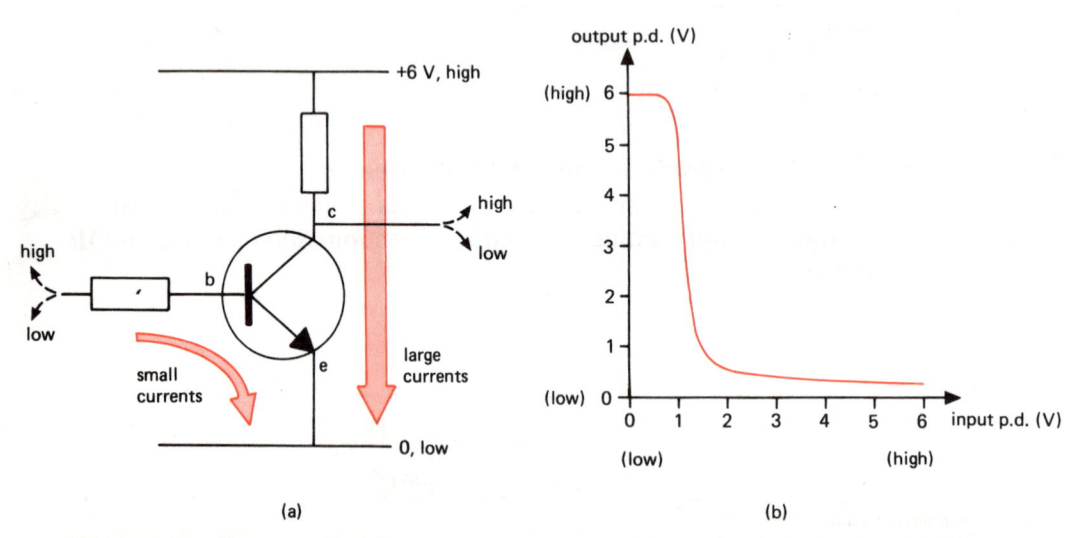

Figure 21.8 Small changes to the base (input) will control large changes at the collector (output)

(b) Controlling the transistor

A potential divider is often used to provide a base signal which varies a little below and a little above the switching voltage. If one part of the potential divider is a thermistor, then the transistor can be switched on automatically by a change in temperature. A divider using a photocell will allow light to control the transistor.

In Figure 21.9 a transistor switch circuit is contained in a grey basic unit box. The output indicator lights when the photocell is illuminated and goes out when the photocell is covered.

Indicator on

Indicator off

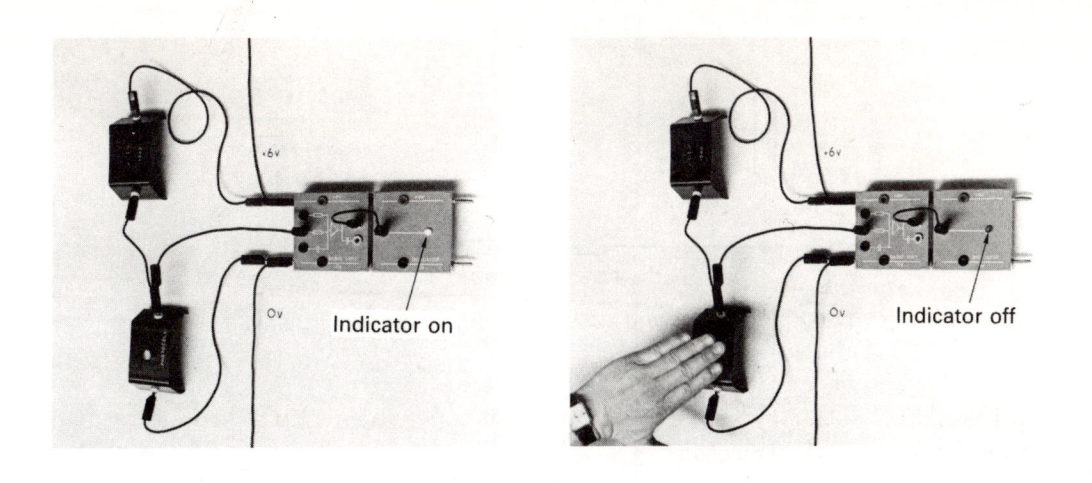

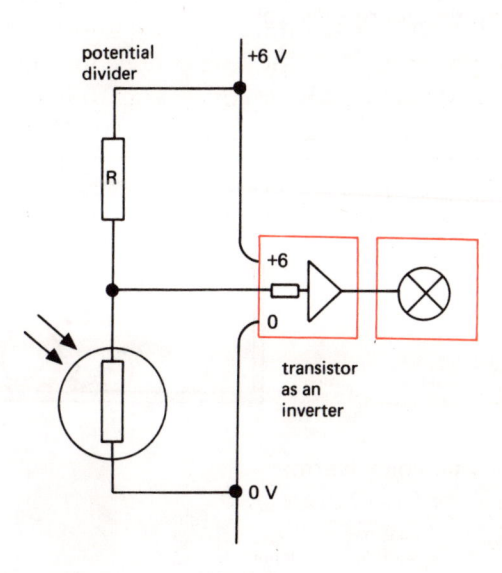

Figure 21.9 A potential divider will control a transistor switch

(c) Some applications of transistor control
Let us suppose that an emergency light was needed in a hospital. It had to come on automatically if the main lighting failed. A solution would be to use the circuit in Figure 21.9 with an inverter to reverse the switching. —see fig 21.10

A second application is to use a thermistor as a temperature-sensitive switch which could switch on a warm lamp in a chicken incubator. The lamp would turn itself off when the temperature reached the required level. fig 21.11

A third application is to use a capacitor to switch on a transistor after a time delay. This could be useful as a home burglar alarm. The time delay would allow you time to turn the alarm off when you open the door. An intruder would start the capacitor charging but would not interrupt it before it reached the switching voltage. fig 21.12

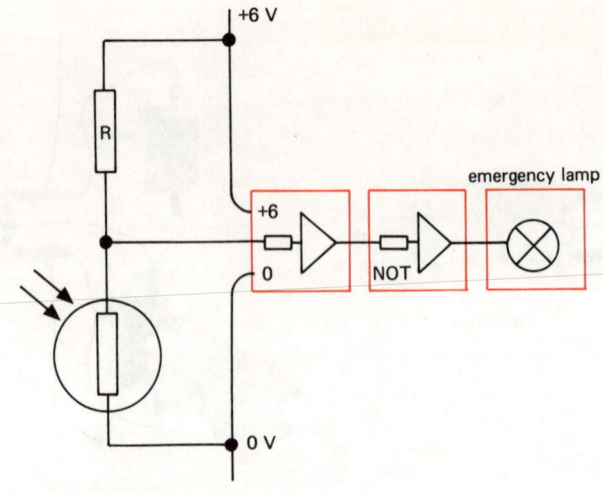

Figure 21.10 An automatic emergency light

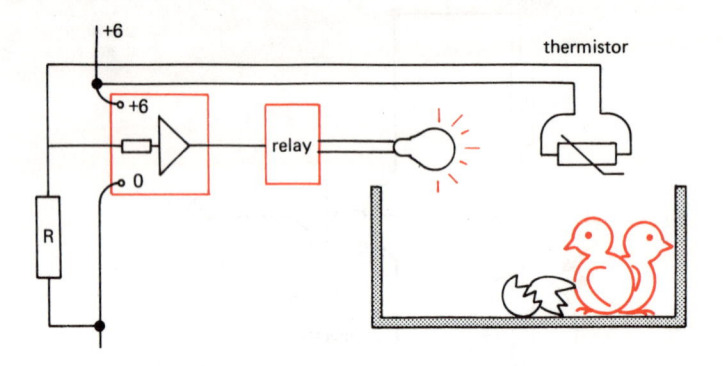

Figure 21.11 An automatic chick warmer

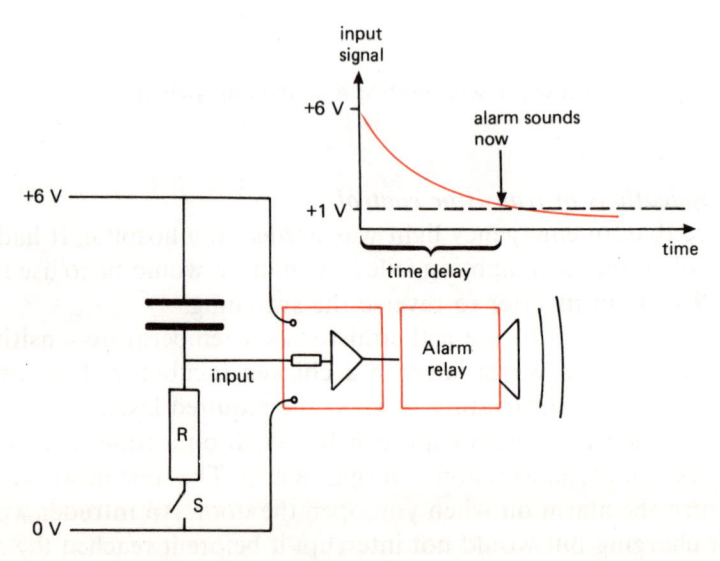

210 Figure 21.12 A capacitor creates a time delay

21.5 The transistor as an amplifier

The transistor can be made to operate in the very small range of input voltages near the +1 volt switching voltage. This is achieved by using a fixed potential divider to hold, or 'bias', the base at about +1 volt. Any small additional signals applied to the base will then appear as larger signals at the collector.

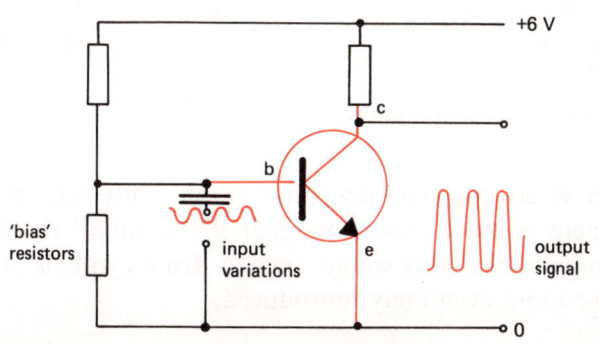

Figure 21.13 Operating a transistor as an amplifier

21.6 Related reading: Electronic pianos and sound synthesis

Look at box X in Figure 21.14. Can you recognise what is drawn inside the box? Now look at box Y. Does the extra information contained in box Y help? Box Z contains even more information. Is there enough for you to recognise the shape of a bicycle?

Whenever smooth, or analogue, information needs to be translated into a digital form, there is a compromise between the accuracy of the translation and the complexity of the digital display. This problem faces makers of electronic pianos when they try to capture the analogue sound of a real piano and store it in a digital form to be reconstructed later when a key is pressed. Rival electronic piano makers use claims like "you can't hear the 'electronic' in our pianos." Recording sound on to compact disc suffers from the same analogue-to-digital problems.

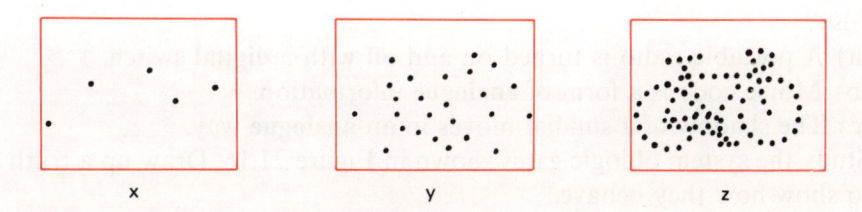

Figure 21.14 Reconstructing digital information

The technique for analogue-to-digital transfer is known as **sampling**. To digitise the sound from a grand piano, the analogue signal is 'sampled' at a high sampling rate, typically 40 000 times per second. The result of each individual sample is

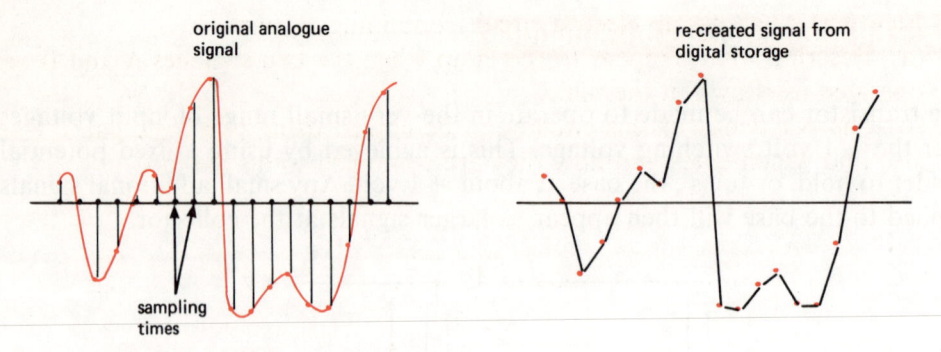

Figure 21.15 Sampling an analogue signal

one point on an electronic loudness/time graph. This information is stored electronically. There is more room for error if the sound to be sampled is a high-frequency, rapidly changing sound, such as drum cymbals. A low-frequency bass sound will be more accurately reproduced.

21.7 Summary

- *Analogue electronics deals with smoothly changing signals. Digital electronics deals with a logic language with only two 'states': 0 and 1.*
- *Logic gates are described by their 'truth tables'.*
- *A transistor may be operated as a 'not' gate or inverter.*
- *The base connection of a transistor controls the state of the transistor switch.*
- *A potential dividing circuit can automatically change the base signal and switch the transistor.*
- *A transistor operating at its switching point can amplify an input signal.*

21.8 Progress questions

1. Here are some statements about information. Which are true and which are false?
   (a) A portable radio is turned on and off with a **digital** switch.
   (b) Morse code is a form of **analogue** information.
   (c) The shadow of a sundial moves in an **analogue** way.
2. Study the system of logic gates shown in Figure 21.16. Draw up a truth table to show how they behave.

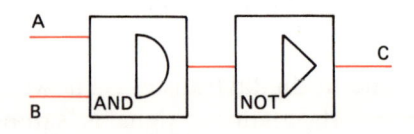

Figure 21.16

3. Figure 21.17 shows an electric circuit containing a lamp.
   (a) Describe what happens to the lamp when the two switches A and B are operated as shown in the table.
   (b) The behaviour of this circuit can be copied using two logic gates. Can you find which gates and how they are combined to do the job?

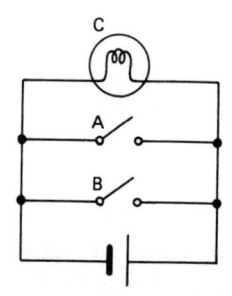

Figure 21.17

4. A butcher would like to know when the temperature in his cold meat store falls below a certain value. Can you design a transistor switch circuit which will automatically sound a buzzer when his cold meat store is too cold?

ASSESSMENTS

22.1 A variety of assessments

(a) Positive achievement

The Introduction to this book referred to the idea of positive achievement. Assessments at GCSE are designed to allow all students to demonstrate what they know, understand and can do. Assessors and examiners will therefore be interested in your achievements rather than your score on some tricky questions.

You should try to look upon an assessment as an opportunity for you to demonstrate what you have achieved in your course. Try not to be too nervous about GCSE assessments. You will be assessed several times so there will be many opportunities for you to show what you can do. As many of your assessments will be carried out by your teacher, it is a good idea to have a chat with your teacher about your worries and about what each assessment will be like. Your

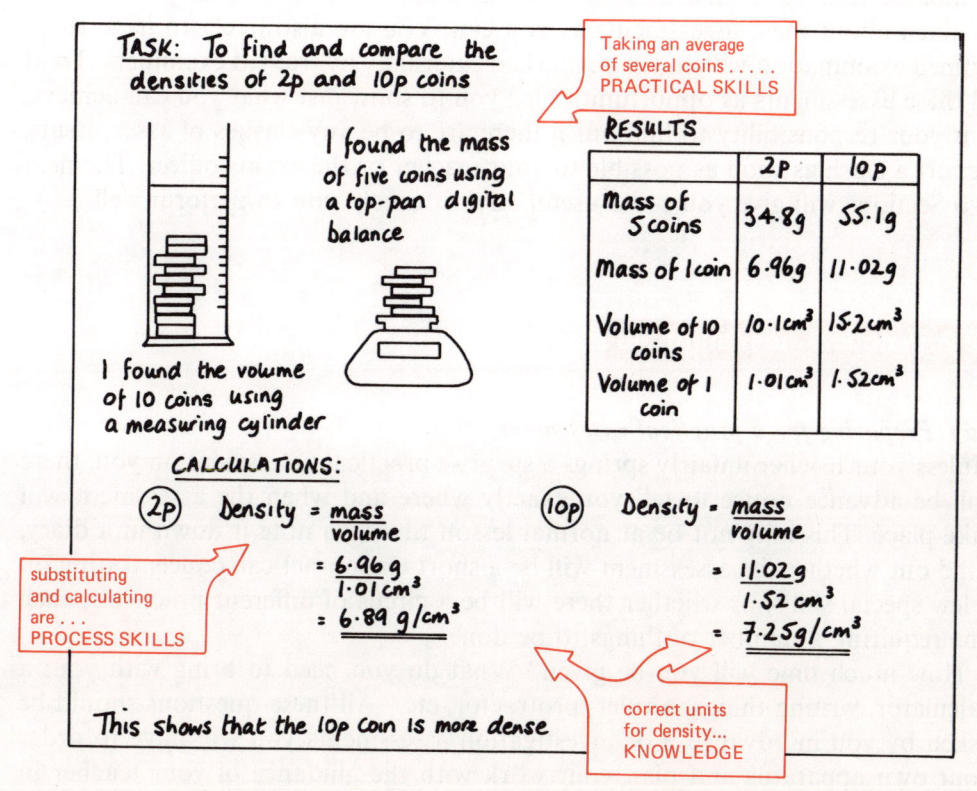

Figure 22.1 A piece of work showing knowledge, process and practical skills

teacher will be able to advise you on your weaknesses so that you can work to improve them.

(b) Skills and abilities

A course in physics will introduce you to a number of new ideas and ways of thinking about situations. You will increase your knowledge about the physical world and improve your understanding of why it is as it is. Knowing the correct units for a quantity such as energy and understanding about energy conservation are examples. Some assessments, usually those requiring written answers, will allow you to show your new *knowledge and understanding*.

There will be opportunities in your course for you to develop particular *practical skills* and be a better experimenter. Skills such as repeating and checking your measurements or following a simple circuit digram are important if you are to succeed with practical physics. You will be able to demonstrate these skills in a class practical or an individual investigation project.

Finally, all physics students need to be able to select the correct principles or mathematical formulae from those available and apply them to what might be an unfamiliar situation. *Process skills* such as these come through plenty of practice in solving problems, both numerical and practical.

(c) Coursework and examinations

Some opportunities for assessment will come during your course. Called coursework assessments, they may be arranged class practicals, a practical circus or an end of module test. Take them seriously and find out in advance from your teacher as much about these assessments as you can. You are also likely to have to sit a timed examination which will be marked externally by trained examiners. Treat all these assessments as opportunities for you to show just what you can achieve. It is your responsibility to find out if there are to be any clashes of assessments. Report a clash as soon as possible to your teacher or the exams officer. The next two Sections will give you some useful advice to help you to perform well.

22.2 Practical assessments

(a) Preparing for a practical assessment

Unless your teacher unfairly springs a surprise practical assessment on you, there will be advance notice to tell you exactly where and when the assessment will take place. This may not be at normal lesson times, so note it down in a diary. Find out whether the assessment will be a short class practical, concentrating on a few special skills, or whether there will be a circus of different practicals, each one requiring a number of things to be done.

How much time will you be given? What do you need to bring with you: a calculator, writing things, a ruler, protractor, etc.? All these questions should be asked by you in advance. For investigation assessments you will have to order your own apparatus and plan your work with the guidance of your teacher in advance. Unit 11 gives plenty of advice about investigations.

(b) The actual practical assessment

Faced with a table full of equipment, the nervous student will be tempted to arrange and rearrange things before starting. Do not touch the apparatus before reading the question paper. It is often the case that apparatus has been deliberately set up to help you to start correctly. If you think that an item of apparatus is missing or is not working, then you should immediately tell the supervisor, usually your teacher.

You will probably be limited for time. Having checked that you are at the correct question for the apparatus, look over the question to see how long it is and then start straight away. Do not be tempted to take an interest in other students or other questions. If you do not spend too much time reading and re-reading the paper, you will find that there is enough time to complete the practical. The instructions are usually very clear. Follow them step by step, doing what is required at each step.

(c) Some useful hints

Unit 9 is devoted to practical work and includes some good advice. For practical assessments some hints are given below:

- *If there is time to repeat a measurement, then repeat it. Write down all measurements and show the assessor that you have considered an average value.*
- *Remember that all physical quantities have units. Do not forget to include them.*
- *Read meters and dials with your eyes placed so that there is no parallax in the reading (see Unit 9).*
- *Connect and check an electric circuit **before** switching on or connecting to the power supply.*
- *Take and record measurements to the accuracy allowed by the measuring instrument. For example, if you use a ruler graduated in millimetres, measure to the nearest millimetre.*
- *If the marks available for a question are shown, use them to guide your answer. A question with six marks available will require more information than a question with only one mark.*

22.3 Written assessments

(a) Preparing for written assessments

You will be given advance notice of the dates and times of written assessments. It is your responsibility to note down this information and be present, punctual and prepared. There is always a problem of remembering the work covered during the course and of knowing factual information. A *revision programme* is an essential part of preparing for a written assessment.

There is no one revision plan to suit all students. Some people find it easier to leave factual learning to the last minute. Others like to start going over work well in advance. Either way you will be faced with a considerable amount of work to read over. It is sometimes helpful to summarise the main parts of each topic on blank postcards. You can buy ready-made physics revision cards but it is much more valuable to make your own set tailored to your course and your needs. The summary at the end of each Unit in this book will give you a guide to help you start your revision notes.

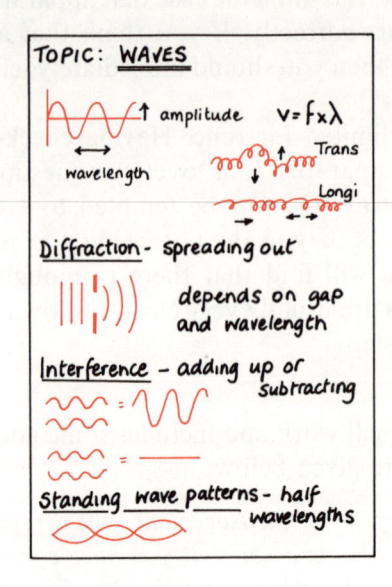

```
TOPIC: WAVES

         ↑ amplitude      v = f × λ
  ↔ 
  wavelength                   Trans

                               Longi

Diffraction - spreading out
                    depends on gap
                    and wavelength

Interference - adding up or
                    subtracting

Standing wave patterns - half
                        wavelengths
```

Figure 22.2 Post cards can form a useful portable revision pack

A copy of the course syllabus might help you. Syllabuses are usually written for teachers, so you must expect to search through a lot of educational discussion before you find the content pages. Send away to the Examination Board for a syllabus.

Revise each topic in turn for a short time. Find a quiet place, at home, in college or in a public library, and decide on a single topic and set a time limit. Have

WEEK STARTING	TOPIC	NOTES
MARCH 7	Particles	✓ done
MARCH 14	Materials	✓ done
MARCH 21	Motion	✓ see Mr. K about terminal velocity ✓
MARCH 28	Radioactivity	✓
APRIL 4	Waves	✓ copy up notes on diffraction
APRIL 11	Energy	✓ done
APRIL 18	Electricity	
APRIL 25	Electricity	
MAY 2	Electronics	
MAY 9	Final look at Term 1	
MAY 16	Final look at Term 2	
MAY 23	EXAM WEEK STARTS	

Figure 22.3 A planned revision programme will help you to feel more confident

your lesson notes, rough paper, textbook and revision cards at the ready, and if possible have some past assessment questions for you to practise. A plan would ensure that each topic was tackled in turn and then revised more quickly for a final time. Take any revision problems which you discover to your teacher. Arrange for an appointment to discuss them, perhaps after lessons or in the lunch break. Take a friend along for support. Some students form small revision groups which meet informally to help each other.

(b) *Doing your best in a written assessment*

If you have arrived at the correct place on the correct day and the correct time with the necessary pens, calculator, ruler, etc., and with enough hours of revision behind you, there is nothing to prevent you from being the best physics student since Aristotle. Well, I suppose there is the question paper.

One of the most important things to remember is that you will be given only a limited time. Know how long to allow for each question and keep one eye on the clock. If you are really stuck on one question, then move to the next. There may be time to return to tricky questions later. The questions at the end of this book will give you practice with your timing.

There are instructions on the front of every question paper. Read them carefully. They will tell you how many questions are to be attempted and in how much time. You will probably be reminded to show the steps in your calculations and to explain answers in clear English.

Success in assessments is about gaining marks for your answers. In many questions, the marks are allocated to particular types of answers which display particular knowledge, processes or understanding. In other words, the examiner knows what sort of answer is needed for full marks. Your job is to read a question and realise just what sort of answer will gain the marks. Will it be a calculation, a description, the stating of a principle or perhaps the designing of an experiment?

To help you decide on just what kind of answer is required, here are two examples of styles of questions with comments. The important phrases and words are highlighted. The answers are not complete but give you a guide.

Question A: 'The diagram shows an electric circuit containing two lamps and a switch. *Calculate* the resistance of each of the lamps and *find* the total resistance of the circuit. Show how you arrive at your answers.' (6 marks)

Comments: There are six parts to this question. The calculations of resistance will probably each have one mark for the numerical answer and one mark for showing how you arrive at the answer. You will lose half the marks if you do not show your working out.

Question B: '"Before a radioactive measurement can be made it is important to measure the background count." This advice is taken from a textbook.'
(a) *Explain* what is meant by background radiation. (2)
(b) *Describe*, using a labelled diagram, how you would measure the background count in a school laboratory. (8)

Comments: Take each part in turn.
(a) For two marks you need only give a short explanation. For example, 'Background radiation is always present around us. It is the constant emission of alpha, beta and gamma radiations given off by isotopes in building bricks, the atmosphere and plants.'
(b) For eight marks you will need to draw a diagram of a GM tube and counter (probably 4 marks) and describe how you would use the readings on the counter (2 marks). If you explain that you would take the average of several minute counts, for example, then you will probably gain the final two marks.

22.4 Summary

- *There will be a number of different opportunities for you to be assessed.*
- *In each assessment what is important is your own positive achievement. This is what you can actually do.*
- *You should find out the date, time and place of each assessment in advance.*
- *Preparing for assessments involves knowing as much as you can about the type and style of assessment, the number of questions and the time available for your answers.*
- *Revision helps you to prepare yourself. A revision plan taken little by little can help to cover what appears to be a lot of work.*
- *Gaining marks depends on realising exactly what the question asks for. Read questions carefully.*

PRACTICE ASSESSMENT QUESTIONS

23.1 Some general points

Each of these questions should take you no more than 15 minutes to answer. Time yourself. They will help you to assess your knowledge, understanding and process skills. Some questions will involve calculations, others will ask for more descriptive answers. If you are finding that you are doing well at physics GCSE, then some of the C to G questions will appear very easy. You should do them and then move on to those designed for grades A to C. You will find the equations in Appendix II might help you. Write all answers on a separate sheet of paper. (Take $g = 10$ m/s^2 = 10 N/kg.)

23.2 Grade C to G questions

1. Figure 23.1 shows a banana being used in a laboratory experiment.

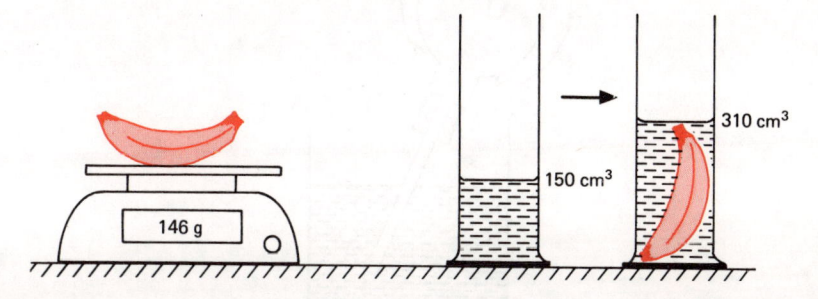

Figure 23.1

   (a) What is the mass of the banana
       (i) in grams? (ii) in kilograms?
   (b) What is the weight of the banana?
   (c) What is the volume of the banana? Show how you found your answer.
   (d) Calculate the density of the banana. Show your working.
   (e) Bananas arive in the market in boxes. The mass of an empty box is

0.3 kg. Each box contains 50 identical bananas. What is the total mass of a full box? Show how you arrive at your answer.
  (f) Do you think that the density of a box of bananas will be greater, the same or smaller than the density of a single banana? Explain your answer.
2. The following results are from a student investigation into the stretching of a piece of elastic material found in underwear.

load (N)	1	2	3	4	5	6
length (cm)	26.0	28.0	30.0	31.2	31.8	32.0

  (a) Plot these results on graph paper. Plot length on the x-axis. Draw a suitable line or curve.
  (b) From your graph find:
     (i) The length of the piece of elastic at the start of the experiment.
     (ii) The load which would stretch the elastic to a length of 31 cm.
     (iii) The **extension** that a load of 2 N produced.
  (c) Another piece of elastic material was found to be twice as stiff as this. Show by a line on your graph how a piece of this new elastic, the same shape as the first, might have stretched.
3. When a glass flask is held under water and heated by warm hands, bubbles appear coming out of a tube attached to the flask (see Figure 23.2).

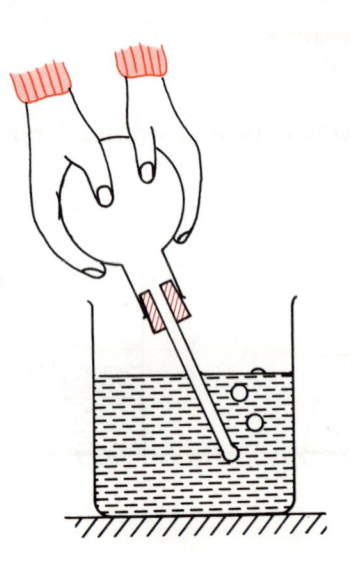

Figure 23.2

Here are some statements people have made about this experiment:
  (i) "The glass contracts when it is heated and so the air is forced out."
  (ii) "The glass expands when it is heated and so the air is forced out."
  (iii) "The air expands when it is heated and so pushes itself out."

(a) Which of these explanations does not explain why air comes out of the tube?
(b) Which explanation explains the bubbles but is in fact not true?
(c) Use your own ideas to explain clearly why air comes out of the tube.
(d) What do you think will happen when the warm hands are taken off the flask? Explain your answer.

4. High divers freely accelerate into water as shown in the sketch. Figure 23.3 shows how the speed of a high diver changes as she dives.

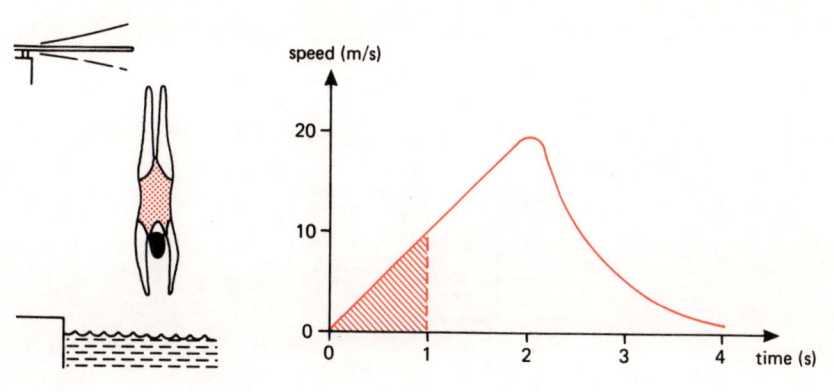

Figure 23.3

(a) The slope of the graph at the start of the dive is about 10 m/s². What does this tell you about the forces on the diver?
(b) How long does the diver spend in the air before hitting the water?
(c) The shaded part of the graph shows how far the diver fell in the first second. How far was this?
(d) Use the graph to find out how far it is from the diving board to the water.
(e) What can you say about the forces on the diver after she strikes the water?

5. Figure 23.4 shows sketches of the same person trying three ways of reaching level 1 of a multi-storey car park. The person weighs 600 N.

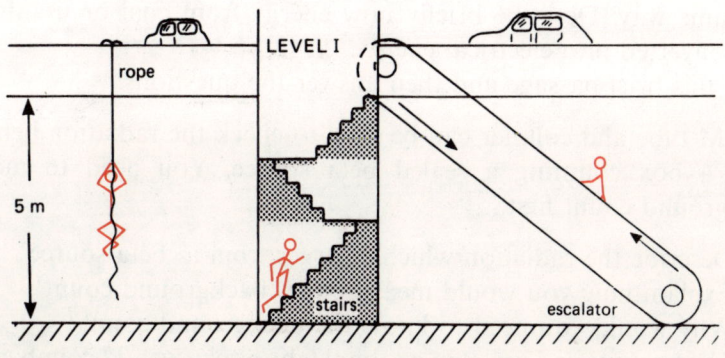

Figure 23.4

(a) What type of energy is being gained in these events?
(b) Where does the energy come from in each case?

(c) Calculate how much work needs to be done to raise the person to level 1?
(d) How much energy is transformed in doing this job?
(e) The escalator takes eight seconds to do this job. Calculate the power of the escalator motor.
(f) What might happen to the escalator or its motor if four people used it at the same time?

6. A car headlamp bulb is shown in Figure 23.5. The lamp has a working life of 1000 hours, or 3 600 000 s.

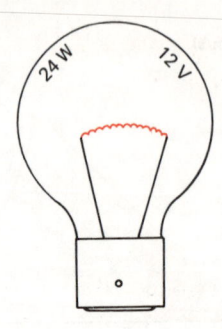

Figure 23.5

(a) How powerful is the lamp when it is on?
(b) Calculate how much energy the lamp will transform in its working life.
(c) Where does the lamp get this energy from?
(d) A fully charged car battery stores about 4 million joules of energy. Why does a motor car need a dynamo?

7. Much of the electrical energy supplied to homes in the country is generated by either nuclear or coal-fired power stations. Nuclear power stations use uranium as a fuel. Coal stations use a crushed coal and air mixture.
(a) Energy is obtained from uranium by a process called fission. Use a diagram to explain what is meant by nuclear fission.
(b) How is the energy removed from burning coal?
(c) Both nuclear and coal-fired power stations generate electricity in the same way. Describe briefly how energy from coal or uranium can be converted into electrical energy.

8. Read this brief passage and then answer the questions.

'A GM tube and counter can be used to check the radiation being emitted from a box counting a sealed beta source. You need to measure the background count first.'

(a) Describe the radiation which emerges from a 'beta source'.
(b) Explain how you would measure the 'background count'.
(c) Why would you need to know the background count?
(d) The background count in a school laboratory was 22 counts per minute. A GM tube and counter near to a sealed laboratory beta source in a box gave a measured count of 25 counts per minute. It this result worrying? Explain your answer.

9. Figure 23.6 shows a light-dependent resistor, LDR, and a resistance meter. The resistance of the LDR changes from 300 ohms in a bright room to 3000 ohms when covered by a hand.

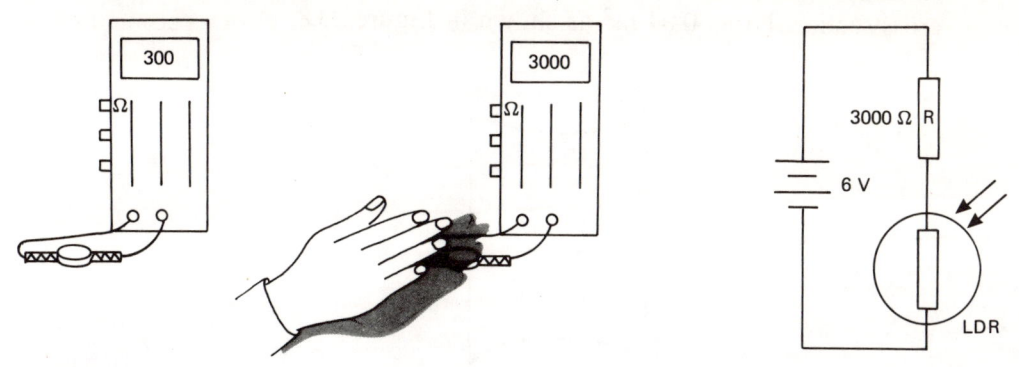

Figure 23.6

In an experiment, the LDR is connected to a 3000 ohm resistor and a 6 volt battery. Electrical connections can be made in series or in parallel.
   (a) How is the resistance meter connected to the LDR in the Figure 23.6?
   (b) How are the battery, resistor and LDR connected?
   (c) The resistor and LDR divide up the 6 volts p.d. between them. Explain why it is that in the dark they each have a p.d. of 3 volts across them.
   (d) What happens to the p.d. across the LDR when the lights are turned on? Explain your answer.
10. You can buy coloured decorative lights for occasions like Christmas from an electrical supplies shop. For 240 volt mains operated lights there are two types of bulb, 12 volt and 240 volt, depending on whether they are connected to the mains supply in series or in parallel.

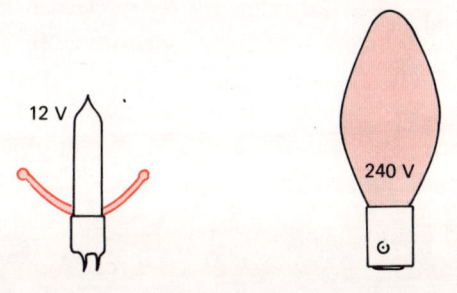

Figure 23.7

   (a) Sketch two circuit diagrams to show how these bulbs might be connected to the mains supply.
   (b) Sets of Christmas tree lights often contain 20 bulbs. Can you explain why?
   (c) What advantages can you seen in the two different methods of wiring lights?
   (d) The working resistance of a 240 volt bulb is 1000 ohms. How much current does one 240 volt bulb take?

225

23.3 Questions for grades A to C

11. A sample of sea water, volume 0.01 m³, was collected in a tube of cross-sectional area 0.04 m² as shown in Figure 23.8.

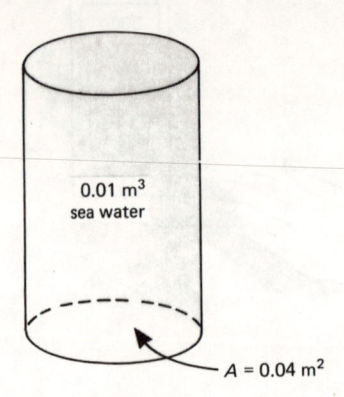

Figure 23.8

The mass of the empty tube was 0.850 kg. When filled with water the mass increased to 10.950 kg. Use this information to calculate:
(a) The density of sea water.
(b) The height of the water in the tube.
(c) The pressure at the base of the tube caused by the water.
(d) How does your answer to (c) compare with the pressure of the water half way up the tube? Explain your answer.
(e) A deep sea diving vessel built to withstand a water pressure of 5 million Pa is lowered into the sea. How deep should it be allowed to go?

12. The graph of Figure 23.9 shows how a piece of copper wire behaved when it was stretched to breaking point. The original wire had an area of cross-section of 1.4×10^{-6} m².

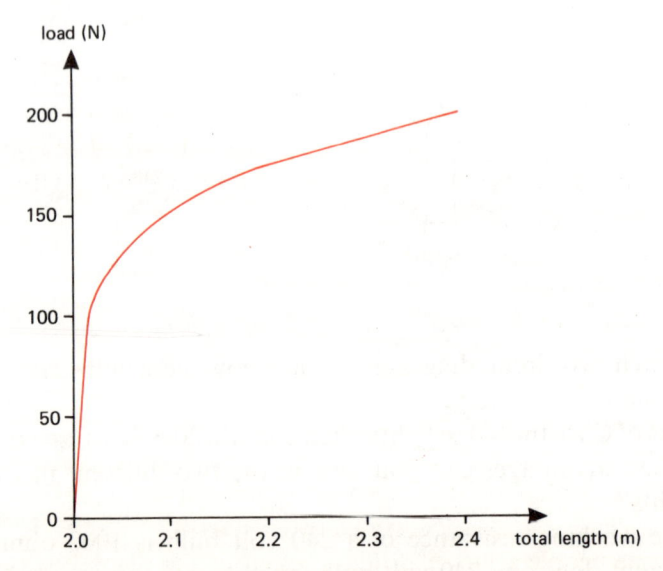

Figure 23.9

Use this information to calculate:
(a) The extension of the wire at breaking point.
(b) The strain of the wire as it broke.
(c) The tensile stress on the wire as it broke.

On inspection under a microscope, the wire showed a narrow neck at the point of breaking.
(d) Explain what was happening to the atoms in the wire at this necking point.
(e) How would this necking effect alter the answer to question (c)?

13. The graph of Figure 23.10 shows how the speed of a hockey ball changed after being thrown vertically upwards at 18 m/s. The mass of the ball was 200 g.

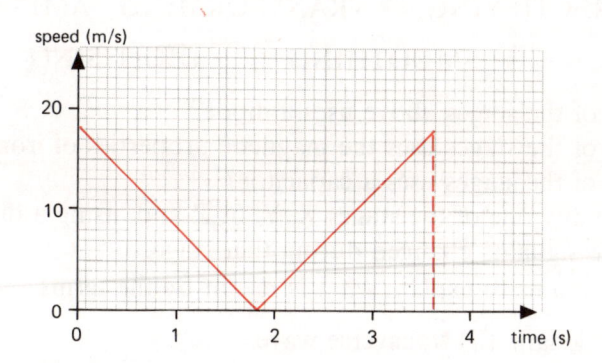

Figure 23.10

(a) Calculate the initial kinetic energy of the ball.
(b) How much work was done to throw the ball?
(c) What height did the ball reach?
(d) How long did the ball take to reach this height?
(e) Calculate the kinetic energy and the gravitational potential energy of the ball after two seconds.

14. A drum containing low-level radioactive waste was buried underground. The waste contained a long-lived isotope with a half-life of 2000 years and a short-lived isotope with a 10 year half-life. The activity of each isotope was initially 400 MBq.
(a) What is meant by MBq?
(b) What was the total initial activity?
(c) Estimate the total activity of the drum after:

(i) 10 years, (ii) 2000 years.

Explain your answers.
(d) If the isotopes emitted a mixture of beta and alpha particles, what would you consider to be a reasonable material for the drum? Explain your choice.
(e) Some people argue that it is a better idea to dispose of radioactive waste

out at sea rather than burying it underground. Explain briefly an advantage and a disadvantage of each idea.

15. A mains adaptor can change high voltage mains a.c. to low voltage d.c. The stages in the operation of a mains adaptor are shown in Figure 23.11.

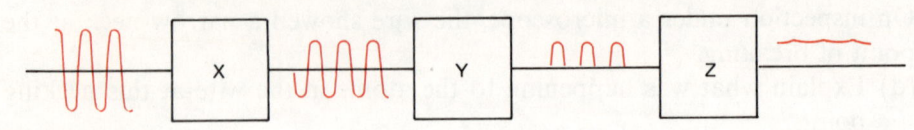

Figure 23.11

(a) Select from the list below a term which best describes each stage, X, Y, Z in Figure 23.11.

RECTIFYING   TRANSFORMING   AMPLIFYING

SMOOTHING   DIGITISING

(b) Which of the stages above uses a diode?
(c) Which of the stages uses the magnetic properties of iron?
(d) Which of the stages uses a capacitor?
(e) Choose any one of the stages X, Y, or Z and, using a diagram, explain why the signal is changed during that stage.

16. (a) Use diagrams to explain what is meant by the terms

(i) wavelength, (ii) transverse wave.

Figure 23.12 is a sketch showing an aerial view of seawater waves near a harbour.

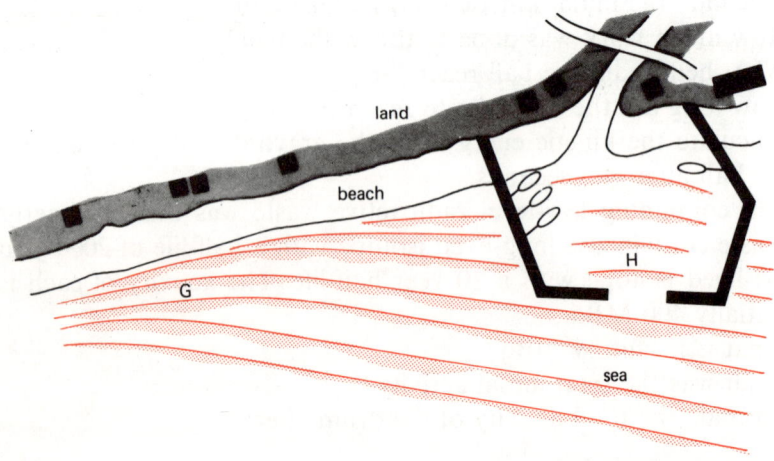

Figure 23.12

(b) How would you describe the behaviour of the waves at points G and H in the sketch?
(c) Why are the waves changing direction at G?
(d) What would happen if the gap in the harbour walls was narrowed?

17. Electronic logic gates can be described by 'truth tables'.
    (a) Which gate is described by the truth table of Figure 23.13?

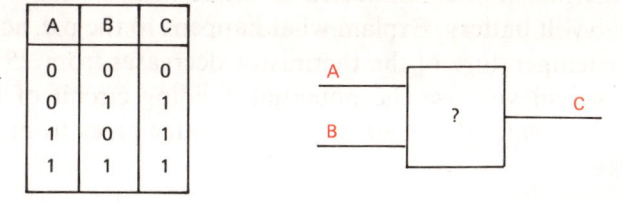

A	B	C
0	0	0
0	1	1
1	0	1
1	1	1

Figure 23.13

The combination of the two logic gates shown in Figure 23.14 could be used as a safety check on passenger ferries:

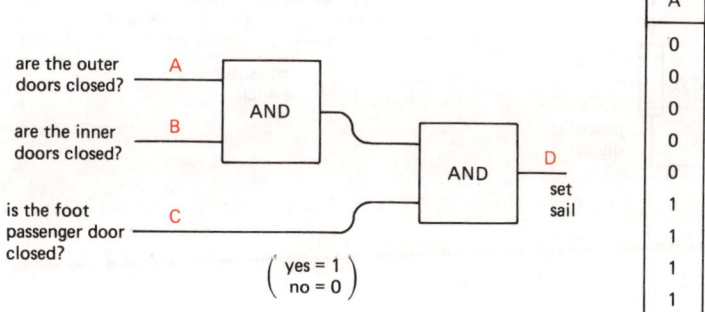

A	B	C	D
0	0	0	
0	0	1	
0	1	0	
0	1	1	
0	1	0	
1	0	0	
1	0	1	
1	1	0	
1	1	1	

(yes = 1, no = 0)

Figure 23.14

(b) Copy and complete the truth table for the gates.
(c) Explain how these gates could help to save lives.

18. Two graphs are shown in Figure 23.15. The first shows how the resistance of a thermistor changes with temperature. Thermistors are made from semiconducting materials. The second shows how the output of a transistor switches as the input p.d. changes.

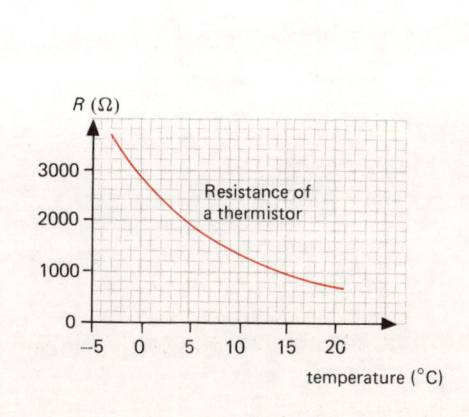

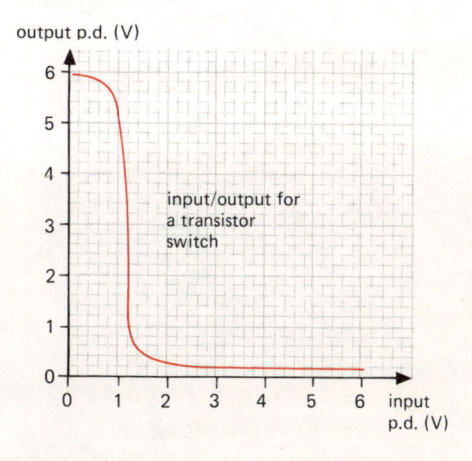

Figure 23.15

(a) Free electrons carry the charge through a conductor. How can a temperature increase change the conducting properties of a semiconductor?
(b) The thermistor was connected in series with a fixed 500 ohm resistor and a 6 volt battery. Explain what happens to the p.d. across the resistor as the temperature of the thermistor decreases from 25°C to 0°C.
(c) How would you use the potential dividing circuit of Figure 23.16 to control a heater designed to prevent water pipes from freezing in cold weather?

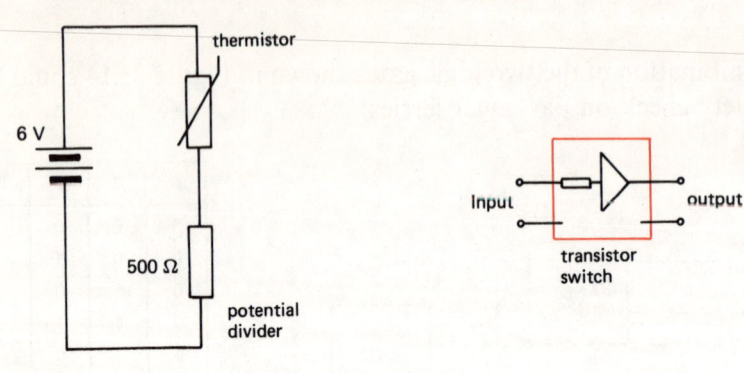

Figure 23.16

APPENDIX I: ANSWERS TO ALL NUMERICAL QUESTIONS

Unit 1

1. (a) 3000   (b) 7200   (c) 2 m/s
2. 6 s, 1200 s
3. 3.85 m/s, 10 s, 48 km, 8 m/s
4. 3600 m
5. (ii) 2.5 cm   (iii) 5 m/s^2
6. about 11.4 kN

Unit 2

1. (a) 14.4 N   (b) 90 N   (c) 225 N
2. (a) 10 m/s^2 (c) 5 m   (d) yes, 1.6 m/s^2, 0.8 m

Unit 3

6. (i) 200 cm^3 (ii) 385 ml   (iii) 2.7 g/cm^3 or 2700 kg/m^3

Unit 4

1. (a) 12.5 cm   (b) 15 cm   (c) 0.4 N/mm   (d) 0.4 N/cm or 40 N/m
2. (c) 3.3 N/m
4. (a) 18 cm   (b) 1.5
5. (a) 360 N   (b) half as much   (c) the thinner wire

Unit 6

1. (a) J (b) J (c) W (d) none
2. (a) 3 kJ
4. (a) 14 kN (b) 112 kJ (c) 28 kW
5. (a) 97.5 MJ (d) PE = 1.95 MJ, KE = 0.39 MJ

Unit 7

2. (a) 0 K (b) 4°C (c) 39°C
2. lead
4. (a) 678 J (b) 1.22 kJ
5. (a) 16.8 kJ (b) 672 kJ

Unit 8

2. (a) 160 kPa (b) 453 kPa
3. 60 MPa
6. (a) 74 cm of mercury

Unit 9

1. (a) joules (b) volts (c) newtons (d) metres (e) seconds (f) metres/second
2. (a) 2.4 A (b) 3 min 10.4 s (c) 75 ml (d) 9.5°C
3. (a) 1 kg (b) 5 min (c) 2 m (d) 100 W (e) 20 mm
4. (a) 46.1 mm (b) 453 mm

Unit 10

1. (a) about 8 (b) about 12000 (c) about 1
3. (a) 4 m^2 (b) 36 m^2
4. 8.3 per cent
5. (a) 38 ohms (b) 383 N/m or 3.8×10^2 N/m
6. (a) 7.8×10^5 (b) 6.6×10^{-3} (c) 2.75×10^1 (d) 9×10^{-10}
9. (a) 0.6 N/cm^2 (b) 140 kN (c) 0.018 m^2
10. (iii) 44.5 mA, 55.5 mA

Unit 12

2. (a) 60 Hz (b) yes
3. (a) 3×10^8 m/s

Unit 13

3. (a) 3×10^8 m/s (b) 1.4×10^{10} m

Unit 14

5. (b) 8 hours
6. (a) 12 (b) 16 (c) about 125 000

Unit 15

5. 24 ohms, 4 volts, 0.06 amp
8. (a) A

Unit 18

6. (b) 0.17 unit (c) 1p
7. £1.47

Unit 23: practice assessment questions

1. (a) (i) 146 g (ii) 0.146 kg (b) 1.46 N (c) 1.60 cm^3 (d) 0.91 g/cm^3 (e) 7.6 kg
2. (b) (i) 24 cm (ii) 3.8 N (iii) 4 cm
4. (b) 2 s (c) 5 m (d) 20 m
5. (c) 3 kJ (d) at least 3 kJ (e) 375 W
6. (a) 24 W (b) 86.4 MJ
10. (d) 0.24 A
11. (a) 1010 kg/m^3 (b) 0.25 m (c) 2.53 kPa (d) 495 m
12. (a) 0.4 m (b) 0.2 (c) 1.4×10^8 Pa
13. (a) 32.4 J (b) 32.4 J (c) 16.2 m (d) 1.8 s (e) KE = 0.4 J, PE = 32 J
14. (b) 800 MBq (c) (i) about 600 MBq (ii) about 200 MBq

APPENDIX II: USEFUL FORMULAE AND RELATIONSHIPS

Average velocity = $\dfrac{\text{distance travelled}}{\text{time taken}}$ $\qquad v = s/t$

Acceleration = $\dfrac{\text{change in velocity}}{\text{time taken}}$ $\qquad a = \dfrac{\Delta v}{t}$

Force = mass × acceleration $\qquad F = ma$

Work done = average force × distance

Kinetic energy = $\dfrac{1}{2}$ × mass × (velocity)² $\qquad \text{KE} = \dfrac{1}{2}mv^2$

Change in gravitational potential energy
 = mass × g × change in vertical height $\qquad \text{PE} = mgh$

Power = $\dfrac{\text{energy transformed}}{\text{time taken}}$

Efficiency = $\dfrac{\text{useful energy output}}{\text{total energy input}}$

Density = $\dfrac{\text{mass}}{\text{volume}}$

Pressure in a fluid = depth × density × g

Stiffness = $\dfrac{\text{force}}{\text{extension}}$ $\qquad k = F/x$

Stress and pressure = $\dfrac{\text{force}}{\text{area}}$

Strain = $\dfrac{\text{increase in length}}{\text{original length}}$

Young's Modulus = $\dfrac{\text{stress}}{\text{strain}}$

Resistance = p.d. / current $R = V/I$

Electrical power = current × p.d.

Specific heat capacity = energy supplied / (mass × temperature change) $c = \dfrac{Q}{m\Delta\theta}$